THE TOP OF THE RAINTREE

Kamalini Sengupta, a former member of the Indian Administrative Service, is a writer, documentary film-maker and freelance journalist and editor. *The Top of the Raintree* is her second published novel.

She also runs an organization working in the field of education, the Surya Trust, which is a passionate commitment with her. Kamalini Sengupta is married and has two sons.

OTHER INDIAINK TITLES :

A.N.D. Haksar	*Madhav & Kama: A Love Story from Ancient India*
Boman Desai	*Servant, Master, Mistress*
C.P. Surendran	*An Iron Harvest*
I. Allan Sealy	*The Everest Hotel*
I. Allan Sealy	*Trotternama*
Indrajit Hazra	*The Garden of Earthly Delights*
Jaspreet Singh	*17 Tomatoes: Tales from Kashmir*
Kalpana Swaminathan	*The Page 3 Murders*
Madhavan Kutty	*The Village Before Time*
Pankaj Mishra	*The Romantics*
Paro Anand	*I'm Not Butter Chicken*
Paro Anand	*Wingless*
Paro Anand	*No Guns at My Son's Funeral*
Ramchandra Gandhi	*Muniya's Light: A Narrative of Truth and Myth*
Ranjit Lal	*The Life & Times of Altu-Faltu*
Rashme Sehgal	*Hacks and Headlines*
Raza Mir & Ali Husain Mir	*Anthems of Resistance: A Celebration of Progressive Urdu Poetry*
Sharmistha Mohanty	*New Life*
Shree Ghatage	*Brahma's Dream*
Susan Visvanathan	*Something Barely Remembered*
Susan Visvanathan	*The Visiting Moon*
Tom Alter	*The Longest Race*

FORTHCOMING TITLES :

Anjana Basu	*Black Tongue*
Kalpana Swaminathan	*The Gardener's Song*
Prafulla Roy trans. John W. Hood	*Freedom's Ransom*
Selina Sen	*A Mirror Greens in Spring*
Shandana Minhas	*Tunnel Vision*
Susan Visvanathan	*Seine at Noon*

THE TOP OF THE RAINTREE

Kamalini Sengupta

*India*Ink

First published in 2006
Second impression in 2007
*India*Ink
An imprint of
Roli Books Pvt. Ltd.
M-75, G.K. II Market
New Delhi 110 048
Phones: ++91 (011) 2921 2271, 2921 2782
2921 0886, Fax: ++91 (011) 2921 7185
E-mail: roli@vsnl.com; Website: rolibooks.com
Also at
Bangalore, Mumbai, Varanasi, Agra, Jaipur

Cover Design: Nitisha Mehta
Page Layout: Kulvinder Singh

ISBN: 81-86939-30-X

Typeset in Garamond by Roli Books Pvt. Ltd. and printed at Anubha Printers, Noida (UP)

Dedicated to the memory of
Deshapriya Jatindra Mohan Sengupta
and
Nellie Sengupta,
great souls
of the era

CONTENTS

Acknowledgements ix

PART 1

The Rajmahal 3
The Book of Nets 18
The Book of Inheritance 63
The Book of Famine 97
The Book of Hope 143

PART 2

Surjeet Shona Moves In 183
Surjeet Shona Moves On 199
The Landlord's Family 204
Surjeet Shona Goes on a Journey 215
Gurdeep Grows Up 225
Ali Mallik's New Formula 235
The Immanent Junior 246
Twice-Married, Twice-Bereaved 254
Heavenly Hetaerae 259
A Love Story 268
The Scarlet Net 279
Memory 284

Credits 292

Acknowledgements

I thank Nadine Gordimer for reading my manuscript and giving me such a detailed and encouraging critique; Shelly Power, my agent, for having faith in me; G.B. Singh and Adesh Manjit Singh for revealing intricate Sikh customs; Kosturi Gupta Menon for checking some chapters; my friends for patiently reading early drafts and sharing their views; and, my family for their enthusiasm.

Part 1

1

The Rajmahal

The Rajmahal rose in 1910, new, creamy white and crystalline on a prime site on Chowringhee. The clear green of the Maidaan opposite and the palladian mansions juxtaposing it served as its setting.

Chowringhee metamorphoses from residential Tollygunge and Alipur at the southern end and breaks up into noisy thoroughfares of commerce further north. Across the Maidaan and out of sight runs the Hooghly, passing first under the partly visible Howrah Bridge, which used to give citizens egress to the main railway station, and then under the newer bridge, Vivekananda Setu. Today it seems astonishing that the northern end of town, the commercial sector and river front, with what was then a pontoon bridge, was the fashionable hub of early British Calcutta, the lawns of the sahibs' mansions sloping down to the water's edge. But Lal Digi, the Dalhousie Square tank, was the chief source of water and it was natural the small British population chose to live near it. The quarter must have been exclusive to the sahibs, with the exception of the scores of local retainers and tradesmen needed to make life tolerable for them, as indicated by contemporary accounts and pictures. It would have been quiet, with spaced-out buildings and sparse traffic, though there would have been frequent flurries when crowds of bhistees carried dripping waterskins from the tank to the mansion of a sahib, or palanquin bearers resting under the shade of a tree rose up with cries and commotion to take up their tasks. As for the Maidaan, it was a marshy jungle infested with crocodile, snake and tiger. When the British swanned about uneasily thus, it is said Warren Hastings went out on elephant back to hunt tiger in the vicinity of the Rajmahal. But things changed as the city expanded and only a few residential buildings, including Government House, continue to exist in the old quarter of the city. The prime locations have, for the major part of Calcutta's history, encroached on the marshes and jungles, shifting further south, over and beyond the Rajmahal. The area around the Dalhousie Square tank has been left to crowd in upon itself and foster the great commercial houses and exchanges, fanning out towards the congested old 'black quarter', while the river front, apart from the burning ground at Neemtolla, has turned into a series of ghats for light craft and, further up in Khiddirpur, for major shipping, most of it ineligible for genteel residential purposes.

The clamour of that part of town was partly buffered by distance from the Rajmahal and reduced to a quiet roar on the Maidaan where Victoria Memorial and the gothic spires of St Paul's Cathedral stood serenely amidst trees, watercourses and green. But the residents had to contend with the noisy Chowringhee traffic, and they often retreated inside to hear themselves think.

The Rajmahal, which was upset at losing its pristine quality after its sale and transformation into a block of flats, had a history replete with the tales of ghosts. It had four floors connected by a vast, soaring stairway, and the heavy wrought-iron balustrades trailed down with festoons of dusty sunlight and pigeon droppings. The iron beams which held up the roof formed convenient roosts for the pigeons and there was a constant bustle, sometimes music, raised voices, a dog's bark, mingling with the pigeons coos and hinting at the life inside the flats. The lobby, at the foot of the stairs, had a graciously proportioned black and white marble flagged floor, barely visible and seductive from the top floor. Within two curved embrasures, naked marble women tilted urns towards basins once awash with water, and a green light filtered through the fan-palms ranged behind them. The stairway landings between each floor were brightened by strips of light filtering through jalousies, glass panes and pillars holding up high windows. In all this great space, the stairs took up only the central area. On either distant side were interior verandahs, looking out at each other between narrow pillars with the stairs sweeping by in between.

The servants' quarters were tucked away on top of the roof, cordoned off from the skylights by a high wall. So they were well out of sight, and their access to the flats was by spiralling iron stairways forming two delicate lacy traceries at the back of the mansion and leading to the kitchens on each floor.

The 'Rajmahal' had got its name from the first owner, Raja Sheetanath. When Sardar Bahadur Ohri bought the property, razed the old building, and built this four-floor beauty, the name stuck, and the new Rajmahal inherited the soul of its predecessor.

Sardar Bahadur Ohri was given his title by the British for his dynamic building activities and his loyalty to the crown. At the end of his long life, he realized the Rajmahal would soon become an anachronism as a single unit, so he arranged for its sale to a Bengali Muslim family, the Malliks. The Ohris retained the ground floor, and the new landlord rented out the four intermediate flats while he and his family chose to occupy the top floor, in spite of the loss of grace after the change of the stairs from marble to wood, and the proximity of the whiffy pigeons.

The original Rajmahal, a palladian garden house, had fallen to wrack and ruin when Raja Sheetanath had retired to the dung beetles and rambling grounds of his estates in Purulia to administer them first hand and introduce reform to his peasant-tenants. He believed the British would never leave unless the people of India, each and every one of them, were made aware through education of their birthright and a revived Hindu pride.

'How can I possibly accept that we Indians are part of a degraded and barbarous society? Am I, as an Indian, to assume I am incapable of appreciating the finer elements of civilization? It's time we woke up!' he would exhort. When the Ohris bought over the site, therefore, they found the furniture, paintings and artefacts decaying in the rundown old Rajmahal, for Raja Sheetanath also found these too glaringly foreign. 'I vow to wholeheartedly embrace swadeshi!' he declaimed. 'And all such alien objects I abjure!'

When the new Rajmahal was built by the Sardar Bahadur, he was already sixty, successful and rich after fulfilling many contracts in the developing cities of the country. His wife, Inderjeet Kaur, was deeply upset at having to move so far away from Punjab.

'Will "he" ever ask my opinion?' she complained to her confidante and maid Heera. 'How does "he" think I can live in the midst of all those Bengalis? "He" could have improved our haveli right here in Saidabad instead, God knows how much it is needed! Or built something in Amritsar.'

The Sardar Bahadur dismissed her by saying, 'The sight of the house will make you change your mind at once, "I-say"! And Calcutta is the capital of India, after all!' A year later, when a royal proclamation said the capital was to move to Delhi, he kept away from his 'I-say' for some days. His chagrin showed only to his sons.

'It was a terrible error of judgement on my part! How easily I could have built a house in Delhi!' he said.

'It's all right, Bhapaji,' was the complacent reply. 'There is nothing to stop you from building another house in Delhi or any other place of your choice!' 'But,' they may have added, 'the Rajmahal is so perfect and Calcutta is so much fun, that we, in any case, are staying put!'

The Sardar Bahadur too couldn't tear himself away. He didn't lose time, though, in bagging some of the prime contracts for the shift of the capital to Delhi.

Raja Sheetanath's family heirlooms graced the new Ohri household. Tables with gilt legs, stuffed sofas and chairs, hunting scenes in over-varnished oil paintings, marble busts, gilt-framed mirrors and velvet drapery cascading from elaborate pelmets, Persian carpets, old armour, tiered cabinets full of Staffordshire china, venetian glass, Chinese vases, candelabra ... From the stuccoed ceilings of the reception and banquet rooms hung chandeliers and fans.

The first floor, the favourite area of the Rajmahal itself, was the Sardar Bahadur's bachelor's retreat which included a conservatory, a Guru Granth Sahib room and a splendid mirrored bedroom. The main bedroom on the second floor, which Sardar Bahadur Ohri occupied with his faithful Inderjeet Kaur, was elevated and separated by a floor from this retreat. He shared the conservatory floor with his visitors and current mistress, of whom he had a succession of three through his years in the Rajmahal, apart from short-term fancy girls. They came up to this floor by the outer verandah stairway, and it was tacit they would never use the main lobby. This was so that the two uppermost floors, the third and fourth, could be kept secluded for the women and members of the intimate family whose importance receded as they ascended. In this, the Sardar Bahadur was carrying on the ancient tradition of courtesans being allowed access to the master's chambers, while the honoured wife was confined to the inner sanctum. It also echoed a tradition among some of the earlier British whose local keeps, while the wives stayed back in Britain, lived in private apartments in the very same building to which they retired coyly at dawn. The conservatory was partly south facing, looking out on to the Maidaan. It had plants of every exotic variety and its windows were lined with flounced silk curtains, which turned yellow and brittle in the sun and came off in flakes. Cane chairs and tables lay scattered on the floor, while a bar was cunningly camouflaged behind a bottle-palm. The rest of the rooms were less elaborately, though expensively, furnished. After the sale, when the ground floor was all that remained with the Ohris, it was carefully altered and re-furnished with the best of these treasures before the rest were scattered to other Ohri establishments countrywide.

Though the Sardar Bahadur identified happily with Bengal and Bengalis, he had never thought of shaving his beard or cutting his hair. And it was natural his origins called as he lay dying.

'I must see the Golden Temple one last time,' he told his doting family. 'See that it is arranged for me to move to Amritsar.'

'What do you mean, Bhapaji?' said an anxious seventy-year-old son 'What do you mean by "last time"?'

'I refer to my impending death,' said the Sardar Bahadur impatiently. 'Please do not make a sho-sha!' he pre-empted, before anyone could protest at the mention of the unmentionable.

It was arranged that he would spend his last days on the verandah of a cousin's home skirting the temple where he could gaze beatifically at the divine Harmandir Sahib afloat in its pool of nectar. His progeny, who kept ownership of the ground floor flat, left it in a chowkidar's care, while they took the air of Chandigarh, Delhi, Jaipur, and, when they could wangle a visa, Lahore. Here, drifting on the fringes of the polo set and driving their vintage Bentleys and Rolls Royces, they preferred to boast about their old palace in Calcutta rather than live in it.

The dejected Rajmahal's spirits had revived only momentarily with the arrival of the first of the fifth generation, Surjeet Shona, who was born just before its desertion by the Ohris. Her birth entitled the Sardar Bahadur to a fifth rung on the tiny golden ladder, prepared to give him an easier passage into the next life. Her parents left Calcutta, taking her with them after the Sardar Bahadur's demise and it was not until Surjeet Shona lost her husband and came back twenty-six years later that an Ohri again lodged permanently in the Rajmahal. So she was destined to inherit at least some of the original artefacts of the mansion, as well as the genes of both Raja Sheetanath and the Sardar Bahadur, for her father, an Ohri, had done the unthinkable by marrying a Bengali woman, a direct descendant of the Raja. It was a mixed heritage of which Surjeet Shona was both proud and well aware.

The Sardar Bahadur's 'I-say' was just as upset when her husband decided to shift to Amritsar and sell the Rajmahal at the tail-end of their lives as she had been decades earlier when she had been uprooted and shifted in exactly the opposite direction.

'Why does "he" have to move again at this age, when it's too late for any good to come from it?' she said despondently to her maid Heera.

'It is of no use to argue, Bi'ji,' said Heera, perfectly familiar with the ways of her employers. 'Think how auspicious it will be to move near Harmindar Sahib!'

'Well, at least "he" is keeping to the lowest floor.'

An elaborate process had to be set in motion. Not only did the ground floor have to be converted into a self-sufficient unit, but the Guru Granth Sahib room had to be moved down too. And the great man intended to see to this reverential task himself. To him, as to all believing Sikhs, the Guru Granth Sahib was more than just the holy book. It was the Guru incarnate. At the sukhasan every night, the Sardar Bahadur himself wrapped the book in its sheet so the Guru could have a comfortable sleep.

The stairway on the ground floor verandah, no longer needed, was broken down to make space for the new Granth Sahib room. No expense was spared and the ceiling and walls were decorated with gold embellished scenes from the lives of the gurus. Rugs were acquired directly from Persia through the Sardar Bahadur's friend, Isfahani, a tea merchant and laid in the room. All was set for the installation.

The Sardar Bahadur had earlier shifted his wife down with him to the first floor once his near-static period had begun, to make going out easier. And Inderjeet Kaur had obediently moved her belongings down to the mirrored bedroom which she had managed to sneak into sometimes for a good pry in earlier times, and which had always upset her by its existence.

'Only when "he" is past it,' she thought bitterly, 'am I to be allowed official ingress!'

She saw to it that the shameful mirror over their bed, which so clearly reproduced their gross, spreading bodies when they lay down, was screened and put out of action. But this didn't stop her from reflecting on fantasies of the old goings-on, based, after all, on her actual witnessing on one tragic occasion, a mind sport set in a tired time warp.

After moving into the Rajmahal in 1910, the Sardar Bahadur had arranged to receive his mistresses at home. His sex life was for him a must, and the best he could do was to keep up the charade for the sake of his wife's dignity. It was obvious he was more concerned with enjoying what he considered his right than protecting his wife's feelings. But in those days, wives also knew they had to keep their mouths shut and be aware of their good fortune in netting such fine manly husbands. Besides, in a joint family household, infidelities by the womenfolk weren't uncommon either. But poor Inderjeet Kaur, though a handsome specimen before perpetual childbirth ruined her looks, had never strayed. The tragedy of her life started, therefore, when she allowed her youth to pass her by in a state of meaningless honour before she first woke up to her husband's philandering ways. The Sardar Bahadur played his role by telling her he needed to spend the night on the first floor whenever business became protracted. He also cautioned her not to enter that floor since she observed purdah and would be sullied by contact with undesirables. She accepted this almost unquestioningly, though she had her first prickle of suspicion. But this was forgotten in her happiness at having the Sardar Bahadur on the premises, promising, surely, a larger share of his time. How was she to know he would straight away acquire a kothéwali who danced for his visitors in the conservatory? Inderjeet Kaur heard the music and the jingling of the dancer's bells and decided momentously, when silence had descended one night, to go downstairs. She hadn't seen her husband for three days, and no one, including sons and daughters-in-law, servants and other members of the household would divulge anything. And their sly looks and ambivalent attitudes were galling.

'All the visitors must have left,' she fooled herself. 'I have not set eyes on "him" for three whole days. Ei Heera,' she called to her faithful ally, 'have all the guests left "him"?'

'Why Bi'ji? You are not thinking of going down, are you?' said a frightened Heera.

Inderjeet Kaur, though a dutiful wife, was far from mousy. She imperiously brushed Heera aside and prepared herself for the descent. The sardarni had made other preparations too, colouring her long thick hair carefully with henna, reddening her fingers and toes with the same herb, and tenting her body with a particularly gorgeous salwar-kameez of a shade of pink bordering on magenta, with silver gota work scattered over it.

She emerged on to the landing of her floor and, reluctant to direct her eyes downstairs, looked first up at the silent and dark landing of the top floor. Then fearfully down towards the ghostly marble ladies dimly spotlighted and blessing the house with the sound of tinkling water. 'Almost like that dancer's bells,' she thought with a sob. Then, clutching her veil to her bosom, she allowed her eyes to reach her husband's floor. Lights glowed behind the heavy curtains of the glassed doors. The ghosts whispered and the house stiffened with suspense. Inderjeet Kaur descended, quivering with each step. On the first floor landing she cautiously approached the verandah outside her husband's bedroom, reciting a prayer as a charm against the unknown. The silver on her clothes flashed on and off, turning her into an exotic traffic warning, and a lone pigeon set up a coo. 'Shut up!' hissed Inderjeet Kaur. 'Bladdy chup rah!' mixing Punjabi with one of the few English words she had picked up from her sons.

Then she spotted a sliver of light between the lowest slats of the bedroom window, waddled to it, took a deep breath and, stooping painfully, peered in. The matter was made more painful by the fact that the slats pointed upwards, so she had to twist her neck to find herself gazing at the ultra clear reflection in the ceiling mirror. Whatever she saw was devastating enough to make her wail in deep contralto, 'Hey Gurujee-eee!' And then she fainted right there on the verandah, making the house wince, and creating such a disturbance with her metallic outfit and bulk of bosom and buttock that the guard came shouting into the lobby, Heera who was peeping from above came running down, and the lord of the house stormed out wrapped in a sheet. He took one look at Inderjeet Kaur and roared, 'So this is how you obey me, oh Mother-of-Rupinder!' He made a magnificent spectacle, his leonine head cascading with hair albeit from a thinning top, his vast hairy shoulders, and the sheet robe. Some of the witnesses imagined they were in a film. They almost expected him to draw a sword from a jewelled scabbard and plunge it into the heaving breast of the equally hugely magnificent figure of his wife sparkling on the verandah floor. When the kotha lady yawned inside the bedroom, as the mischievous mirror recorded, she seemed contemporary and two-dimensional by contrast. She dressed, knowing by experience that the frolicking was over for the night, and picked up her discarded bells, jingling them contemptuously before putting them away in a bag. Then she sat down, made herself a paan, and chewed while awaiting developments. But she was not to be one of the Sardar Bahadur's major loves, and he sent her away in his carriage that very night, one of the rare nights he forgot to pay homage to the Guru Granth Sahib and bestow on it a serene sukhasan.

❧

Now, three decades later and on the eve of their final departure, Inderjeet Kaur had to join the Guru Granth Sahib's re-installation procession with her husband. She was a good five years younger than him, but that made her almost ninety and she didn't look forward to negotiating the stairs. She waited patiently while the Sardar Bahadur got himself ready, in spite of his dangerously enfeebled state and the dissuasions of his family.

'You must listen!' his favourite great grandson, Satinder, pleaded. 'One of us can do it for you. Choose whoever you wish. And we will carry you down so you can watch everything in calmness. But do not try to do it yourself. It will be too much.'

He was right, but the Sardar Bahadur's passion carried him through the occasion. Just. Pulling on his elaborate and much too tight achkan-churidar, sash and medals, he ended up blue in the face and had to sit down heaving, fanned and fussed over. Fortunately, the ceremony demanded bare feet, though the jooties, which went with the formal wear, had been cleaned and kept ready. When his normal colour returned and his breathing calmed, he was hauled up and with an anxious procession supporting him staggered into the old Granth Sahib room. Here he picked up the book, placed it on his head and summoned the family bhaiji to follow him down the staircase with his yak-tail whisk. The Sardar Bahadur was of a great bulk, and it was hard for him or the procession to proceed in spite of the soothing vocal passage of the musicians summoned to sing shabads and the attempts of the house and ghosts to cushion him. Inderjeet Kaur preceded her husband while her great grandson, Satinder, walked by her holding the pitcher from which she would sprinkle water to purify the path ahead of the book. Thus, sprinkling and whisking, they took off. It was a painfully slow progression. The Sardar Bahadur's arms trembled under the weight of the book and Inderjeet Kaur found both sprinkling water and walking down sideways almost impossible at her age. The installation was miraculously achieved and the musicians surpassed themselves with their impassioned singing.

The hymn they sang was the same as was sung on the day of the Granth Sahib's original installation in the Golden Temple.

'... the wondrous deed is done
Satisfied are all desires.
Filled is the world with joy
All pain ended
Complete, pure, eternal.'

The Sardar Bahadur had by then passed out in a dead faint, beginning his own end-to-pain. Inderjeet Kaur sat by him and fanned him, fearfully aware that the inevitable had been put into motion, while a huge feast for all continued under a shamiana in the garden. The old man recovered in the evening, but stayed on in his holy room, feverishly anxious to move to Amritsar.

So, against the doctor's advice, he set off just two days later, to achieve his final aim in this life, seen off by the sorrowing house and its ghosts.

He had ensured his peace of mind. After his arrival at Amritsar he was carried on a stretcher straight up to the verandah of his relative's house, where he opened his eyes briefly to look upon the Golden Temple. Then he was laid finally on the floor.

In a feeble voice yet with the familiar commanding authority, he confirmed that fifty cows with gilded horns along with gold sovereigns were to be distributed among the temples and gurudwaras listed by him in Amritsar, Calcutta and Saidabad, his birthplace. 'Be kind to your wives,' he said. 'And be devoted and dutiful to your children and grandchildren. You must carry on the family traditions and enterprises and bring further glory to the house of Ohris. And above all, remember to honour and worship your mother.'

'What about all the times he forgot to honour and worship me when he was tangled with his bawds?' thought Inderjeet Kaur. But her heart weighed like a lodestone in her breast.

The Sardar Bahadur breathed his last that very day, while the evening hymns filtered to his brain via his impaired hearing, and his soon-to-be widow wept and fanned him with a hand pankha, though an electric fan revolved adequately above them. The evening hymns rose above his death rattle, and as they reached a crescendo the rituals began. The room was prepared for the procession of mourners who began to file past as soon as the signal was given. Before it was laid in state, the body, including the scanty but long hair, was washed in curds by the men of the family. Inderjeet Kaur begged to be allowed to help, but her emotion and age overwhelmed her and the job was finished in no time. Not before she could view her husband's bare form, the distended flesh, rolling about as it was washed, the hirsute chest and arms with the sagging breasts, the wobbling dome of the belly. Then her eyes were drawn to the folds of flesh hiding the almost invisible worm of the penis and the wildly swinging scrotum distended by late life hydrocele. She had never looked on all this because, till the end, her husband had bathed himself, and they had always had sex in the dark on her insistence. She wished she had seen him in the clear light of the days of their youth, when her enclosing arms could feel his muscular fat-free body and his penis was more like a snake than a worm as it bit its way into her womb. Then he was washed clean of the curds and made decent again in pure white clothing, with a colourful turban gracing his head. Tubs of ice were brought in and placed next to the body, while fans were set up. Earthen lamps were lit and a pitcher was filled with water with a coconut at its mouth and placed near his head. He lay there all night, covered in white, while a senior temple priest chanted prayers, placing a fragment of gold in his mouth, touching him with the little golden ladder. The family were silent, stoical, neither sad nor happy, including Inderjeet Kaur who had become quiet. When mourners came in beating their breasts and wailing loudly, they were chided by the sons. The Sardar Bahadur had reached a ripe old age with glory and left a long line of successors, and this wasn't the time for lament. Soon after dawn, in the room which was thick and unpleasant with incense smoke and sweat, when the sun was already broadcasting its unwelcome heat, the bier was put on a carriage pulled by one of the family Rolls Royces. The Sardar Bahadur's white shroud, which would turn orange with sprinklings of saffron water on its way to the burning ground, was carefully decorated with flower garlands and gilded coconuts. The bier left the house in a shower of silver coins and golden petals eagerly secured by the waiting crowd. Watching the procession trickle out of sight through the broader routes of the old city from a terrace, Inderjeet Kaur could feel the cold grip of death on her heart as her life's companion tugged hard at it. She vowed to stay on in Amritsar, to give up the mansion in Calcutta where she had reigned over her family, with the fast vanishing figure on the bier.

❧

Whenever any of the Sardar Bahadur's progeny returned and entered the Rajmahal lobby, they found it sad and strange that this once sparkling area with the playing fountains, statues and palms should be so sadly divested of its crystalline aspect. The reason was it was now open to the public. Refinements such as running fountains and flowerpots offered themselves readily to the indescribable muck-trailing postmen, tradesmen, servants and other casual visitors. The new landlord tried his best by keeping up a minimum standard with annual whitewashing, daily floor sweeping and swabbing and removal of pigeon droppings. Inside the flats, however, the sparkle was kept up by its particular and rich tenants.

The original privacy of the upper floors was violated when the central stairway became public and the building was turned inside out as a block of flats occupied by unconnected tenants. But by now, most of these tenants knew each other's idiosyncrasies by rote, and with their ageing faculties didn't feel any more comment was needed. This ageing also made their bones creak and lungs whistle as they trudged up the stairs, particularly the upper floor tenants. A querulous rumble could be heard about the need for a lift. The landlord ignored this, knowing well the aged ones had no choice. In a city where such accommodation was precious, his tenants' yokes to these flats would loosen only with death. The result was some of the tenants were forced into seclusion and gave up the idea of ever stepping out.

The Rajmahal was concerned, first and foremost, with Sardar Bahadur Ohri's family, to whom it had transferred its loyalty from Raja Sheetanath, and secondly with the new landlords. As to the ghosts, these it welcomed and encouraged. But the Rajmahal strictly curtailed their haunting activities, and the ghosts amused themselves by appearing sometimes to the guards in the lobby and frightening the pigeons.

The Rajmahal observed the negotiations with the new landlord warily. A Muslim in that privileged position was a distressing departure from sanity, was its initial reaction. But what choice did it have? The ghosts were getting hysterical as it was. Both the Sikh and Hindu ghosts, earlier busy being vicious to each other, now showed how virulently anti-Muslim they were, based more on in-built prejudice than any thought of having to encounter those alien beings. The Rajmahal had to strain itself to the utmost to contain their agitation. And soon, when the second, could it be called defilement? was in progress, as major alterations went under way, its confused efforts at resisting got it nowhere. Though it tried in the best way it could by releasing a loose brick here, pushing a pillar out of alignment there, springing a leak in this bathroom and bulging out the plaster in that ... But with all the building frenzy no one noticed, and the work went on relentlessly, soon there was a plethora of new families, atmospheres, sights and sounds, leaving the Rajmahal dazed for a good half year and silencing the ghosts.

Six families now inhabited the Rajmahal, the remaining Ohris in their ground floor flat, and the Malliks, the new landlords, at the top. The four families who rented the split middle floors were a mixed lot, British, Bengali, Anglo-Indian and lastly Russo-Bengali. At the start of this story, the British couple, the Stracheys, were still there, as were Proshanto and Mohini Mojumdar, the Normans with their widowed sister and the Petrovs. The abrasive eldest son of the landlord, Junior Mallik, had taken over the running of the Rajmahal in place of his retired father.

After its recovery, the Rajmahal continued its sharp observance of ghosts and goings-on. It had shuddered at its first loss of innocence, when Raja Sheetanath had deserted it to a Sikh family. But it had recovered in that incarnation in spite of the shattering nature of its earlier decrepitude and destruction. And here it was in yet another guise, as a block of flats with a Muslim master. Fortunately for this third incarnation, it would grow to learn to appreciate the Malliks before long, but it couldn't avoid the inevitable disappearance of its inhabitants one by one, and violence, before its day was done.

2

The Book of Nets

The Stracheys lived in Number 4 Rajmahal, a handsome sized flat though it occupied only one half of the second floor. The most remarkable set of rooms was the main bedroom, dressing room and bathroom, the Sardar Bahadur's marital suite. The bedroom was largely occupied by Raja Sheetanath's double bed, made of carved oak, with caryatid pillars and frolicking winged cherubs. The ceiling above held a silken canopy with mosquito netting which could be pulled up and down by a chord. At the centre of the canopy was a ceiling fan, which sometimes caught and tore the netting to shreds, and this was one aspect of its original fittings which the Rajmahal wished could be replaced. But the Stracheys appreciated the antique value of the fan and had the wooden blades shortened rather than replaced with a modern version. Their bathroom held another beauty from the original Rajmahal, a marble open-oyster-shell shaped shower in which the bather was sprayed deliciously from neck to foot through rungs of perforated pipes. In those days, Calcutta had centrally supplied gas from the Oriental Gas Co. and gleaming copper geysers were installed for the supply of hot water during the chilly winter.

Jack Strachey worked for Sharp and Co., a managing agency with offices on Clive Street. Sharp's imposing block stood close to the grandiloquently pillared Royal Exchange, which housed the

Bengal Chamber of Commerce and Industry, an offshoot of the old Calcutta Chamber started by the traders of the East India Company. Sharp-owned jute mills stretched along the Hooghly, and Jack spent his early years in the Sharp's mill at Nagarpara. Most of the mills were run by Scottish engineers from Dundee. And 'Little Dundees', with nostalgically named pubs, 'Honey Bee', etc were set up inside their well-insulated compounds, essential for the game of pretend. At the right time of year, haggis and other Scottish delicacies appeared, and Highland flings were danced by unhealthily ruddy women and their sometimes kilted husbands. So India was warded off, allowed to impinge only from a remove, riverine images framed by verandah pillars. Semi-naked coolies chanted and spat and loaded bales on to barges which swarmed the jetties at the factories' sides, scenes which the 'mems' could snootily ignore as they idled along the river banks of their secure compounds with their ayahs and perambulators. But in another world were the hot and humid spindle and loom-filled factories, sweat amidst hanks of the golden fibre, flying particles settling like threshings of locust wings on every surface. Here Jack and the rest of the white management were forced out of their chastity belts into sweaty intimacy with the country's private parts. But locks hastily clicked shut against one last nightmare, the living quarters of the workers and their families, the 'lines', which existed across the road and away from the river.

Myrna Strachey, like the other 'mems', made rare forays out of the magnificent residential compound of Nagarpara Jute Mill. She was careful not to look beyond the back of her chauffeur's neck while the black walls and slimy drains of the mills and 'lines' passed by. And she held her breath when they passed the stinking raw jute which lay drying by the roadside ditches in the retting season. These forays could be to a neighbouring white residence or to Calcutta to British friends' houses or to clubs with all-white memberships. When the Stracheys shifted to Calcutta, they were the ones visited by these doughty Scottish families at their Rajmahal flat. Here they would gather around the piano while corseted matrons sang Scottish ditties and pressed tins of shortbread into their hands.

Myrna Strachey was a long-limbed, dark-haired English beauty. She liked to spend endless moments in the nude before a full-length mirror, examining her figure for flaws and curvetting to maintain the perfection. The children of the Rajmahal felt a rising excitement every time the Stracheys' son, Martin, came back from boarding school for his holidays. They would find excuses to make Martin speak to her and crowd around him when he knocked on her bedroom door. This stratagem was used after the one-time luck had favoured them. Myrna was holding her door slightly ajar hiding behind it to speak to her son, and Martin was jostled out of the way by the others craning their necks and yearning for forbidden ephemera. This yielded nothing more than an impression of perfumed and shadowed pinkness in a distant mirror. It created a bond between them and they would often remember this, their first glimpse of a naked adult woman, and then each other, and a softnesss would enter them for old associations in the security of the Rajmahal. The gang would hang around in the Strachey flat, waiting to see Myrna emerging from her room in a mist of scent, her face flushed with make-up. She would hug her little boy, and sometimes one or other of his fortunate friends, and run down the stairs on confident high heels.

Jack Strachey adored his wife. He was a large square blonde Scotsman with an accent countered by English and Indian influences, an effect cultivated by him to put him on par with the superior English up at the head office. 'They're ridiculous!' he would say, defensively offensive against both Scots and Indians striving to get the right accent. 'I had to interpret between Chatterjee and Mackintosh again, and they were both speaking English!' Myrna, English by birth, kept judiciously silent.

When Jack Strachey moved on to the head office in Calcutta to become one of the youngest directors, it was commonly expected he would end as chairman and managing director of Sharp and Co. This would lead to the presidentship of the Bengal Chamber and a knighthood. But Jack had to face the ultimate dishonour of being superseded by an Indian. Peculiarly, he used this failure to justify his staying on in India after retirement. In reality, he had never intended to return to the stifling suburbia of his background. His father, a carpenter, though a superior one with his own furniture business in the end, was originally 'Skiddaw', not the regal sounding 'Strachey'. Jack had no hesitation in changing his surname when he was of age. Myrna, with her upper-class background, tilted the balance in his favour among the Calcutta British, who were mainly English. But trends in post-Independence India added to the convolutions and Jack was right for the job at the wrong time.

The Stracheys spent seven years in the jute mill out in Nagarpara before moving to Calcutta. During this time, Myrna was submitted to the exaggerated pampering of her ayahs. They massaged her with creams and kept her cool with delicious iced drinks and seasonal summer fruits, laying out fresh cotton dresses lovingly laundered, and sheltering her from the extreme heat. But this bored and sickened her in the end. The savage, squalid country, the digs at her as an alien in the predominantly Scottish compound, were at first less relevant than the growing ties between her and Jack. But being kept out of the big bad world outside, cramped, created a resistance to having children. It was only after five years into her marriage that she gave in and had Martin. And then, the life instilled a stupor in her, till one day it seemed she was trapped in a shrinking glass bubble. She lay inertly on deck chairs, staring across the muddy Hooghly at scenes she had once observed with such fascination. The changing moods of the river, the magnificent sunsets, bloated half-burnt carcasses floating by after nominal cremations, tidal bores knocking the small craft about, capsizing a ferry once and drowning its passengers before her very eyes. When the war came, amphibian planes landed on the water and khaki amphibian tanks droned across the river and crawled miraculously ashore as if earth and water were one element. But she was simply a viewer, not a participant, and the scenes remained what they had always been, vignettes framed between the verandah pillars of her prison.

When a trio of British air force officers was billeted on them Myrna was astonished to hear herself say, 'Eenie, meenie, mynee, mo, catch a man... who should it be?' She smiled wickedly to herself at the first of the many anticipated thrills before a liaison. 'Tom, Dick or Harry?' Ironically, she alighted on the oldest, who had so far shown no signs of facetious flirtatiousness. The lover-elect was cynical, the affair was brief and almost unpleasant. But Myrna felt liberated, as if she had smashed her way out of the glass bubble. The shift to Calcutta came like a rescue air raid, one of the miraculous planes screaming down under strafing fire cover, and sweeping her away from that terrible place.

Jack and Myrna examined many alternatives before settling for the Rajmahal. They ignored the advice against moving into a block tenanted by Indians. 'In Alipore,' they were told, 'you'll get a house to yourselves and a garden, and you'll be close to all of us. Everyone lives in Alipore, or Ballygunge or Tollygunge …' 'Everyone who's anyone, as well as white,' they may have added. But the thought of continuing within semi-rural limitations filled Myrna with dread. She needed desperately to be in the thick of things, centred.

Jack didn't mind either way, and the Rajmahal was that much closer to his office. He may have regretted it later when he saw the latitude it gave Myrna for her liaisons. But he couldn't have foreseen and planned so clearly into the future.

As for the Rajmahal, it felt both tentative and excited about the Stracheys, never having dealt with British tenants before. And it had also to deal with the ghosts who were frantic at the very thought of sharing their spaces with white people.

'Mlechchas in our midst!' shouted a Swadeshi ghost. 'Our purity will be sullied!'

'What purity?' said a tart Sikh ghost. 'You know nothing about this city. It's a real hotchpotch! Wait till you see what comes next.'

'We never thought we would have anything but upper-caste Bengalis,' said the Swadeshi ghost, recklessly calling to question the aristocracy of the venerable Sardar Bahadur.

'Keep shut! *#@+!!xx# Bengalis … Black, skinny creatures from the gutters…,' more unprintable words followed from a middle-aged Sikh ghost and the house had to intervene. The ghosts had begun to tussle with each other's disembodied forms and utter little screams, which would soon escalate into shrieks, and this always permeated the atmosphere and affected the inhabitants' nerves. But the Sikh ghost was right. The post-Ohri Rajmahal would truly see a 'hotchpotch' of tenants within a very short period. And what with calming the ghosts at each new incursion, and grappling with its own confusion, the house had already entered its half year of frustration. It was only after things had settled down that it could follow its natural inclinations of concern and affection towards its inhabitants. 'They are upper class, anyway,' it would try and soothe the ghosts. 'And variety is the spice of life,' it added feebly.

Jack Strachey had been full of zest during the early jute mill days. Life was good, work was hard, and the big, hot country was getting him in its grip. As long as he had no contact with those stinking 'lines' across the road …

All employees at Sharp's, British employees, were sent on regular furlough to Britain to stop them from curdling, convulsing with colic and draining away. Too many succumbed to the enervating air with its cargo of mosquitoes, the muggy water with its infusion of microbes. The other objective of the furlough was to ensure British employees married British. A handful had gone native and acquired Indian wives, exotic creatures perfumed with oriental attars, their foreheads adorned with vermillion. A girl from home was so much more befitting. Jack had been seen with beautiful Bengali companions for a while, causing a ripple of anxiety at Sharp's. 'See that young Strachey goes home. Needs a bit of a change…' Obediently, Jack Strachey, in the end unaffected by the Bengali beauties, the malaria and the microbes, picked on Myrna. Sharp's congratulated itself when he returned from that furlough with his young bride leaning with him over the rail of a steamer.

The Stracheys had decided to stay on after Independence, a minority among the British. Why should the proponents of the colonial power subject themselves to their country's erstwhile subjects? Yet some, a few, did, unwilling to give up the ineffable qualities built up over the centuries. Like the Stracheys, they 'stayed on', as some well-known writers have expressed through their fiction. The best in that fiction is exhibited in the reality of old age. Of British people who grew old in India after Independence. And of such were the tragic Stracheys ... Un-understanding of the Indian ethos, sympathetic but un-understanding. However much Jack Strachey may admire charming Indian women, or Myrna have sensual Indian lovers, or both enjoy the rhythm of the seasons, they couldn't encompassingly rap with Indians.

'What rapport?' you may ask. 'Isn't it a bit too much to expect of a couple who stayed on just because they felt like it? Why all this sermonizing about "rapping"?' Rebuke accepted. It is in the na ure of things that such lack of understanding must be. And for that matter, most Indians, whether from one extreme of urban-upper-class-westernized or the other of rural-poor, have their binoculars turned in on themselves. Apart from knowing little about the larger country, they can rarely rap with anyone outside their own confined groupings. So let's not waste time on all this and go on to the dilemma or situation of Jack and Myrna Strachey as among the few British who stayed on till the end.

When it came to lovers Myrna could rap with white and coloured, European and Indian without discrimination. She was the mistress of men in an outré sense, having, by the time she had reached fifty, slept with almost any man who took her fancy.

And once, a visiting and elderly Ohri, had stayed for a time in the ground floor flat belonging to his family, long before Surjeet Shona came back to settle in the Rajmahal. 'I wonder if all Sikhs carry the "five k's",' Myrna had always wanted to know. And when she saw the handsome Ohri downstairs she had smiled to herself. Apart from the kesh, the kanga, the karrha, the kirpan and the kachcha, she also longed to know if true Sikhs were forbidden from 'interfering' with Christian women, white Christian women, just as they were instructed against Muslim women. Some of the older Sikh ghosts could have enlightened her, but they couldn't read Myrna's thoughts.

'Oh Myrna,' her long-suffering and adoring Jack had thought, 'why do you need so badly to explore everything in the world to its very core, why are you so curious about life you big beautiful thoughtless woman? Where does he keep his dagger, his "keerpawn", Myrna? Did you find it pinning his under shorts together? Or tucked into his uncut pubic hair?' He reprimanded himself for this uncharacteristic burst of spleen. He knew he was lucky to be exempt from jealousy. 'And no,' he thought smiling to himself when by the end of the millennium everyone was racing to the dhobi ghat to wash their dirty linen in public, 'I'm not like Mountbatten.' He referred to the assumption that the last viceroy must be homosexual because he didn't have jealous tantrums at his lady wife's allegedly wild love life, including her affair, platonic or otherwise, with Pandit Jawaharlal Nehru. Jack couldn't remember if the insinuations included Lord Mountbatten himself being in love with Nehru, in which case he ought at least to have been jealous of Edwina for having smitten the one he was smitten by … Yet he seemed to have expressed only true warmth and friendship for the ever-so-romantic Nehru, providing no hint of the sexual leanings suspected by the Freud-seekers.

Mountbatten came to a sticky end, an extremely sticky end, but that was caused by an outside agency unconnected, to-date, to Freudian patterns. So, blessedly, Jack Strachey was absolved of the endless pain his wife should normally have caused him. In retrospect he would classify these rare mental outbursts as spiteful objectivity rather than anything baser. And never would he express these thoughts out loud. But he recognized he was lucky not to suffer from jealousy.

At fifty, Myrna still continued with her curvets. She still had a slender figure, though it was getting harder and harder to trim the thickening waist. Her last affair had bored her and for the first time she asked herself the question, 'Why do I do it?' And then she corrected herself, 'Why do I have to do it?' But she couldn't get beyond the simple question. She couldn't ask if it was an inherent urge to power or pure sensuality, and the corollary that no one and nothing should stand in the way of its impulses. The more she continued, the more compulsive were those impulses, all the classic signs of an addiction. She would continue her aberrant behaviour, a pure hedonist one moment, a loving wife the next, like a yo-yo in a typhoon, up, down, whirling, out of control, but attached with that string to Jack's strong finger.

The first turning point was when the British Raj was taken over by the historical compulsions of an ancient and humiliated people. When the transformation had been heralded by an unprecedented year's carnage, abruptly ending on the eve of Independence, 'a miracle' as Chief Minister Hasan Surhawardy had whispered to the fasting Gandhi. When death and deepest degradation had raged in and around Calcutta during the Great Famine four years earlier. When a flood of refugees had poured across the new partition line between the two halves of the country. As if the terrible reluctance of the colonial power in withdrawing had left as its reaction, a vacuum so fierce it had sucked in the world around it, whipping itself around and around into the spiral of a potent tornado. And yet, researchers would be dejected to find so little in the personal records of the Rajmahal tenants and their ilk to reflect those cataclysmic events. They would eagerly scan the pages of the dusty, browned diaries of the Stracheys flipping to 15 August 1947 and finding nothing out of the ordinary. Nothing to reflect the banner headlines screaming INDEPENDENCE!! FREEDOM!!! in the newspapers.

'But they weren't official chroniclers,' you may say, 'or self-conscious celebrities hoping their private papers would one day be published.' For instance, Myrna Strachey's diary said 'Coffee party, 11.00 a.m. Lady Bannerjea' 14 August, and it also said, 'Dinner, Roys, 8.00 p.m.' Was that dinner party organized specially to usher in Independence? At midnight Pandit Nehru was to hoist the flag in salute to that long-awaited day. Did the Roys, who were the hosts that night, wait with the string of the furled new flag in their hands, radio on, for the signal to pull that string? And did the Indian guests go crazy, their tears dropping with the flower petals from the unfurling flag? But then, why wasn't it mentioned in their diaries? They would have to be content with the records of the great, such as Pandit Nehru, whose pocket diary said 'The appointed day!' Pandit Nehru must have known his destiny and that the diary would be eagerly scanned by future generations. But, whether noted or not in their diaries, the Stracheys must have recognized that the changes had to come. That the tortuously built-up bastions on which their empire had rested couldn't bolster the new India forever. The changes would take place gradually but necessarily, for now the incumbents of Writers' Building had brown skins, wore dhuties, with the reverse sartorial snobbery, and spoke a language which had remained a mystery to their British predecessors, allowing the healthful self-respect to flow back into the enervated Indian body politic. The changes would slowly impinge on the Stracheys and alter the texture of their lives in ways they hadn't foreseen when they had made their choice. That day, 15 August 1947, most of the Rajmahal tenants must have gone out on the streets to taste the air rich with the resonance of crowds, jammed into trucks, waving from tricolour-draped balconies, chanting 'Jai Hind!' The Stracheys hung no tricolour from their balcony. But they leaned out and waved and smiled at their friends and the crowds, joining in with the 'Jai Hinds', jostling unknowingly with the merry ghosts. And when the joyous temple bell rang and conch shells blew, the Stracheys even felt a thrill, perhaps mixed with their first inklings of discomfort.

❦

Long after Independence, when Jack was poised for the final push to become chairman and managing director, he was pipped at the post, as loyal friends put it, by a man who didn't deserve a clerk's job, a covertly apartheid remark. The culprit was a brilliant Indian, backed by the newly powerful Indian lobby with strong nudgings from the government. 'I'll have to resign,' Jack declared impulsively. But he pulled up short when friends alerted him, 'They'll think you object to working under an Indian.' Jack didn't admit this was another sticking point. That year, the presidentship of the Bengal Chamber was also given to Jack's rival.

Independence had knocked down one of the British Raj's bastions as it was doing everywhere. The chamber was to decline gradually and lose its pre-eminent position. Sharp and Co. dwindled after being dogged by scandal and with the government squeezing it through new laws. The British knew their time was up, and Jack Strachey's pipping was accepted with resignation by the beleaguered community. He toyed briefly with the idea of joining one of the big Indian business houses, but the thought to him was in the end nonsensical.

After all the lost chances Jack Strachey became introverted and his adoration for Myrna intensified, part of a new siege mentality. Myrna's remorse grew. 'It's time,' she said. She didn't articulate to herself that the arrival of menopause was the pushing factor. 'It's time I looked after Jack,' she said righteously. This was made easier by Jack's gentle nature and perennial good looks. While most of her other men friends had become ugly and cantankerous, here was her Jack, as impressive as ever. 'How could I have had the heart?' she wondered. 'How could I?' The regret grew and then faded with time. Now that Myrna was in extreme old age her faculties were sharply reduced and such niceties non-existent. She was instead wedged on top of a mountain of resentment which translated into a general vengefulness. She bragged endlessly about her beauty and her betrayals, as if there had been no choice. 'How could I not?' she said now. She was convinced she had some legendary role to play in the sexuality which writhed like a hidden turbulence under Calcutta's surface. This is what she thought that day looking at Jack leaning on the rail of their verandah, presenting his rugged octogenarian profile to the South breeze muggy with unshed rain. 'I know,' she thought. 'But what could I do?' The ghosts were pensive. After all these years they had acquired the same feelings of concern and protectiveness towards the 'mlechchas' that they felt towards all the tenants, including by now the Muslim landlord and his family. And the Rajmahal kept as calm as it could, recognizing that it could do nothing while Myrna's ageing reached an extreme of disharmony.

Kuldip Chopra was the high flyer who did Jack Strachey out of the chairmanship of Sharp's. This was the second turning point. Jack, though steady, just, and steely, was without brilliance, as everyone at Sharp's regretfully noted. Regretfully, because he was popular and respected. But with Independence, the bosses, though still British, had to show their bona fides to the independent Indian government, and discrimination had to be seen as ended. Getting their own to come out to India was a vanishing option, and Indianization was unavoidable. So when the brilliant, flamboyant Kuldip Chopra created ripples, there was already a buzzing in the wings that if anyone was to signify the new order, it had to be him. Kuldip had shocked his white colleagues when he had first strolled into their offices, coolly plucked cigars from their humidors, sat back and hiked his well-shod feet on to their desks. Before Independence. But this didn't stop him from taking the company surging forward with inspired management. Until that stage, very few Indians had been accepted into the covenanted ranks, and Kuldip was one of those few. He had a genuine pukka accent after a long education at Harrow and Oxford, a fine dress sense, and a sophisticated wife and living style, easily equalling his most fastidious British associates. Jack was a grammar school boy and had trained at Dundee for the jute mill floor and factory management, risen 'from the ranks'.

Myrna was gnawing her nails and pouring herself too many whiskies on the expected day when the phone rang. She snatched at it eagerly, thinking, 'He's lost it, I'm sure he's lost it.' She could feel her energy draining out while she listened to Jack's laborious words. The ghosts were listening in too, eagerly, and they sighed collectively when they heard the news. 'So it's him after all, Kuldip Chopra!' she exclaimed when he came home. Jack's mind lurched and he wondered for a nightmarish second if Kuldip had been one of her lovers. His eye met Myrna's at the same moment and realizing what was going through his mind, she shook her head slightly, the first such acknowledgement between them. This was when the bell finally tolled for her illicit affairs. Her heart went out to Jack, the predictable, unpretentious husband, her life's stable rock, so crushed by this blow. Indian policies and politics had to be transformed at this time of all times, just when it would hurt him most!

'At least he won't be knighted,' said Jack.

'He can't be,' said Myrna, her small triumph being that Kuldip was the loser somewhere for not being British.

Kuldip Chopra became president of the Bengal Chamber later, a position that was no more the preserve of the British.

Then what, one might wonder, made Jack Strachey stay on? Was the ignominy of losing to the outstanding Kuldip Chopra, of not being knighted, of seeing his wife's ex-lovers flitting around him till the end of his life, of living among subject people cocky with freedom, not enough to drive him away, join at least one of the later streams of returning Britons? And if the attractions of staying on, ineffable or otherwise, had been so overwhelming, why was it that most other Britons thought and decided otherwise? Demographers, sociologists, psychoanalysts, historians, political scientists may have come to the conclusion that this was the inevitable pattern when colonialism was ending, when, usually, the approaching end of an alien rule braked the ruling expatriates' ideas of putting down roots, turned their eyes homeward.

It is difficult to say, except that going back unbearably depressed Jack. Not even the attraction of Martin's nearness could turn that depression around. Underlying this choice was the memory of that cold, grey Skiddaw world, the formal distance between people in that small space. Here, there were all the other advantages, the automatic assumptions of the-ones-who-had-ruled, and the infinite and tender arrangements for leisure. And his commonsense told him that in spite of the grumblings of other expats, they were still well-off, and life would still remain 'good'. As for the Indians being cocky, Jack knew his Indians. Kuldip Chopra would always behave decently with him, and a subtle superiority still clung to the expats as long as they had money. He convinced himself Calcutta society inherently knew an injustice had been done to him. How could he face the idea of Kuldip Chopra being the better choice?

❦

When the Stracheys' son, Martin, came back to Calcutta with his bride, Proshanto Mojumdar, the first floor tenant snatched at the excuse to indulge in his favourite pastime, hosting an entertainment. 'We shall go to the theatre!' he enthused. 'And then to the *300*!'

Martin's bride, Gwendolyn, was a scholar of European music, a subject far removed from his own. He was an academic too, specialized in nineteenth century British colonial history with Calcutta as his focus. Martin, who was more than normally promiscuous, had been Surjeet Shona's lover for a while. But this affair had been too zippy and had all but zipped out of his mind. Occasional visions of their intimacy sometimes came into his memory, but divested of feeling. Gwendolyn had knocked Surjeet Shona and everyone else off his mind, and they were too lost in a blinding meeting of bodies to worry about minds. She was just the intellectual, yet passionate, blue stocking he had always wanted to marry. However, a shortcoming Martin hadn't anticipated was her antagonism to India. The signs were visible on the drive in from the airport. Gwendolyn was a petite blonde, her long hair plaited and wound around her head, a delicate Renaissance painting, but churlish. As they headed for the city, her lips clamped together tighter and tighter, till they became a thin sealed line. Martin did his best to distract her with hurried chatter. But he couldn't block her view of a naked boy selling newspapers on the roadside. He groaned when Gwen unstuck her lips and hysterically stopped the car. Before he could think, he found himself helping her buy a cheap set of clothes at a nearby stall. She raced back flushed with her deed and presented the clothes to the astonished boy. A crowd immediately collected. Gwen, reeling with shock when she saw a pair of young men blithely holding hands, plunged back into the car. The young men peered through the car windows and planted their fingerprints on the panes, scattering when the chauffeur shooed them away. When one of them scratched his private parts, Gwen shivered, already down with mental malaria. Martin's lips were tightly clamped now, but to dam up the laughter. He said nothing when the shirt was hauled off the little boy to the amusement of the victim. Just as he didn't point out that being naked, even because of poverty, was pleasanter in the heat than being burdened with sticky clothes. Or that the young hand-holding men weren't homosexuals. Or that in India, when you itched you scratched ... What was the use, he groaned, of trying to remind her of their jointly mocking at white missionaries for clothing, civilizing and Christianizing 'naked savages'. 'They are savages!' hissed Gwendolyn, startling him.

Proshanto Mojumdar asked Martin to make a choice of entertainment, a regrettable move, he felt, because Martin lighted on *Neel Dorpon*, a historic and controversial play, unflattering to the British. He suggested safer alternatives. 'Your wife is new to this country,' he pleaded, 'she may find it embarrassing ...'

'Why? It's history ...'

'But nevertheless, do you not think we should try something lighter, *The Pirates of Penzance* at the New Empire, for instance?'

'*The Pirates of Penz* ...!' Martin was outraged. '*The Pirates of Penzance*! Come on, Pro. This is India!'

'No, but seriously ...'

'But I am being serious. Don't you understand? *Neel Dorpon*'s from my area of specialization, nineteenth century colonial Bengal. I never dreamed I'd get a chance to see it. And Reema Devi's acting at the Petrovs' own theatre! It's too exciting.' He spoke of their neighbouring tenant, the Russian, Anatoly Sergeivich Petrov, who was married to the celebrated actress of the Bengali stage, Reema Devi. The ghosts were excited. 'I wish I could see it too,' enthused a grandmother ghost from the Sheetanath family. 'I remember what an uproar it caused when it was launched! In the early days of our wonderful theatre ...'

'These Bengalis are always showing off about literature and drama and art!' said the tart Sikh. 'As if they are the only ones who are cultured! What do they know of a good robust Heer, or a manly bhangra. Hunh!'

Finally, Proshanto Mojumdar gave in. 'Very well,' he said glumly. 'The evening is in honour of your bride, and it is, after all, your choice.'

Martin was being partly dishonest. *Neel Dorpon* per se wasn't as exciting to him as testing his bride's reactions, and, even more exciting, indulging in the erotic prospect of teasing her. His mischievous intellect at work. 'It must provoke her, one way or the other,' he thought.

Neel Dorpon, in its English version, was brilliantly done and the audience watched Reema Devi's rendition with hushed awe. Reema Devi Petrov was in her fifties, yet as the young victim of rape her bulky body was transformed in effortless illusion. Her small, mysterious smile, hardly visible to the audience, seemed enlarged by a non-existent projector on to a non-existent screen, and each member of the mesmerized audience felt its quality. When the dastardly English planter, played with a combination of bombast and lasciviousness, threatened to rape her, the laboured breathing of the audience turned the hall steamy.

'To speak to me is like throwing pearls before swine!' spewed the planter, convulsed with laughter and brutally flailing the victim of his lust with a whip. 'We indigo planters are the companions of death! We can beat ten women with the Ramakant!'

While the swooning Reema Devi – the victim – lay face down awaiting the lashing leather thongs of the 'Ramakant', Martin felt his arm gripped by Petrov, at the very moment the would-be rapist shouted, dropped his whip and fell. The cause was a black shoe which had gone arcing through the air to strike him on the head with an audible clunk. The audience roared, and Martin, jerked out of his trance, said to Petrov, 'My God, they'll lynch him!' But the lights came on, the curtain dropped and the roar diminished as suddenly to a loud murmur. Petrov had vanished and Martin turned to find Gwen glowering at him.

'How can you sit and watch this, this …!' She couldn't finish her hissing sentence and turned towards poor Proshanto Mojumdar. Brilliantly and smoothly, Martin hustled her out of her seat. Every time she turned to him to speak, he silenced her by urging her forward. As the Rajmahal party inched its way out, it caught the announcement that the play was indefinitely postponed. Planter Rogue had suffered an injury to his person which had caused 'concussion and incapacitation'.

Proshanto Mojumdar squirmed at this post-Independence rudeness to his British guests, so abhorrent to his exaggerated notions of politeness. Though it was only a few weeks earlier that he had helped break the 'whites only' taboo of a swimming club, his sensitivity was far from contradictory. At the swimming club it had been the righting of an anachronism, when racism (surely the very anti-thesis of politeness!) was supposedly justified in the context of ruler and ruled. When 'natives' weren't allowed into the exclusive pool of the whites. ('Did they think our colour would come off and stain their pool? What about sharing the water with people who only use bathroom paper ...! Chichi!' the minister who led the party had said.) Once the ruler had left, the racism lay exposed and had to be excised. It was the racism, which had been 'impolite'. But this in no way justified his, Proshanto Mojumdar's, reverse impoliteness to members of the offending race who were here as his guests, when most of that had been put away in the past.

It was later that Petrov, who had gone backstage, would tell them of the ironic parallels between this incident and the happenings at the first staging of *Neel Dorpon* nearly a century ago. That during the rape scene, a shoe had been thrown at the offender, it is said by the great Vidyasagar, to opposite effect, because the flattered actor, unhurt, had taken a bow! The incident is a legend in Calcutta theatre circles.

'Poor Pro!' exclaimed Martin in the privacy of the Strachey limousine. 'What a disaster!'

Gwen's rage simmered down to a squeaky indignation and she suggested boycotting Proshanto Mojumdar's party.

'Oh come!' protested Martin. 'You'll break old Pro's heart. Besides you must go to the *300* at least once before it folds up.'

'Of course she must!' enthused Myrna, who couldn't bear to miss a party. 'The *300*'s such fun!'

'Is it?' said Jack.

The play had left him dejected, adding to the weight of a sadness he didn't want to analyse. Every dismal event sharpened his sense of failure, shrinking his ego, leaving him only with the natural aversion to letting go.

Martin hadn't given up. He planned to persist with Gwen's indoctrination. Tonight he would tell her of the Jallianwala Bagh massacre, when the odious Dyer had ordered his men to fire mercilessly on an unarmed and cornered Indian crowd, killing hundreds. He would tell her of the same Dyer who had ordered that Indians would be whipped unless they crawled on their stomachs when they were in a particular lane, because an English woman had been attacked in it. Martin would then take her to dine at the Bengal Club, just up the road from the Rajmahal. There, he would point out the entrance gates which the British women of Calcutta had picketed in 1919, demanding a collection for the disgraced Dyer. And then he would point out the valuable paintings in the club, its history of the colour bar, and finally soothe her with the magnificent Anglo-Bengali smoked hilsa fish. He wondered if her intellect would allow her to accept what he told her and she would get her balance back, or if she would get squeakily indignant again. His erotic fancies were aroused by thoughts of provoking his petite intellectual.

At the *300*, Myrna almost fell in love with Proshanto Mojumdar as he swept her on to the dance floor and surpassed himself, pressing his right hand firmly into the small of her back and holding her hand high with his left, fox-trotting and quick stepping with authority, sideways, backwards, swaying and gliding, waggling his backside for the rumba or twitching his shoulders for the cha-cha-cha. It was a good thing they would dance less and less frequently. Who could imagine them replacing these structured dances with the grinding of the grunge generations? This was one of the last times the Stracheys would visit the *300*. The Russian couple who had contributed to its special quality had already left, and the *300* was to follow Martin's prophecy and fold up. That night, in spite of Proshanto and Myrna's wonderful exhibition on the dance floor, the

Rajmahal party stayed sombre, and the characteristic gaiety of the club went missing.

❧

Martin could see his dream of staying on in Calcutta receding. After his persistent and desperate attempts, he recognized the futility of persuading Gwen. 'Lucky Petrov,' he thought, filled with a genuine and deep envy, and he often sought the Russian's company.

'You don't miss Russia, Europe, the language, the people ...?'

'I have been on visits,' said Petrov. 'What is there to miss?'

'Do you still think in Russian?'

'No, no,' Petrov shook his head. 'I realized some time ago that I now think in English, and sometimes Bengali. Very rarely in Russian!'

'What about the food, the culture ...?'

'I adore Bengali food. And I can have Russian food in a restaurant here. I can see European theatre, admittedly only occasionally. Listen to European music ... In fact, I am planning to go to a film on New Year's Eve. I do not usually go to films, but this one is a must. It is a film on the life of Glinka, the Russian opera composer. Well? Interested?'

'Glinka!' said Martin. 'Well. I shall certainly mention it to Gwen. Her field's music, and she's sure to have heard of, er, Glinka. As long as it's nothing to do with India!'

'You will be going to an Indian picture hall,' warned Petrov. 'More correctly a Calcutta picture hall! On New Year's Eve!'

'Oh yes!' said Gwen when Martin broached the subject to her. 'Glinka's a particular favourite of mine!'

'Mother, Father,' called Martin unbelievingly. 'Have you ever heard of Glinka?'

'I've heard him mentioned,' said Myrna vaguely. 'But we'll go to Prince's after the film, dear.'

At 11.00 p.m. on New Year's Eve, the Petrovs and Stracheys walked into the Globe to watch *Glinka*.

The hall was abuzz with an unnaturally excited chattering and a raffish element had occupied the cheap seats in the stalls, closest to the screen. The Rajmahal party sat upstairs in the plush Royal Circle. In spite of the cool Calcutta winter, it was stuffy in the hall without air conditioning, and the raffish element had divested itself of its shirts, which hung limply on the proscenium. 'What interest can they possibly have in Glinka?' wondered Martin. He saw his father nudging his mother and heard him whisper, 'Can you imagine them when the singing starts? What will we do with our Gwen? Shall we leave?' And he was delighted when Myrna whispered back, 'No no. Let's watch the fun.'

Inspired by this remark Martin applied his diversionary tactics to Gwen again, murmuring to her and nibbling her ear. 'It's our last night here, after all. She owes it to me,' he thought.

Gwen woke up when the first cracker burst against the screen with a greenish spark, bang! followed by a cheer from below. There was a hush when the film began. But it was clear this would be no ordinary viewing. Half an hour into the film, myriad little paper crackers were exploding and sparking against the screen while the actors went through an inaudible mime. The mob downstairs wildly imitated the arias, and when there was any suggestion of a kiss they erupted with smooching noises and pranced joyfully in the aisles. Plucking their shirts off and swinging them about their heads, they continued to fling endless salvos of paper crackers with inspired frenzy at opera stars, amorous couples and the miraculously unharmed screen. Petrov shot out a swear word and Martin turned to him with his face split in a grin. In the end, the Rajmahal group was shaking with collective laughter. They watched the pale magnified figures on the screen and the thin dark Bengalis writhing in the pit below. 'I'll send you some Glinka records from London,' shouted Gwen to Petrov. 'You can listen to him at home!' 'Yes, let's go to Prince's,' said Myrna quickly. 'It's New Year's Eve! Come on!' They left their second aborted theatrical entertainment in a month, and crossed the street over a carpet of expended paper crackers. Just outside the Grand Hotel and Prince's, above the sounds of merriment, they heard the ships' sirens hooting as the year turned. Martin swung the car on to the edge of the Maidaan and they all got out inhaling the smoky, chilly air. Then they stepped on to the grass, crossed hands and moved slowly around in a circle singing *Auld Lang Syne*.

❧

'Penny for your thoughts, Jack Strachey,' said the very old and India-haggard Myrna, joining her husband on the verandah balcony.

'None,' promptly. 'I have none at the moment.'

The only secrets Jack had from Myrna were *her* secrets, *her* affairs, the knowledge of which he had always kept hidden from her. He guessed at most of them, wondered how far she went, and stopped worrying. He knew she must come around, some day. Confronting her, giving her ultimatums, all that was never an option. Myrna knew he knew. She also knew, deep down, that he could never betray her. Why did she deserve such devotion? she often paused to wonder. Straying was so zealously surveyed and expected in their society.

Away from it all at this age, her nagging drowned such considerations.

'Why?' she said, pulling at Jack's arm. 'Why should you have no thoughts?'

'Petrov, it's Petrov who's inspiring me. He's teaching me meditation. You have to stop thinking, that's what he says.'

'It isn't that, of course it isn't!' Myrna Strachey, nowhere near as gentle-minded as her husband, still fretted at the loss of the Sharp's chairmanship and its follow-up of honours. 'Sir John and Lady Strachey!' Not to be, not to be …

'We should have gone home of course, left this ungrateful country and this, this puerile city and gone back to our proper places. We can still go home. You never talk of going home any more!' Myrna's high-pitched voice was a direct contrast to her stately body. 'Her voice …!' Jack quickly disciplined himself against blasphemous thoughts.

'I thought you liked Calcutta …'

Myrna catered to the common view of their peers that India, and Calcutta, of all things, couldn't possibly hold a candle to the imaginary Britain with a big ballooning 'B'.

Jack half listened to her and mentally listed the plus points of their staying on. The Rajmahal with its congenial tenants, the luxury of servants, the friendly Indians, the blissful Royal Calcutta Golf Club and the Tolly, with grounds more reminiscent of English country estates than the paddy fields, fish ponds and banana groves typical of Bengal. Top-notch partying with industrialists, diplomats, the governor of West Bengal who continued to include them on his guest list. The races, where they preened with maharajas. The air conditioning and the annual sojourn in the hills to combat the hiatus of the hot weather. And the verandah views of the ceaseless activity of the Maidaan, the cricketers, the yogis and ear cleaners, the Jain monks feeding ants early in the morning. Distanced from the people, yet in touch through the Maidaan's spectacular rallies. Monsoon rains cascading and sweeping over green, ghostly tree forms through wind-blown mists.

But friends dropped off as the Stracheys lost their glamour. Martin visited them less and less, discouraged by a wife hostile to India and his parents. Then there was Petrov-across-the-landing, turning peculiar, and Proshanto Mojumdar, dozing off in the middle of his scatty chatter.

'It's the tropical climate.' Myrna complained. 'Brains get addled.'

The Stracheys no longer holidayed in Britain. How could they understand that ageing and its refinements were universal?

Jack was urged by many to write his memoirs. He was a prime witness to the loosening and final removal of the jewel from the British crown. But the Great Famine and Great Killing, most of all the Raj's abdication, its indifference to these major disasters, with first its priority to the war and then the immensity of its impending colonial finis, took Jack through trances of disbelief and shame. This reaction he camouflaged, then forgot and raking up its memory was too painful to encourage the writing of memoirs. The rest of the tale, too, was full of dubious merit. Jack Strachey saw, as India and Indians became more and more his, that though it was a tale worth telling if honestly told, he couldn't bring himself to do it.

It was easier to poke fun at quaint Indianisms, to decry the persistence of the poverty and illiteracy of Indians, the corruption, in which he was enthusiastically echoed by his Indian friends. He couldn't resist the assumption of a distance and superiority without any reference to the British role and responsibility even so soon after the break.

His work had helped him carry on, and he had been spared from direct attacks on his conscience when Indians died in their millions from starvation and in their thousands from violence for reasons beyond his wish to comprehend.

The Stracheys were already in the Rajmahal when the Great Famine hit. The gross reality had been right there, in front of their eyes, under their feet, surrounding them. But it was impossible to pull out of the inertia imposed on them by their origins. Before going into Firpos one evening, they had come across a scattering of skeletal bodies on the pavement. Jack had swerved to avoid a comatose woman while an emaciated child tugged at the breasts flapping over her ribs. He had turned sharply to see if Myrna had noticed and saw her face set resolutely towards the brilliant lights of Firpos. Taking her by the elbow he had walked her up into the palatial Italian restaurant where he had cleared his mind of this scene with a stiff drink.

During the Great Killing, after Direct Action Day, when Hindus and Muslims were blasting each other with bombs, and hacking and sawing at each other like mad butchers in a slaughter house, Jack had been caught behind the office district and would never forget the wracked bodies and faces of terror. But, like the mems of the jute mill compounds, he had stared steadfastly at the back of his chauffeur's neck and urged him to drive away.

He once caught a glimpse of Mahatma Gandhi addressing a vast crowd on the Maidaan. The Mahatma was sitting on a dais surrounded by the Indian leaders of the time. He was at a great distance, but Jack focused on him through his binoculars and imagined he could feel the Mahatma's power. The little shrivelled man was to receive a bullet in his heart a few years later to slump gently over into eternal rest after his hectic sad life.

And there were the times the distance dropped away, bringing unsettling close encounters. The time after some disturbance involving white sailors misbehaving with local women, when Jack had been hauled from his car to chants of 'Shala white monkey! Ba'dor! Shala!' jostled and made to kneel on the pavement, till Proshanto Mojumdar, his neighbour, had rescued him. Proshanto himself had been threatened because he was fair-skinned and wore a tie. But he had soon pacified the crowd when he spoke in his native Bengali, and they were spared after their ties had been yanked off, stomped on and spat at. That ties had little to do with sailors was not the point.

He sent Myrna and Martin away to England at the time of the killings, but they had come back in two months when it was clear the killings would go on and on, off and on, as they had done for an eternity. Yet, like the famine, the mayhem all around had hardly impinged on the Stracheys' domestic front. In the Rajmahal, nothing was felt of the terrible wounding in the body of the foetal country nearing the end of its gestation. Just as she was to be far removed from the savagery between Hindus and Muslims on the western border, Myrna scarcely witnessed anything out of the ordinary right here in Calcutta or knew much of what was happening in Noakhali in the same province she lived in. Even when Gandhiji arrived to exhort the mad populace with his toothless heart-wrenching whispered utterances.

❧

Jack watched Calcutta shifting gears repeatedly till it lost its industrial supremacy, and the flight of capital created a vacuum in the city. A city which had all but forgotten its glory days as the second city of Empire and the capital of British India, but which continued with its seductive club life. At eighty Jack still, though less and less, limped around the greens at the Royal with his clubs, or visited the stables of the Tolly to look at the horses.

Both the Stracheys were lovers of 'curry' and when the clubs were taken over by Indians, the insidious difference in the food provoked an indulgent nose-wrinkling by the British. But really, they couldn't resist a good curry, and Jack Strachey's face broke out in a heavy sweat and turned slowly red as he bit pleasurably into the spicy mouthfuls. The Stracheys had only westernized local friends, and hadn't explored the intricacies of Bengali cuisine, which no restaurant served in those days. But the hybrid developed during the British Raj, epitomized by the skills of the Chittagong Mog cooks, smoked Hilsa fish, 'cock-up' in tartar sauce, prawns baked inside tender coconut and a version of lobster thermidor, not to speak of caramel fruit baskets, soufflés and gateaux, made for intensely pleasurable eating. And they were among the few privileged still with a Chittagong Mog cook.

Jack Strachey sank sometimes into nostalgic memories, of Lys and Lyn shimmying on Maxim's floor, of Angelo Firpo charming his way from table to table, kissing ladies' fingers, of the band led by the romantic Francesco Casanova. The Blue Bell girls would never again dance at Prince's and Scherezade, and the choicest hors d'oeuvres and ice creams of Firpos had become a legend like the defunct restaurant. There was a gradual narrowing down and loss as the international quality deteriorated, then dwindled, till the last tawdry belly dancer from Australia performed in a restaurant on Park Street. The razzle dazzle of a city set up as a trading post by Job Charnock with Armenian, Jewish, Persian and Chinese settlers, attracting a top-dressing of international buccaneers, apart from missionaries, civil servants and boxwallahs, was to go through a ravaging yet revitalizing transition. Calcutta had to grow out of its rumbustious past to redeem itself. And the denizens of the erstwhile 'black township', the 'natives' of those days had this responsibility.

Myrna looked back too, but chiefly at her conquests. Her first lover after their shift to Calcutta, for the brief period of two weeks, had been a newcomer at Sharp's, a mere boy. Myrna couldn't resist his limpid brown eyes and dark hair, though the boy was ten years her junior. He came from a robust middle-class Punjabi family. 'Oye, Oye,' he thought to himself. 'Who is this firangi stunner?' The ghosts, still to learn about Myrna's weakness, held their breaths, wondering what this 'mlechcha' would be up to. Before long, Myrna was driving frequently to the young Punjabi's small flat and the Swadeshi ghost was congratulating itself, 'See? I told you!' 'What?' said the tart Sikh. 'Have you forgotten the scandal of your Indrani ...?' The Swadeshi ghost subsided, but Myrna's behaviour continued to thrill and shock the ghosts. The Punjabi retired and settled in Delhi, and was in his sixties when last seen, unrecognizably coarsened, with a thick scarred face and paunch, his liquid eyes sunk into fat, his dark hair gone.

The British were plagued by the devaluation of the rupee, and only a few of them still thought it worth their while to continue in India. Jack Strachey regularly discussed and kept up with developments, but his mind was made up. The city was now his city for the rest of his life, as much as any Bengali's, and his body, when lifeless, would be given to its soil. Sharp's had vanished, an unimaginable development, and he was saddened to see the decline in local industry.

And now old age claimed the prime attention of this couple. Both were completely white haired and though Myrna used corsets in cooler weather and they tried to keep themselves trim by walking briskly on the Maidaan and golf course, they couldn't hide the facts that their bodies and faces had thickened, their hair had thinned, and they found it more and more difficult to negotiate the stairs.

The progressive mental decline of their friends had a poignant effect on Myrna, and she worried incessantly she would go the same way.

'What if I don't know, if I don't realize it?' she asked Jack that day, after they had decided yet again not to return to England. 'What if I get senile, how will I know?'

Jack decided to face her questions. Myrna had that effect on him. When she persisted with something he, who took her every utterance so much to heart, was quickly convinced. He remembered the Wentworths in their crumbling house on Lansdowne Road. The house had been under endless litigation, and the neighbouring guards had had to chase away the landlord's thugs when they had tried to create a disturbance. The litigation had reduced the Wentworths to a state of penury and they had only one erratic servant. When he stopped coming, the Wentworths didn't eat but drank endless cups of tea. When that was beyond them, one of them would totter across the street to a tea shop in the wall and fill up an old kettle with steaming, milky tea, pick up a spicy samosa or two in tendu-leaf containers. And magically, there had always been alcohol in some form, devolving from rare scotches in their heyday to Indian whiskies, gin, vodka, beer, country liquor, and finally to poisonous concoctions which almost turned them blind and certainly speeded up their end. The building had become decrepit and dangerous and they had moved out into the garden permanently, taking shelter in an abandoned outhouse. The British community, including Jack Strachey, had tried to help through the Society for the Aged run for Anglo-Indians. But Mrs Wentworth had driven them away, screeching at them in her own version of Hindi, and brandishing her stick at them. The Wentworths had died, half-starved, filthy, their bodies dropsical and barely clothed, not a possession to call their own, except the rusted kettle and kerosene stove in the kitchen. Their servant had made off with whatever little of value lay in the house, the litigation was at a standstill, and the landlord, patiently waiting, reclaimed his property and completed the demolition of the building.

No one knew or remembered if the Wentworths had children and, if so, why they hadn't come forward.

Seeing Martin's impossible distance, Jack Strachey realized the fragility of their state. And here was Myrna, possessed, impossibly abrasive. He fought the certainty that this was the very thing she dreaded.

It was just after the monsoons. The air was pleasantly cool with stirrings of the South breeze, which made the verandah such a blessing. 'What if I get senile without *knowing* it?' said Myrna, again.

'Why should you?'

'Have you forgotten the Wentworths?'

Jack winced at this evidence of their coinciding thoughts.

'I must write to Martin,' he said, trying to steer the conversation away.

'Martin! As if he'll do anything! It's because of you that Martin is what he is! How can you let him treat us like this?'

Jack turned from the balcony and limped to the sofa, nursing a sore knee.

'What could I do?' he protested feebly. 'He *did* ask us to come to London, to live with him. It's we who refused. You know that!'

Myrna followed him obsessively to the sofa. 'He *knew* we wouldn't come! Can you imagine Gwen accepting us? What's more, you *knew* he knew!'

'What's that dear? You're confusing me!' Jack tried facetiousness as another escape.

'Martin asked us because he *knew* we wouldn't come.'

Jack thought how her vocabulary limited itself once an idea took root. 'Soon, she'll be reduced to one word which she'll repeat endlessly, like duckspeak.' He lost himself in a game where he settled on a word and imagined her repeating it in all its versions. 'Know, knew, knowing, will know, did know, must know, quack, quack, quack …' Downstairs, the lobby guard stretched his limbs before coming on duty. He heard Myrna's fearful voice through the sounds of the traffic. 'Poor Strachey saheb.' His breast filled with pity.

'Well, at least you're still clear enough to make such statements, dear!' Jack's voice trembled.

'You should have given Martin *some* of your money,' Myrna went on relentlessly. 'You haven't given him *any* yet! He has to have *some* money to face that Gwen! Money gives you confidence!' Their daughter-in-law was a subject Myrna always alighted on with verve. 'No wonder he's so disappointed in you. He's just hiding his disappointment, wondering where all your money went …'

'Money, money, money,' Jack hummed, and thought, 'I cannot pass on any of our assets or give power of attorney over any of my affairs to Martin. How can I take the risk? And who knows what Gwen might get up to?'

'Time enough for Martin to enjoy our money once we're gone,' he muttered. And he added in sudden fear. 'We have each other, don't we my darling?'

He looked at his beloved wife, at her lined face with the heavy jowls, the wrinkle nest around her eyes, the carefully blue-tinted hair held in place by a fine net. He looked over her once exquisite body, the stiff waist encased in its corset, the hard-looking well-bound breasts which had long ago lost their natural shape, the blue-veined legs. A thought took shape in his head.

'*Qui hai*,' he called out in Hobson-Jobson, and added, 'we must get that bell repaired.' He went on calling, his voice getting louder and louder, mingling with Myrna's shrill calls. Their old bearer, Abdul, came in.

'Where were you Abdal?' Myrna scolded. 'Have you gone deaf? Or were you loitering in the *bobachee connah* instead of laying the table? Go on! Answer me! Are you deaf?'

'Enough,' Jack murmured. 'That's enough, dear. Abdal's here.' Carrying on before Myrna could interrupt, 'Abdal,' to this toothless old man with the round eye glasses, 'two whisky – *bilayatee-pawnees* please. Doubles. And tell *consommah* to give us our supper half an hour later today.'

'Yes huzoor,' Abdul cackled, a lately acquired nervous habit. 'I get whisky-soda.' He cackled again, showing red paan-stained gums.

'You've been eating betel again,' scolded Jack mildly. 'And tell ayah to come. Bring memsahib mora for feet and give massage. Wouldn't you like that, darling?'

'What? What was that?'

'A massage. For your feet, and a nice whisky!' He put his arm on Myrna's back and stroked it. 'Ayah's coming to massage your feet with a little powder. You'll like that, won't you?'

The ayah came in. A wizened little Bengali woman in a plain white sari. Her head, though covered by the sari, was clearly cropped. A widow following the orthodox Bengali tradition, shaving her head, giving up meat, and wearing white. Initially the ayah had discarded the wearing of blouses too, thus sometimes inadvertently exposing a shrivelled breast, like a famine case out of '43. Myrna had firmly opposed this. Now the ayah sat demurely bloused, next to her memsahib's feet, which were stretched out on a cane stool. She took them in her lap one by one and massaged them with talcum powder dabbed on with an enormous puff. There were little cries from Myrna when a tender spot was touched.

Abdul came in with the whiskies on a silver tray, and deposited them by his masters.

'Remember *lawl shrub*? And evening time *hugger*?' Jack said to Abdul. 'Lawl shrub' the Anglo-Indian for 'laal sharaab', red wine, and 'hugger' the Hindi hukkaa, hubble bubble. 'Remember?'

'Of course, huzoor. How I can forget? So nice, huzoor, in British time. Everything gone now'day'. No good …'

'Yes, yes. Quite. But at least you don't have to wash ice with soap any more, eh? At least you have good fridge, and making nice clean ice. That's better than before, eh?' Jack, laughing, watched Myrna out of the corner of his eye, hoping she would be amused enough to join in. This was the sole purpose of the contrived conversation with Abdul.

'When, when? I didn't see him washing ice!'

'Oh come, darling. Surely you remember that morning. There was Abdal, out on the lawn at Nagarpara, bright and early, scrubbing away at the ice block with soap …'

But Myrna was distracted by the ayah. 'You can go, ayah,' she said. 'Enough, enough. Bones old. Hurting you know. Bones old like yours, and such hard pressing not good, not good. Bas! Enough!'

'Good enough, good enough, basbasbas,' repeated Jack.

The ayah malevolently applied a final pressure of the thumbs to her mistress's ankle. Myrna cried out and lashed at her with a tremulous palm. The smack sounded resoundingly on the ayah's shaven sari-covered head. She jerked back, her sari fell off her head and trailed on the floor, exposing the stubble on her head and dark brown nipples dangling below her short blouse. The glass-powder bowl spun across the floor and shattered as it struck the wall. The sweet scent of talcum powder increased and tears streamed down the ayah's cheeks.

'Jao!' Myrna cried half in shock. 'Out! Get out!'

The ayah tottered up and out, nattering to herself and weeping.

Jack usually ignored such outbursts, but today a spark of anger was ignited. 'You shouldn't have slapped her, Myrna! Why did you have to slap her like that?'

Myrna cried, softly keening and Jack was instantly contrite. He stroked her and soothed her. 'I'm sorry, Myrna. I said I was sorry. Ayah was in tears too, and you must have hurt her.'

Myrna mumbled, sounding remarkably like the ayah, and Jack swallowed the lump in his throat. The ghosts for once were too sad to make any comment. Instead, they helplessly bowed their heads.

Abdul came in and without looking at his master and mistress shakily swept up the shattered fragments and powder with a brush and dustpan, leaving some behind.

'Cheerio my darling!' said Jack, after Myrna had become quiet. He put her glass into her hands, holding up his own, and clinking it gently with hers. 'Here's to the future!'

'Future indeed!' Myrna snorted, her tears forgotten.

Jack put his glass down carefully and leaned across. Taking Myrna's glass and setting it down, he held both her hands in his. 'Listen. I've been thinking of something, something important, and the time has come to talk about it. Are you listening to me, Myrna?'

'Of course I am.'

'We have to make a pact, a covenant with each other. Do you understand?'

'What *are* you on about?'

'It's to set your mind at rest. Do you follow? I want to set your mind at rest, my darling!' Jack took a deep breath. 'Tell me. What do you worry about most these days? What were you talking about a short while ago?'

'I was talking about getting senile,' said Myrna promptly. 'Getting senile, forgetful, incontinent, all those things. And I said I wouldn't like to live if that happened. If I were to get senile.'

'And …?' Jack prompted, hope surging back at her coherent reply.

'And what?'

'You said something else as well …'

'I, I don't remember! Oh my God, it's started … Jack! It's started!' Myrna's voice was dry, hands up at her throat.

'There's no sign of it at all,' said Jack, taking her hands and clasping them again. 'Your mind, at the moment, is as clear as a bell.' He willed himself to sound confident.

'Then what was it I said? What was it?'

'Just this, my darling. You said, "What if I become senile and don't realize it." That's what you said …'

'Yes. I remember,' Myrna whispered. 'I remember. But that's true, isn't it? It's true. If I become senile *I'll never know*, will I?'

'And I? Have you thought about me in the same predicament?' Gently.

'Of course I have. I don't know if I'll have the strength to look after you. I'm not so strong, you *know* that! You *know* I have angina …'

'I'll tell you what. I'll tell you exactly what, Myrna.' Jack's voice became thinner, the tremor in it increasing. 'Look. It's hardly likely that we'll both go down the hill at the same time, is it? Tell me,' urging, 'is that likely?'

'I suppose not, no, I suppose not.'

'Well. In that case, the answer's clear.' His grip on her arthritic hands became painful. Myrna snatched them away.

'I'll make the arrangements, and I'll show you what I plan.' Pausing. 'We'll have to promise, solemnly and honestly, to help each other, Myrna.' Pause. 'And the one who remains normal, in control, will have to promise to help out, by, by …' He came to a standstill.

'By what? What are you on about, Jack Strachey?'

'By helping the other to end it all!' blurted out Jack.

'To what?'

'To end it all!'

'You don't mean …'

Myrna's mouth had fallen open, her face was contorted. 'But that's *murder*!' Her voice was thin and tremulous too, like Jack's. 'How do I know you won't *murder* me? You, you evil man! I'm going home before you murder me. I don't care if you stay on here. I'm going to, to Martin! Oh you *evil* man …'

The ghosts were equally distraught. 'What is to happen?' they muttered.

Jack tried to embrace her again but Myrna pushed him away in an extravagant gesture of panic, dislodging the delicate arrangement of her hairnet. Her hair fluffed out exposing bare pink patches. She struggled to get up but fell back heavily. She talked on, demented, incoherent, continuing to struggle in her seat. Jack stared at her aghast, and swallowed fearfully. A refrain went through his head, 'Murder evil, murder evil.' Listening to her and looking at her, his face slowly suffused with blood. 'But where is she trying to go? Where *can* she go?'

❧

The light trom the verandah haloed Myrna's white, blow-away hair. It was yet another languishing day. She sat in a chair with the television on in front of her, talking incessantly. Jack sat next to her, paying attention to the TV and responding with practiced fluency. Today, instead of saying anything abrasive or accusing she was reminiscing, recollecting the early days of style and splendour. Jack gave up watching the TV to listen to her.

'Who would have thought men could be so manly with jewellery and perfume and kohl! He was so handsome, Jack, wasn't he? Wasn't he handsome?' Her reference was to an ex-lover, the Maharaja of R.

'Why don't I have such memories?' thought Jack. 'Don't I have an erotic side? All I can remember is Abdal out on the lawn, washing the ice with soap … That's all I remember … Silly old Abdal out on the lawn, washing the ice with soap …'

'Do you remember Abdal, washing the ice with soap,' said Jack out loud yet again. 'In the garden … Remember?'

'Oh yes! Wasn't that funny! And shaving you in bed, every morning …'

'Before his hand started shaking … And talking of luxuries, there was "Lady" Myrna, reclining in bed with ayahs massaging her from all ends!'

And then Myrna laughed, a natural, easy laugh, putting him into a state of painful suspense, suspense that her mood must soon return to normal. 'No, not "normal",' he corrected himself, '"usual".'

The distinction seemed clear for the moment to Jack, whose mind broke up in confusion over two things, Myrna and his failed career. The latter lurked hidden, bursting out sometimes like a monster from a cave. Myrna overpowered most of his waking moments with her vexation and her emotion. When she screamed at the servants, he forced himself to remember her innate kindness. Servants were by definition imperfect and for compensation perfect whipping boys. But Myrna had always looked after them, hadn't she? Clothing and feeding them, spending freely on them. Martin, a native born 'Anglo-Indian', understood. Poor boy. How he had loved his India, Calcutta in particular. But … back he'd gone, and rightly … Is that what they should have done? Gone back?

'Oh but yes, yes,' said the Swadeshi ghost, gently for once. 'You would have been so much better off!'

At the bottom of Jack's decision to stay on was the fear of an uncared for old age, accessible to Martin but neglected because of a strong daughter-in-law's dissent. Was it the right decision? Here they were, with an inaccessible Martin, plumb at the end of that old age. Was that better than the neighbourhood neglect he had feared from his son? Who was there to care for them here? The servants? Did he feel secure? Would he feel secure anywhere? Wasn't old age the ultimate insecurity, the end without solution? Did he subconsciously hope that by staying on he could take on the enviable attributes of an Indian extended family, loving care till the very end? What of Myrna's mental state? What about all the cajoling for her to just step out of the flat, through a stream of invective, complaints about the heat, about the cold, about a weak heart, the stairs …? But Jack was glad of the stairs. He took a sadistic pleasure in hauling himself up. It proved him still active and able, didn't it? Even if obscured by stopping often for Myrna, which gave him a rest too, a rest to prolong the anticipation of re-entering their last refuge, their flat.

Summer, winter, monsoon, the flat was perfectly attuned after decades of organization. In summer, the khas-khas tatties replaced the verandah chiks, with the breeze carrying in the zest of the wet reed. The dust scent settling under the first rains became a pleasant cliché for Jack, and if he had known, he would have bought the attars sold on street corners promising the bottled essences of khas khas and rain-dust. The potted lilies prepared to bud and flower white against the dark of the khas-khas tatties. Solutions were endlessly attempted against one of the few faults of the Rajmahal, the low plinth of the lobby floor that led to flooding. During early days, the Sardar Bahadur, always elegant, had shallow ducts carved to drain into the fountains. But rainwater during a Calcutta monsoon is jealous of elegant solutions and it had never worked. The Rajmahal tenants would be almost immobilized till the end of the rains. The house knew this disregard of old age underscored its decline as it shuddered and picked up its metaphorical hem. When the waters receded, a clayey lining was uncovered with little colonies of tadpoles and other slimy creatures of the wet. The Rajmahal suffered the clinging staleness of mildew and mould, straining to evict any organic remains after the post-monsoon cleansing.

But the monsoon was a season Jack loved, and the outer verandah had always given him just the exposure he needed. He would venture out and peer around the chiks to enjoy the thunder and spray of the heavenly Niagara. Then the rains would come to an end. 'Perfect,' he would sigh as the weather turned dry and fine and fans and air-conditioners were stilled. The renovation season would come around, and the 'little men' appear. The polishing wallah to sandpaper and re-polish the teak and rosewood furniture and floors, the pleasant smells of spirit polish and beeswax spreading their fragrances. The masons to scrape and repaint the damp patches on the walls, sometimes to redecorate a whole room. The tailor to stitch new curtains. The upholstery wallah to re-cover the chairs, Myrna overseeing their rearrangement with renewed pictures, lamps and polished silver. The newness would inspire vases full of flowers, early roses and chrysanthemums.

But the movement of time came barging in, disrupting the harmony. The 'little men' vanished, shifting away from traditional avocations. Water no longer flowed on demand from taps. Power breakdowns meant the installation of noisy generators. The khas-khas tatties vanished. The tolerance to heat diminished with air-conditioners. The floor waxing was short circuited after Myrna slipped and fractured her ankle, and the sparkle of seasonal adjustments all but disappeared. With them disappeared a civic feature unique to Calcutta, the washing down of roads with high pressure hoses by superhuman little men, deftly aiming their water jets to avoid cars and passers-by.

The human contents of the Rajmahal, Jack's companions over the decades, were fading like the building. Sightings of Mohini Mojumdar were rare as she took to her bed. Then there was Petrov-across-the-landing, turning peculiar, and Proshanto Mojumdar, dozing off in the middle of his scatty chatter. The landlord hardly came down though he and his wife waved sometimes from their landing. And Jack would reproach himself when he was occasionally asked to help an ageing co-tenant. 'Of course,' he would say guiltily. 'Certainly. It's the least I can do. I've been so …' And he would add, his conscience heavy, 'I didn't realize …'

One of the all-year-round activities involved the war against malaria-bearing mosquitoes. This was romanticized by Jack through the mosquito net which swirled down every night from the ceiling. Jack retreated into his bed, pulled at the strings tied by his side, and shut his eyes as the soft netting encircled him and Myrna, holding them in its protective embrace. That cloudy world gave Jack a feeling of intimate safety, like the net spread below trapeze artists, cocooning them in their aerial spaces. His worst moments came when the fan, still the crazily impractical fan with the wooden blades, tore the mosquito curtains when the delicate balance was upset. Each time, he saw to it that the netting was immediately replaced. The very worst was the day of the Bad News, when Myrna had lunged at the netting, tearing it from its moorings. Jack had felt as if he, a trapeze artist, had fallen from the high swings through a hole in the safety net, ever-dreading the fatal impact to follow.

He felt the same dread again, though the net was as secure as it had ever been.

Petrov, the Russian tenant, kept a diary in which he made philosophical observations, which he shared only with Surjeet Shona, his eager acolyte: *What are the Stracheys doing here in this crazy, filthy, smoggy, out-of-control city? Do they really need this flat, this Rajmahal, these ancient toothless servants, just for the sake of a view of the crowded Maidaan, an access to a few shabby clubs, an idea that their Raj is still here? How do they face the sly hints about the greed of the British during the Raj, their savage revenge after native uprisings? I have heard them being taunted about the famine. Have they forgotten how they went skipping across starving bodies on their way into Firpos? What about all the writing on this British indifference, the writing which reviles it? What about Jack Strachey's own true background? (I know what this means, after all, though I was so young when I left Russia. Jack Strachey was a full adult when he left his country.) A 'true' background means a wholeness which can never exist in another country, in spite of a long life's association. It means knowing people of your own family, your region, your background … It means recognizing who you are and what you are, your true level … Ah! There I may have hit upon something. Perhaps Jack Strachey's level in England is the problem…*

Small differences with the Indians on which Jack and Myrna had commented and laughed over the years were now like monster barriers.

'It's rude to tell the truth, but not to yawn, spit and burp.'

'And fart too.'

'What about nose picking?'

'Have more, naa, please, but you must …'

'No thank you …'

'Are you sure …?'

'Of course I am, I said so didn't I!'

Exasperating. Maddening. As if one doesn't know one's own mind.

'Look at him Jack, piling my plate, it's monstrous!'

'Shshsh. Just eat as much as you can …'

'Myrna, give Mr Ghosh another helping …'

'I just asked him, he said "no"!'

'Myrna! Insist, go on! Or you'll offend him …'

But Jack knew the Indian experience would deny him simple solutions, that in the end he could not have re-adjusted his personality and status-consciousness in Britain. Here his level was intact and understood. He was himself now and till the end.

Myrna's familiar quack-quacking penetrated.

'What dear?' he said mildly.

'How do I look?' Myrna said in that anxious tone close to hysteria. 'How do I *look*, Jack? You're not listening!'

'Oh no. She's started again!' moaned the ghosts.

How did she look indeed? Jack realized he hadn't looked at her recently, because of her incessant natter, because of his incessant concern for her. 'You …' automatically, knowing his best strategy. 'Darling, you … look … just fine …'

'Don't lie! I don't believe you meant a word of that!'

'What dear?'

'I used to be so sexy.' Myrna's voice took on a mewling tone.

'Don't I know it!' Jack dutifully lunged at a heavily corseted breast.

Myrna slapped him away. 'Stop it!' She started crying, turning Jack's heart and lowering his resistance so painfully that he groaned out loud.

'Oh Jack, I don't know how I should do my hair, and what I should wear … It's so hard …'

'Hush.' Jack's voice trembled. 'Hush …'

'I can't decide! Should I dye my hair? And look at these stays, they hardly make a difference. It's too awful of Martin to forget the new ones … And, and, should I dye my hair? It's *awful*.' Desperate. 'You aren't saying anything. Should I *dye* my hair, Jack Strachey, should I dye it, so they'll look at me again …'

'I love you.' Jack was saying under his breath, all this while, like a mantra. 'I love you. Hush, hush.' He held Myrna in his arms. 'I love you,' he said, repeatedly, while Myrna sobbed her soft pretty little sobs.

Sitting apart again, Jack stroked his wife and held the usual evening panacea, a weak whisky, out to her.

'They say it's good for the heart.'

'The same words she repeats every evening, every single evening without fail!' muttered the ghosts.

'I do look forward to it, I really do. It's just the thing for my angina.'

'But you don't have angina, dear. The doctor just said …' Jack realized too late he had set Myrna off yet again. He consoled himself that most things said, or not said, would set her off …

'You'll believe how bad it is when I'm gone.' Myrna swallowed the pretty little sobs. 'The doctor *said* I had angina, he said it just last week. It's serious, angina, and it's so painful. I could go just like that, in a second …'

Jack breathed hard to hide the deep distress he always felt when Myrna talked of death. He took his whisky glass with him and walked over to the balcony. He leaned over, not seeing the pale orange sunset, not seeing the smoke hovering in its evening pall. 'Why does her death bother me so much?' he thought. And then, while listening to Myrna's complaints, his heart thudded loud and fast. He remembered the pact he had suggested not so long ago. Jack shivered in the descending cool air. Was he afraid of dying, of death, for himself? He remembered incidents of violence in this city, when he was the victim.

There was the 'white monkey' street attack. And once, when he was visiting a Sharp's jute mill, the workers had kept him gheraoed for forty-eight hours. He had used his waste paper bin as a urinal, and somehow refrained from doing the other thing. No harm done in the end. When things had gone back to normal, and he was back at the Rajmahal, the workers had again become the anonymous nonentities they had always been. Strange. Neither of these incidents recurred much in Jack's memories during those sightless lookouts over the Maidaan. It was other remembrances, of the many times pedestrians had banged on the bonnet of his car angrily with an umbrella, briefcase or bare hands, to tell the man in the car to stop for him – the righteous pedestrian-citizen. For a while, Jack had thought this behaviour was reserved for the whites. It was in a way justified they should feel, 'Simply because you have a fine car and I cannot, oh foreign upstart, you do not have priority over me in my own country!' While in that helpless position, looking on meekly at the militant pedestrian, he would think, 'If he attacks me, he'll be joined by all the others, and they will kill me, an intrusive white man milking them in their poverty.' It was with the deepest shock that he witnessed the same violence done to a car driven by an Indian.

'Look, look!' he exclaimed to his chauffeur. 'They are attacking an Indian man's car?'

'Bangali babu,' the up-country chauffeur laughed, missing the point. 'He doing it everyone. Sahib not remembering, he doing it us too many time?'

But that memory, of frustrated aggressive faces and reverberating bonnets, stuck in Jack's mind. Its association with death, his own possible death. He felt no fear, felt none even the very first time. It was the phenomenon of Death, with a capital 'D', that was frightening, not his own death.

Jack had always been proud of his physical courage, his fearlessness in the face of danger. Death when deeply feared was of others. The death of Myrna, or Martin, or Gwen, his grandchildren. He brought his mind back to the 'pact' with an effort. Myrna was surely well into the dreaded state. Jack looked at his hand as he raised the glass to his lips and tried to stop it from shaking. He was afraid. He physically lacked the courage to carry out his own pact. He was not a brave man! Myrna was in her hell, yet he, Jack Strachey, was completely helpless. He was unable to put an end to it, in spite of his own pact. He remembered the evening of proposing his 'pact' to her when she had suddenly seemed so clear and normal. Yes normal. Not her 'usual' incoherent shrill self …Yet she had instantly regressed when he had made the proposal. 'Evil!' she had shrilled. 'Oh you evil man, you want to murder me!' She had tried to get up from her seat and her hairnet had come off, releasing her soft, fluffy, white hair.

Tears came to Jack's eyes and he turned to look at his Myrna, a Myrna without a hairnet, for she had never retrieved or replaced it. Difficult as it was to get from moment to moment, where was the time to think of hairnets and such …? It was as if his suggestion had precipitated her decline.

Myrna was quacking on again about the Bad News, and Jack felt a sinking feeling mixed with the familiar confusion. He was over eighty. The area of confusion covered the period when he was still in his early fifties, and it was about an unethical action of his at Sharp's. When he had deliberately passed over a bright young Indian, who was due for promotion to a position still well below the glass ceiling put up for Indians. In his place he had pushed in a younger Briton newly arrived in India, by exaggerating his qualifications and 'misplacing' a file. The Indian had left in frustration without creating a fuss and gone on to greener pastures. Jack had always felt that this act had forced him to meekly accept the takeover by Kuldip Chopra, the brilliant Kuldip Chopra who had finally brought Sharp and Co. to its knees. Carrying out, it was rumoured, much that was unethical along the way, and thus keeping Jack's fall within the realm of the angels by comparison. Still, there was a clear guilt attached to his own lesser, though unethical, act. In trying to forget, he allowed his priority anxiety to dominate, his anxiety for Myrna. And then, from the premise of guilt, he moved on to the guilty area in his relationship with Myrna. In which his guilt featured, not Myrna's. Myrna's guilt was a given. He sighed, his mind teetering on the threshold of his other guilt. Though the lesser emotions of jealousy and revenge had never troubled Jack consciously, his ego's bruising, crudely put, his male ego's bruising, had resulted in the need for violence. He had never recognized this deeper impetus, but he had felt the need to be violent to Myrna during the sexual act. In what he was convinced was a purely sexual context. 'Nothing,' he told himself, 'nothing to do with her other men, just a, a sexual thing.' But he had always controlled himself, only rarely allowing a snarl to escape his lips while making love in that strong and passionate way, yet smouldering and holding himself back from actually tearing into her, making her bleed, cutting her and raping her. Myrna, never the most sensitive of persons, had loved this contained force in Jack, not for a moment suspecting the cruel battle he fought each time, the battle to hold in his fangs and talons.

'But in the end,' sighed the spent octogenarian looking ironically at his blunt nails, 'I held back, didn't I?'

His mind sank again into confusion and escaped to the immediate scenes down below outside the Rajmahal, the crowds queuing up at the planetarium and the ever-so-slow revolution of the Venus on the Victoria Memorial dome. And he wilfully blurred his mind to his impotence, the cruel fallout of a prostrate gland operation. The doctors had suspected and then confirmed cancer of the prostrate gland when Jack was seventy, a late discovery. He and Myrna had flown out to London, and with Martin to support them the operation had been performed by the best surgeon available. But none of this could avert the aftermath of the surgery, the impotence.

'It's partly because of your age,' the doctor had comforted him, 'and partly because it was discovered so late ...'

'Too late,' thought Jack.

And he had to console himself. 'At least I'm released from my devilish desires ...' But he forgot that much before the operation, his 'devilishness' had retracted, and the loving couple had long decreased their sexual activity to suit their age.

Although Jack's own death may not have frightened him, he was filled with terror by Myrna's incomprehension when he talked of his health. 'Oh Jack, don't say such things. Don't say such things. You're *such* a hypochondriac! *I'm* the one who's ill!' She would clutch her bosom and call for her medicines and Jack would instantly forget his own problems. After a few moments Myrna would say, 'Call the doctor Jack. I don't feel at all well, not at all well.' He knew then the uselessness of calling on her for support. Another operation was unthinkable.

He tried his best to clarify his thoughts. 'How will she cope if I go first? Who'll care for her when she has an attack of angina? Ayah? Bearer? How can I place such a burden on them? Should I call in Martin? But what about Gwen, and the children and all their problems, who's lucky enough not to have problems ...?'And then, before he could go on to the next logical thought, of him being left without Myrna, his mind broke apart and refused to come together.

More and more, he had blank periods, when days coalesced into forgotten intervals. And then, while thus torn and anguished, he convinced himself he could recognize the recurring symptoms of his cancer.

He remembered the pact with Myrna again, and his plan took concrete shape.

It must be at the end of the perfect day. Nothing must go wrong on that day. When the miracle took place, as if willed by him, the very next day, he felt hopeful again. 'But she's fine,' he thought. 'Look at her! She's beautiful. Just like old times!' There had been visitors, Surjeet Shona and some of her friends, and the eminently sane, intelligent and good-looking Rajmahalians enlivened them so much with their warmth and humour, and they laughed so freely, that nothing seemed amiss.

But later that evening, Myrna threw endless tantrums, bathing herself in tears and unleashing bitter streams of invective on the servants and Jack. When he saw Abdul and the khansama signalling to each other in the pantry and laughing at Myrna's buffoonery, he knew their laughter was more from perplexity and pain than from amusement. He decided to act before the suffering became pure hell.

❧

The mosquito netting was still up, and Myrna was sitting on the edge of the bed trying to kick her slippers off her swollen feet, a task made more difficult by her tipsiness that night. Jack had given her three stiff drinks, accepted eagerly by her each time. Even the semblance of vigour shown by her kicking off her slippers, her quivering bosom, gave Jack a twinge. But he too had numbed himself with whisky. He diverted his attention to his meticulously rehearsed actions.

Myrna would be drowsier than usual tonight, and he must act quickly. Once she fell asleep it would be impossible to go through another interval of anguish and invective, another agonizing struggle to get to this point. Conscious of the affection accrued over the years between him and the servants, and their devotion, he had given each of them large sums of cash to avoid cumbersome wills. And he had made elaborate arrangements to free them of involvement in the sleeping pills he had bought, a circumspection inspired by reading countless Agatha Christies.

A talkative ghost tried to say something, but the mansion sushed him.

'Can't you keep quiet for once!' the other ghosts added. 'Look at poor Jack's anguish!'

'This is the beginning of the end,' insisted the talkative ghost. 'Just you wait and see.' But silence soon descended, as the talkative ghost finally recognized the solemnity of the occasion.

Jack walked over to Myrna's side of the bed and prepared her medicine as he did every night, carrying two glasses this time.

'Here's our new tonic, my darling. Come on. Down the hatch!'

He handed her a glass and drank from the other, matching sip for sip while he watched her over the rim. But Myrna, with the liquid half drunk, put down her glass. Jack didn't trouble to hide the tears streaming from his eyes. Myrna would never notice them … Before she could draw up her legs he sat by her side and held her in an embrace. 'I've drunk it,' said Myrna slurring her words. 'Go to bed now and let me sleep. I'm awfully sleepy you know. They say one must have a good night's sleep, especially with angina …'

Jack felt a painful throbbing in his head together with a familiar feeling. The corners of his lips trembled, then drew back to expose his canine teeth. He snarled, a deep growl emanating at the base of his larynx, and viciously wiped the tears from his cheeks. His grasp on Myrna tightened and he held her up with uncharacteristic force.

'Come on old girl!' he snarled. 'Drink up!'

The ghosts left one by one, going back to their normal haunts where they huddled in sorrow.

Jack felt his head exploding, two horns emerging from the top and dislodging his thin hair. He knew his eyes were getting bloodshot and slanting upwards at the corners and his feet were developing cloven hooves. He forced the shocked and weak Myrna to open her mouth and, while her teeth clacked against the glass, he poured the liquid from his glass into her mouth, forcing her to swallow, again and again. The glass cracked and a sliver came off. When he put the glass on the table her upper lip was torn and bleeding. He missed the suffusion of red in her face, the look of utter terror, and the bubbling heave of breath before she fell back on to the bed, her after-all susceptible heart at its final standstill. Jack felt his own heart becoming impossibly heavy as he recognized what had happened. The unspeakable, that he should suffer for the shortest second from her loss … And from the very terror of discovery he blocked out all thought, feeling for her pulse and confirming what he knew. Summoning his strength and sanity, he wiped Myrna's lips and chin, and with the same manic precision pulled her legs on to the bed and arranged them in a seemly fashion, covering her upto the neck with a quilt. His movements became heavy as he picked up the other glass, earlier hers, shambled over to his side of the bed, and gulped down the remains. He put the glass down, pushed the slippers off his feet, lay down and pulled the double-sized quilt over himself. He manipulated the strings on the wall and the mosquito net slid gently down, enveloping them in its loving mist. He pressed the light switch dangling behind him. In the darkness he felt for and found Myrna's hand, and softly taking it in his, just managed to close his eyes.

3

The Book of Inheritance

Proshanto Mojumdar, scion of a rich zamindari family, had the good luck of bagging the flat on the conservatory floor of the Rajmahal. It included the Sardar Bahadur's favourite bedroom, heavy glass panels embossed in the contemporary European style of the Rajmahal's construction year, peacocks trailing their showy tails in turquoise blue and the clear ceiling mirror over the bed.

After graduating from the Imperial College in London, Proshanto had been recruited straight away by the Peninsular and Oriental Steam Navigation Company as an engineer. During his childhood he had been taken on the annual seaside vacation to Puri, and to the Sagar Mela where the many-headed Ganga lay dynamically sprawled, its mouths fanged with mangrove and crocodile. The boundless seascape made him dizzy with longing and a shipping career became his goal. When he started travelling up and down between India and England on P&O liners as a student, always first class thanks to an indulgent father, this goal became a passion. To him, the ocean liners were miraculous, floating skyscrapers voyaging between the ends of the rainbow. The luxury thrilled him then spoilt him, and he longed to spend his life skimming the high seas in this softly lit encapsulated world, tinkering with engines. When he took his flat in the Rajmahal he would dream of all this in his bedroom, which bore such a close resemblance to the grand interiors of the liners, the blue-green luminescent waves roaring and pounding outside the tall bedroom windows, flecking them with foam. But conditions at work were far from this secured luxury, and Proshanto had to sleep in a sultry bunk room while the sweat poured and cold drinks were no help against the pulsing air of the engine rooms. 'Even the Calcutta heat is better than this,' said Proshanto, when his ship drifted on the Red Sea or scraped between the sand banks of the Suez Canal. As a 'blackie' he had to face relentless racial barbs from his mates, though he won their respect with his sharp ripostes. He was more assiduous than the rest in his work, for defensive reasons too, and soon, he was promoted and given a small cabin of his own. It wasn't yet like the luxury he expected, but the cabin would keep improving as he rose. And then he came face-to-face with the ultimate bitterness, discrimination, when a junior, an Englishman, was promoted over his head. The directors ignored his complaints, and highly aggrieved, he simply resigned. 'This takes things beyond the acceptable,' he said to Mohini. 'I have no need of a livelihood from them anyway!' It wasn't a bad choice at a time when large passenger liners were in decline after the leap into air travel.

When the newly married couple had first moved into the Rajmahal, Mohini was still a dewy teenager, and the mirror was witness to god knows what concupiscent activities on the part of this nubile couple. Mohini used to often join Proshanto on his voyages as a paid passenger, anticipating the future revival of these liners for luxury cruising. It had allowed her to devour the plays, concerts, food and culture of other countries, and indulge in shameless leisure. The ship's captains disapproved of all this, but Proshanto persuaded them she had every right to be there as a paying passenger. It suited him fine, as he could share her cabin, and life became so romantic they were convinced that Mohini could conceive on board if nowhere else, not even in the mirrored peacock bedroom at home. But it didn't work and they were destined to stay childless, which though saddening, allowed Mohini the freedom to travel.

They missed the old life after Proshanto's resignation, but he couldn't bring himself to take up a job with an Indian company. 'I am reluctant to change at this advanced age,' he said. 'The contrast will be too great.' He wasn't that old, but other Indians of his generation suffered from the same plight.

'You should have joined an Indian company at the very beginning,' said Mohini, 'instead of going for the first offer.'

Mohini Mojumdar was from a wealthy family and with her dowry and the Mojumdar riches, Proshanto could have lived a life of retired leisure. But his father encouraged him to work, just as he pushed him into marrying the right wife. Proshanto could have insisted on a love marriage, which he once almost did with a girl he had picked up with in Gibraltar. No one could have been more unsuitable. The house rejoiced in the old custom, of the bride holding a bowl of water with a fish in it, and stepping into a basin of milk at the threshold of her new home, to the lusty blowing of conch shells and ululation-uludhwoni of the females of the family. When she held the fish in her hands as custom demanded, she cleverly slipped it back before it had a chance to flip out of her hold, thus ensuring a faithful husband. But the house mourned when the symbolic ritual failed to give them the blessing of fertility.

Mohini and Proshanto settled down to a comfortably compatible sex life, with a passion fired by pill-less, condom-less concerns because it was Proshanto who was sterile, though far from impotent. But it was intensely galling to Mohini that he got carried away by any new belle he encountered well into their married life, and that these belles were always in their twenties, while the two of them grew older and older. 'Can't even get me pregnant, and he's off every week on some new crush!' she thought angrily. She wasn't to know he never carried his crushes further than the moony behaviour. Ever polite Proshanto had suggested adoption. 'Why don't you stretch the limits of politeness and hire a stud for me then?' she almost said.

She had once allowed imaginings of such a stud to manifest. The medical facts had just clarified, and then Proshanto had gone off over a nubile newcomer. 'How dare he when he's the one with the shortcoming!' snorted Mohini. She knew Proshanto's sterility, or his presumed infidelity, were strong grounds for divorce. But it was still early days, and revenge seemed sweeter. Her French class provided the chance, with the stud manifesting as a co-student from, of all places, Bulgaria.

'Wait till I produce a blue-eyed baby!' fumed Mohini. 'What on earth made me think I had to depend on that dolt of a husband!'

The Bulgarian sat next to Mohini, then a voluptuous young woman with an enchanting smile and glossy black hair which flowed down her back. Her large eyes turned soulfully towards him often, and he found himself stutteringly addressing her at any excuse in his poor English and poorer French in order to have that pleasure. Mohini at first found him hilariously funny with his easy blushes, but when she saw the unmistakable invitation in his blue eyes she felt herself blushing back. The Bulgarian became more attractive in an inspirational flash when her thoughts of revenge clarified. She allowed their arms to brush and soon, the pleasure of this contact became a game with them. One thing led to another and, heaving with guilt and excitement, she found herself one day in those familiar arms in his lodgings. The Bulgarian, no fledgling, plunged into the sexual rites he was used to, and before pulling her down on to the bed put a hand on her breast and brought his face close to hers with his tongue suggestively darting in and out. Mohini kept her lips tightly sealed and held her breath, fearful that the Bulgarian would have stinking breath, with shreds of beef rotting between his teeth. And suddenly, his appearance became so abhorrent, the satyr grin on his face, the darting, snake-like tongue, that she panicked, picked up her things and fled. She was reminded of scenes of bacchanalia from the paintings of the European museums, and the Bulgarian was transformed into a hairy Pan whenever she thought of him. She never went back to the French class, terrified of encountering the poor puzzled Bulgarian again.

Dream-mirages of the Sardar Bahadur's mistresses whose bedroom the Mojumdars now occupied, evoked bawdy scenes from the *Arabian Nights* of Mohini's mind. Her psychic vision was especially activated when old Inderjeet Kaur's ghost arrived all the way from Amritsar and appeared in the ceiling mirror above her bed. One night, when the mirror clouded and frothed with white clouds, partly the mosquito curtains in fact, partly the fumes of delusion, while pink and silver flashed in the dark, Mohini nudged Proshanto awake to share the vision with him. He opened his eyes briefly, blinked several times, and then scolded, 'Put off the light!' It was the mirror above, staging the cameo scene of the sardarni's night of spying. And it was this ghostly floodlit drama that Proshanto Mojumdar had mistaken for the bedroom light.

The vision, engineered by the house, did immense service to Mohini Mojumdar, setting her balance right and allowing her to regard objectively the comedy of her husband as exemplifying this life and its inexplicable yearnings.

She had, after that one little incomplete rebellion, resigned herself to childlessness. Not so Proshanto, who started off on a search, lasting years, for a remedy. It was a pity test-tube babies, sperm banks and surrogacy came too late for the Mojumdars. Proshanto went through all the available medical and pseudo-medical practices, faith healing, allopathy, homeopathy, ayurveda, Unani, and all the quackeries that came to his notice. But he wasn't destined to achieve an increase in his sperm count.

And then, in middle age, he was overtaken by feverish fears about his decelerating libido. 'Male menopause,' he convinced himself. 'That's what it is, male menopause.' In his anxiety to end the pause before it became a full stop, he embarked on another long and weary search. Cures for 'sex weakness, hormone imbalance and secret diseases' in the sex clinics of Calcutta.

His desperation went on other tangents, making a jagged many-rayed star around that insecure phase of his life. He put an announcement in the matrimonial columns of a leading Bengali newspaper, partly honest: 'High-caste widower, 55, wealthy, vigorous, handsome, fair, six feet tall, seeks lively, unencumbered out-going lady. Widowhood, caste, colour, no bar …' Somehow he balked at 'marriage'.

He furtively collected the responses, a total of six, from an anonymous post box and kept photos of these hopefuls in his wallet. He would look at them and fantasize, hoping for a revival of his libido. 'Any one of them could be mine if I wanted,' he assured himself. But instead of replying formally, he bought himself an expensive toupée and feeling uncomfortably tight about the head, traced an address to a back lane in a distant suburb. There he waited in vain for his fancy to emerge. Thus began his surreptitious loitering in obscure lanes observing the prospects, always disappointing. When the last of them turned out to be a transvestite, Proshanto was so depressed he threw the photos into the back of a drawer. Mohini came across them and managed to prize out the truth. She shrieked with laughter and embarrassed Proshanto by making the venture the prime story at any event. Proshanto was provoked to helpless anger by this disloyalty and had to make the best of it, stiffly smiling with the rollicking gathering. It was Mohini's revenge. 'Just imagine, he killed me off in his ad, became a widower!' she would announce during her exposés. When the toupée needed a wash, Mohini soaked it in such strong detergent that it shrivelled and shrank into a hairy spider. After listening tight-lipped to Proshanto's scolding, she contemptuously flicked the spider into a waste-paper basket. Proshanto rescued it but when he tried it on its suction end came unstuck with a slow hiss and leapt off, producing another burst of hilarity from Mohini. He compensated by demanding that Mohini should dye her hair. 'You still have such a young face. It will be entirely suitable!' he said. His reason for saying this was complex. It wasn't simply to show a complementary approval of his own moves, but that a youthful-looking wife, by reflection, would shore up his image. Anyone looking at her should imagine a still active sex life with a still desirable partner. And in order to live up to these assumptions, his libido might revive! But Mohini was having none of it and, fed up with Proshanto's crazy behaviour she became more stubbornly set in her gracious ageing. Proshanto's loitering-in-obscure-lanes ended with a last visit to a sex clinic. His choice, a doctor of 'discrete and famous reputation', turned out to be a huge Pathan sort with bristling moustache and wig, the latter easily diagnosed by the experienced Proshanto. He clung to his dignity and submitted to the intimate probing and testing, receiving as a reward a packet of expensive magic made from crushed tiger bone, ginseng, and other uncertain ingredients. He also carried a package of physical aids, which he examined minutely in the privacy of his car and then flung into the nearest dustbin. 'What would Mohini say if she ever found them?' he thought, shuddering with relief at his timely action.

When nothing worked, he became overactive to make up for the tumult in such an important area of his life. He and Mohini spent long periods on his estate near the East Pakistan border, involving themselves in the land reforms of the newly elected government. They had a quaint mansion overlooking low hills and surrounded by Santhal villages. Sitting on their verandah next to a well shaded by papaya trees and biting into ripe guavas just plucked and dealing with the paddy crop, seasonal labour and other farming matters, which took up much of their time, was diverting. At first, the division of lands among the landless gave Proshanto Mojumdar a purpose in life. He had old friends among leftist politicians, and felt secure that the size of his own land holdings, which had dwindled after division between himself, his brother, and a few cousins, would protect him from any such takeover. When a band of party workers and peasants militantly armed and waving red flags oversaw the handing over of a portion of these lands to the landless, he was outraged. But after spending fruitless days in Calcutta trying to reverse the situation, and sleepless nights agonizing over justice and injustice, feudalism and egalitarianism, he realized how hypocritical he was. 'Why did you think you would be immune?' Mohini asked him. 'Just because you knew some politicians?' She felt, strongly, that the redressal of centuries of inequality by losing their lands was irrelevant when they were childless. This ideologically mixed thinking confused Proshanto, especially as his nephew Rudrangshu was to be his heir. 'Rudro will have more than enough with whatever is left,' chided Mohini.

The land redistribution left Proshanto feeling aggrieved and ill-done-by on the one hand, and swelling with righteousness on the other, till one day, his remaining lands slipped out of his grasp while he stood by helplessly like his body.

But Proshanto's libido was soon to be reawakened by a zealous minister friend's ideological activities. Busily erasing colonial memories by renaming streets and replacing monuments, the minister decided to end the white segregation still continuing in some clubs.

Proshanto Mojumdar, imbued with a deep sense of politeness, always squirmed at manifestations of racism (surely the very antithesis of politeness!). How could it be justified, even in the context of ruler and ruled, that 'natives' should be barred from the exclusive haunts of the white man? Surely, once the ruler had left, the racism lay exposed and had to be excised. But things were changing fast. There were so many ironies, small and big. There was poor Jack Strachey's supersession at Sharp's by an Indian, to match Proshanto's by an Englishman, one before Independence and one after.

'Viewed within the context of our lives, it seems somewhat like rough justice,' said Proshanto in his pedantic diction.

'"Justice" because both of you have suffered for the colour of your skins? They cancel each other out?' his wife retorted.

Proshanto didn't reply. He knew it had been the injustice of racism and ruler-ruled syndrome which had taken away the final promotions in his case, and a righting of these imbalances in Jack's.

'What you are saying is "it serves him right!"' continued Mohini.

'Not him exactly,' said Proshanto, 'but the British generally for what they did to us.' He should have added that he still felt sorry for his neighbour.

The minister chose the Swimming Club for his first assault, and called on his friend Proshanto Mojumdar, a good swimmer and versed in the ways of the West, to join in the direct action.

'They are in for a shock,' said Proshanto, excitedly.

'Why shock?' said Mohini. 'Those places should have been taken over with Independence.'

Proshanto agreed with her for once.

He decided to wear a dhuti on the occasion, for the first time since his wedding, but had to take his upstairs neighbour, Petrov's help. The Russian had worn dhuties off and on for years. His Bengali academic and theatre world friends had never thought of abandoning their native dress, unlike Proshanto, who moved in different circles and had lost the habit. But he thought the occasion called for some such statement.

He remembered the Englishman of noble descent employed at one time at Sharp's. The Englishman was forced to resign when he began appearing in office swathed in a dhuti-Punjabi. At the Strachey's one evening, it was ironical that the only two people in Bengali dress were two white people, both of noble descent, the maverick Sharp's ex-employee and Petrov. Was it their noble birth which allowed them to carry off their 'fancy-dress' with such élan? The jokes which followed couldn't hide the earlier hegemony of the colonizers and their indelible imprint on sartorial mores.

The minister friend, a group of young swimmers, and Proshanto Mojumdar, his over-starched dhuti beaten into shape, set off in a cavalcade of cars. Inside the club, the minister's group brushed past the stunned members and marched into the changing rooms, whipped off their dhuties and, clad in a medley of swimming trunks and loincloths, reached the pool and plunged in. This was the time the minister, who was watching from the side, made his famous remark. 'Are they afraid our colour will roll off our skins and stain the water? What about sharing the pool with people who only use paper! Chichi!'

Proshanto, in the meantime, was filled with a euphoric triumph. At the same time, a feeling of unease lurked deep inside him, which he realized amounted to shame. Shame that his people had allowed themselves to be stripped of their dignity by the colonizer, and a deeper shame that they had allowed the British to continue in their assumptions of reverse untouchability so long after Independence. He reminded himself, as he had always done at such moments, that even before Independence, at least one leading Bengali, Deshapriya Sengupta, had started a racing-rowing club, the Lake Club, where whites were excluded, right next to the existing whites-only Calcutta Rowing Club, and that too in spite of his having an English wife, Nellie. But Nellie was an honorary Bengali, who had taken readily to the sharee, spoke fluent Bengali and went to jail, like her husband, while fighting for freedom for her husband's people from her own. He felt better while stroking alongside the champion, pushing away the bitter truth under this thin salve, while he worried, 'How am I to re-drape that complicated length of starched white cotton again without help?' He came out of the pool still worrying, to find flashbulbs popping while the members and club officials stood by, bewildered. Proshanto Mojumdar marched heroically into the changing rooms again, and wound his still starchy dhuti around himself, somehow getting to his car intact where he couldn't stop it from coming undone again. He arrived at the Rajmahal with the difficult garment bunched up in place by a string, and was greeted by Mohini's familiar screams of laughter. 'We succeeded anyway,' said Proshanto Mojumdar proudly.

That night he had the first of his laughing dreams, speaking incoherently yet jovially in a deep nocturnal voice while Mohini watched in amazement. She shook him angrily and was more amazed when he turned to her and made love as never before after a gap of six months. While lying under him, she cast her eyes up at the mirror above to watch their middle-aged bodies at this ritual which had started such a long time ago. Something brushed her lightly and a pink flash told her the ghost of Inderjeet Kaur was smiling down on them, and showering them with a benison of silver gota.

With Proshanto's complete sexual revival he had already reached the end of his desperate search. He and Mohini spent a lively swan song, punctuated sweetly by those idyllic laughing dreams. Their only sadness, which they philosophically quelled, was their lack of offspring. Then Mohini's ill health overwhelmed her and she took to her bed with palpitations, migraines, everything weakening – digestion, limbs and organs, the inexplicably swift onset of premature ageing. And its grand culmination.

'Maybe we shouldn't have had such enjoyment at this age,' her ghost sometimes thought. But she convinced herself her reasoning was faulty. No overseeing power could grudge them the compensation of good sex when they were denied its natural outcome.

The Mojumdars had seriously thought of adoption as an alternative, and family circumstances made the choice for them. When Proshanto's brother, Shudhangshu, was deserted by his wife, he had a nervous breakdown, leaving his young son Rudrangshu a virtual orphan. It was natural for Proshanto and Mohini to take him into their care. Their affection for Rudrangshu, a handsome, gentle youth, grew over his long stays with them between returning to his father's care. He became their legal heir. But Proshanto's desperate search of the earlier years interfered with his attention, leaving room only for affectionate rather than intense concern. The intensity was his brother Shudhangshu's parental preserve. Shudhangshu, jobless, heart-broken at losing his wife, squandered his inheritance on alcohol and travel, and was left with little but this intense concern. After his initial neglect, his son became his obsession.

Now, he was bent on wresting Rudrangshu's inheritance from Proshanto, to set him up in business, buy him a job, make him a landlord, anything. Rudrangshu was indifferent, inclined to indolence and a complete lack of ambition. Unfortunately, his loyal and loving uncle's memory had stalled permanently into a running marktime, a stuck record, dating back to Rudrangshu's school days, when he had done well in his exams. All recollection of his miserable performance in university, his joblessness and fecklessness, had evaporated with the onset of senile forgetfulness. 'Ah, that boy will make us all proud one day,' he would say repeatedly to his impatient younger brother, ignoring all hints at Rudrangshu's need for a fiscal injection.

Rudrangshu continued living in the Rajmahal after Mohini's death. His father visited frequently between disappearances to the decrepit family home on the edge of their former estates. One morning, when Proshanto came out of his bedroom, he heard Shudhangshu's voice.

'Hello Dada!' it said.

'Shudo!' Proshanto looked at his younger brother's face with the bulging eyes and shaggy moustache.

'Don't be surprised Dada. I came in late last night.'

'Ah, you must have met Rudro.'

'Last night. When I came in.'

'Where is the dear boy. Rudro, Rudro!'

'He's still asleep.'

'Ah yes. Young people! They indeed need great quantities of sleep. And where is Bonzo? Bonzo, Bonzo!' he called feverishly.

'If you mean your dog, Dada, his name is Rover!'

'Eh? Where are the servants? Bearer, bearer!'

'They're out. One fellow's taken Rover for a walk and the other's gone to get some sausages and bacon. You know how I love sausages and bacon! I'm planning to stay with you a while, Dada. Does that suit you?'

'Yes, yes, of course. You are most welcome. Tell me. Is your wife all right. Er …' He had forgotten her name altogether. He had also forgotten that she and Shudhangshu were divorced. 'Body odour,' the wife had snapped succinctly when pressed for her reasons.

'I … what wife? Have you forgotten? Ruby left me years ago!'

'Ruby. A gem, yes, a real gem. Er … how is she by the way?'

'Divorced, we are divorced!' Shudhangshu shouted.

Proshanto nodded and went back to his bedroom to dress. When he came out, he found Shudhangshu sitting comfortably at the dining table wolfing sausages, bacon and eggs with relish. 'Come on, Dada,' he said magnanimously. 'Make yourself at home!' He laughed obnoxiously. Everything about Shudhangshu was obnoxious, including the clinging body odour. 'Hope you don't mind, I've started breakfast. Very hungry, especially after the late night …' He stopped abruptly and bit his tongue. Why remind Dada that he had come in drunk and helped himself to giant pegs of whisky till Proshanto had fallen asleep in his chair?

'What, last night …?'

'Found you fast asleep in your chair in the drawing room, and dreaming. Something funny. You were laughing away most loudly. Gave me quite a fright, by Jove. There you were, mumbling in your sleep and laughing. Couldn't make out a word you were saying. I had to carry you to bed. You need looking after Dada …' Shudhangshu, wiped his mouth with a napkin. 'Ah! That was delicious! Try some, Dada!'

One of the servants arrived with a plate of fried eggs on toast and put it down in front of Proshanto. He ate neatly with a fork and knife and with a concentrated frown. When he looked up again his eyes encountered Shudhangshu and he gave a start. 'What are you doing here, Shudo?' he said. 'Are you planning to stay?'

'I just told you,' said Shudhangshu irritably. 'Of course I'm planning to stay. I need your advice about Rudro …'

Proshanto Mojumdar's infinite reserves of courtesy came into known territory again with a grateful leap. 'Oh but of course, of course. You must stay. And as long as you wish. Where is the dear boy? And where is Bonzo?'

'Dada,' said Shudhangshu with extreme circumspection. 'You know Rudro is still asleep. And, it's not Bonzo, it's Rover, Rover!' He found himself shouting and lowered his voice with an effort. 'Bonzo was your last dog, the bulldog, remember? He died at least twenty years ago. This one's a doberman. His name is Rover, Rover!' This was a mistake, because Rover had returned from his walk and answered the call. He came bounding in, a monster clothed in a sleek brown body, bristling and growling at the presence of this intruder. Shudhangshu cried out and sprang up, another mistake. The dog leapt at him ignoring Proshanto's calls, and clamped his jaws on his arm. A servant, already on course with a jug of water, threw it instinctively at the dog. The water cascaded on to both dog and Shudhangshu and the temporarily shocked Rover was held back by the servant. 'Damn monster!' growled Shudhangshu at the confined dog, chained and being pulled out of the room. Proshanto looked on with a dropped jaw. 'I cannot understand it,' he said. 'What is the matter with the dog?

Where is he? Bonzo, Bonzo!' he called. The dog bayed from the next room.

'Oh god, Dada! You're the limit!' Shudhangshu's arm dripped with blood and water.

He called to the servants, 'Where have you tied him? You should have tied him up earlier. You know he bites. Be sure he's kept out of my way!' Fuming, he left to have himself treated. Inoculations, bandages and pain didn't encourage a feeling of kindliness towards the dog.

Soon, Shudhangshu was settled into the Rajmahal, constantly aware of the dog's menace, and trying to work out ploys to relieve Proshanto of his money. But controlling his irritability was a hard task, especially with Proshanto's insistence on calling out to 'Bonzo' at regular intervals. The dog's baying response resounded in reply. 'It's too much!' fumed Shudhangshu. 'Dada's gone off his rocker!' And he held his head and shook it morosely. 'I have to stop shouting at him! Come on!' he exhorted himself. 'Control yourself!'

'Dada,' he said. 'You must allow me to pay you for my board here. As it is, you are being so kind to Rudro.'

The clever move wiped out Proshanto's confusion. 'Pay? Of course not! Have you forgotten you are my younger brother, and Rudro is like my son! Have you taken leave of your senses?'

'Far from it, Dada. I'm in close contact with my senses, I can assure you,' and Shudhangshu laughed his uproarious laugh. 'But … I'm having some problems with my health … My heart …,' he added vaguely, refusing to divulge anything further in spite of repeated pressing. This additional nuance further pulled his elder brother to him through dutiful anxiety, and in time Shudhangshu's health became an obsession with Proshanto. Shudhangshu's feeling of power grew. 'It's so easy to manipulate him,' he thought. 'Why can't I get the old skinflint to part with his money?' And again he held his head and shook it, his frustration bursting out in a growl to match the dog's.

He stayed away from alcohol to help his self-control, yet at the back of his mind, he knew his addiction would return, which it did in just one day. 'A noble drink indeed,' he said, happily draining plentiful draughts of superior malt whisky again. He ordered it by the crateful on his rich brother's account, after convincing him it was essential for his heart. He also took the cunning course of encouraging his brother in his campaign for a lift.

Proshanto Mojumdar's memory contained a scattering of clear points in the fog of forgetting. Among these was the matter of the lift. Whenever he mentioned it, which was often, Shudhangshu enthusiastically supported him. 'It is time to prepare for old age before the stairs create an insurmountable barrier to the world outside,' said Proshanto. Repeatedly. The other tenants supported him, including Surjeet Shona, in spite of her flat being on the ground floor. They banded together and tormented Junior Mallik, the landlord's son, who had charge of the building. Loud arguments could be heard from the Mallik flat, dominated by Junior's harangues. 'Can't you understand climbing the stairs will give you exercise! Don't you see it's a must ...!'

Bravely brushing aside Junior, his father Ali Mallik acquired a prized antique lift. 'What do you think?' he said to Proshanto Mojumdar, when the lift was unloaded outside the lobby. 'It's a copy of the Government House lift. If it's good enough for the Government House, it should be good enough for us, don't you think?'

'What! That "birdcage"?' roared Junior, arriving magically.

'A brilliant move!' enthused Proshanto Mojumdar.

The Rajmahal could hardly contain its excitement. When had such a technological revolution been promised in its interiors? What, how, when, was it going to enjoy this stunning, electrically worked contraption of such delicate proportions, a veritable fairy goddess with its curvaceous roof and wrought metal filigree, its trellised designs of rings, curlicues and flower bouquets? For the Rajmahal had fallen in love with the little creature. 'I want you!' it sang, silently and frustratedly to itself. 'I want you!' It almost had an orgasm, stopping itself just in time when a beam nearly snapped out of position.

Junior was outraged, but could do nothing when his father stood firm. 'Very good,' he said, clapping mockingly. 'Congratulations, dear father, on your enterprise. I only hope it works!'

His words, uttered with such bad grace, sounded the death knell for the enterprise, and the lift would never be installed. It was discovered there simply wasn't space enough in the stairwell. Small as it was the birdcage was too wide by almost a foot. And attaching the lift to one side of the lobby raised grave problems of symmetry. The Rajmahal found its desire to embrace the flighty little creature dissipating. Any suggestion of creating a lop-sided aberration, pretty though the cause may be, was too upsetting to the confirmed bachelor returning to his senses.

'I concede,' said Proshanto Mojumdar despondently to Ali Mallik, after the birdcage had been evicted.

'Sorry old chap,' muttered Ali, wincing as he contemplated the long years of toiling up the stairs with gammy knee joints.

But with Shudhangshu's continuing support, Proshanto defiantly installed a dumb waiter from his first floor verandah to the lobby floor, his last major, coherent act, a cogent one. Junior Mallik trembled with rage and helplessness at the desecration of his lobby, but stopped from taking out a court injunction when the other tenants showed such a sickening solidarity in the matter. Though it shuddered to the cornerstone of its conservative structure, the Rajmahal, remembering the birdcage, was excited again by this belated introduction of technology. It felt in its bricks that soon, surely, the real sleek thing, of which Proshanto Mojumdar had many brochures, would be installed. The dumb waiter was announced by Proshanto Mojumdar as a warning. Either this aberration or the real thing. Proshanto's victory filled him with indulgence towards his ally, his younger brother.

Now the latter could say, tongue-in-cheek, 'Has Rudro talked to you yet? Wait. Let me call him.'

Rudrangshu, who was combing his hair in front of the mirror in his bedroom, came in reluctantly, saying privately to his father, 'It's embarrassing, Father. Why can't you leave the old bozo alone?'

'Shshsh,' cautioned Shudhangshu. 'Try and behave yourself. A lot depends on your uncle.'

Rudrangshu was a youthful forty, with beautiful hair which bounced healthily and swept his brow. The slight raising around his eyes, an acknowledgement of his father and uncle's bulging eyes, gave him a look of innocence. His generally pleasing aspect was reduced by a lazy-looking plumpness in the stomach region. Rudrangshu was too intelligent to imagine he could beat his laziness, and had long ago decided to spend time travelling without purpose, a pursuit for which he had a real bug, fed by two sea voyages with Proshanto and Mohini, the high points of his life so far. He spent time fantasizing about these voyages while constantly combing his superb hair and trying to work out the problem of finance. Even so, he was too guileless and too fond of his uncle to covet any inheritance from him. He resented his father's desperate tactics to take control of his life, convinced he was depraved if not downright wicked. He had his own theory that the emanation of Shudhangshu's characteristic body odour was the devil's sulphur.

After his mother's desertion of him in the same package as the smelly Shudhangshu, Rudrangshu gladly accepted Mohini as her replacement, his Maami or 'Aunty', and began calling her Mini-ma, after her nickname 'Mini' and sometimes 'Little Mother.' When his father summoned him in that significant way to talk to his uncle, therefore, he called on his late aunt for help.

'Mini-ma,' he called, feeling the psychic emanations which sometimes overtook him, 'Mini-ma. What am I to do with this father of mine?'

The house guarded its tenants zealously, keeping the ghosts from getting hyperactive. It knew that, contrary to the vague belief among mortals, ghosts couldn't be omnipresent, omnipotent or omniscient since that would make them gods, which they surely were not. It was more likely they were prescient rather than omniscient. So, Mohini's ghost, which was in a state of suspended prescience at this moment, had to be prodded by the house, and she gladly responded to Rudrangshu's mental summons.

'Dada,' Shudhangshu was saying, 'It's time Rudrangshu set up something on his own. What do you think?'

'Eh? Excellent, excellent!' said Proshanto. 'But he is such a clever lad, he will always make excellent progress!' And he looked beamingly at his nephew with the innocent eyes and cute mop of hair.

Rudrangshu, seeing what his father was up to, said, 'Certainly Uncle! I have your blood after all!'

'What about my blood?' said Shudhangshu, obviously hurt, and triggered to aggression he added sharply, 'It's the capital! Rudro needs the capital to set up ...'

'Credit me with some intelligence, Father ...,' butted in Rudrangshu. 'Look Uncle ... I've made my own arrangements. I've already told Father I don't need capital,' and he looked triumphantly at his poor odour-emanating father who would find it difficult to come to the point again.

'No need to doubt the boy, Shudo. Let him stand on his own two feet. Are you sure it is not you who are in need of cash, eh?'

'No, Dada! Credit me with some concern for my son,' said Shudhangshu, fuming privately, 'By Jove, that boy's sly!' And then his anger melted as he looked at his son's charming face, the only souvenir of his wife Ruby whom he so devastatingly loved and missed.

But with a strange cussedness, Proshanto Mojumdar simply couldn't get the point. 'What is to become of Rudro's future? Who knows when Dada's going to kick the bucket? People live till they are ninety these days. Look at old Petrov, still going for long walks and so forth. Rudro will be destitute and dead before Dada! He's forty already. Rudro, forty! By Jove, he doesn't look it!' And smiling fondly, Shudhangshu got lost in thoughts of his darling son merging into the persona of his darling ex-wife.

Inevitably his frustration brought him on to the expensive whisky with increased ardour, and his impatience reached frenetic levels. 'A precipitation,' he soothed himself. 'That's all it needs. Nudging on the inevitable. Why not? What a precious thought!'

'Swine!' the prescient ghost of Mohini swore, certain her husband's life was in danger. And then she urged her husband, 'Oh, get on with it! Can't you win this race? Can't you either just give him what he wants, now, or die quickly and peacefully in your bed!'

And thus a terrible tussle took place, between Mohini the anxious, hovering, waiting ghost and her desperado brother-in-law, while the obtuse Proshanto Mojumdar chewed the cud. Rudrangshu was uncharacteristically busy trying to buffer his uncle from his father. 'What happened to all that "Mini-ma" business?' wondered Mohini. But abandoning his laid-back attitude for the present had exhausted Rudrangshu too much for psychic games.

It was a measure of Shudhangshu's repulsiveness that no one and nothing, neither his son nor his brother, nor the prescient ghosts, nor the house, had an inkling of his true motives. For, to be fair to the malodorous father, he would only rest happy if his son, his ego's extension, was successful. And, like most of the world, he assumed success meant happiness.

But Shudhangshu possessed dithering desperation, not the required ruthlessness to achieve that end. This wasn't the opposite of, but obliquely separate from, self-centredness. His assumptions about success were so uncomplicated that he couldn't imagine his son could be indifferent to moneymaking. His machinations would precipitate Rudrangshu into uncharacteristic action.

Forced out of his inertia and compelled to protect his uncle, Rudrangshu's laid-back lay-about life was disturbed, and he decided on drastic action. He activated his intelligence to focus and reached his version of a compromise formula. It was, in the end, uncompromising, because it involved abandoning his old uncle and cutting out his father's interference in his life. It was, within the parameters of his character, ruthless.

One fine day, Rudrangshu Mojumdar picked up his possessions and left the Rajmahal, ran away. Figuring out that the pursuit of happiness was the only worthwhile course, he applied to a luxury ocean liner company for a job and found himself employed. The ship was to set off from England, and he complacently approached his uncle to fund the journey. 'Rudro my boy!' beamed the loving Proshanto. 'I'm so glad you asked!'

'I'll return every penny of it to you, Uncle, I promise you!' Rudrangshu could feel the familiar frisson of Mohini's presence and smiled happily to himself. 'Goodbye, Mini-ma, Little Mother,' he said. 'Knowing you are there, I won't grieve when Uncle goes. He goes to infinitely better company than he has here!' And he added,

'You at least will understand and approve of what I am about to do.' Mohini Mojumdar's ghost whooped with joy. Shudo, she thought, having lost control of his son, would be distracted from murderous inclinations.

Rudrangshu's disappearance upset both father and uncle. Shudhangshu made weekly entreaties to his son through the personal columns. 'Dear Rudro, Where are you? I anxiously await news. Remember I am on your side. Please come back, or failing that, please write. Your anxious Father.' Proshanto, on the other hand, felt his nephew's absence as a hollowness which couldn't be pinpointed. The hollowness was increased by the absence of the dog from his usual position by his side. The frustration of these feelings brought his forgetfulness into full spate, and smothered his kindliness. 'Where is the dear boy? And where is Bonzo? Rudro, Rudro! Bonzo, Bonzo!' was his constant, maddening call, followed by the chained dog's baying response. Shudhangshu, inebriated and combative, was riled beyond forbearance and foamed and raved. The Mojumdar flat became the noisiest in the Rajmahal, and the other tenants refrained from complaining only because they had grown old with Proshanto.

When Rudrangshu wrote finally, his letter was addressed to his uncle. Proshanto cut open the envelope and a cheque fell out. 'When did Rudro leave? I do not remember extending a loan to him!' He automatically had the cheque dispatched to his bank and kept the letter aside, pleased his nephew had taken to a life at sea. 'I knew that boy would come good,' he mused happily. 'I wonder what post he holds … Ahh! God is kind.'

His frustration receded but came up again when Shudhangshu appeared in the doorway and flopped into a chair. 'You must go on a diet, Shudo,' he said. 'What about your cardiac problems?'

'Ooof Dada. Do you have to say the same thing every time you see me, every day five hundred times?'

'But you are much too stout for your age! Look at me!'

'Yes, yes!' said Shudhangshu. 'I've been looking at you for weeks. And listening to you too.' He stopped abruptly when he saw the envelope and recognized Rudrangshu's handwriting. 'By Jove, he's written!' he shouted. 'Dada, why didn't you tell me?' He pounced on the letter.

'Dear Uncle,' read the sweating and trembling Shudhangshu.

'I hope you are quite well. I for one am positively flourishing. You will be happy to hear that I have joined shipping and that I am aboard the *Queen Elizabeth II* at this very moment, about to dock outside New York! Surprised?

'I have enclosed a cheque for the amount you so very kindly and generously lent me. I have Mini-ma and your portraits with me. As you know, you are like parents to me.

'Speaking of which, is my parent still with you? If so, do give him my salutations and tell him I am very happy.

With respect and affection

Rudro.'

Shudhangshu gnashed his teeth in extreme chagrin, that his son had addressed his uncle, not his own father. But the relief at knowing his whereabouts cancelled the chagrin.

'What should Rudro be, given his intelligence, Dada? Purser at least?' he asked proudly.

'What?' said Proshanto. 'Could be, could be, yes. He has a strong head for accounts, has he not?'

Shudhangshu wondered where his brother had found this nugget. Rudro couldn't distinguish a crore from a lakh, let alone add single units. But that was typical of Dada. He could re-invent life and events easily with his atrocious memory. Shudhangshu hummed, what luck, what luck for his darling boy. By Jove, he could relax at last. At last. Shudhangshu gave vent to a huge sigh, his paunch subsiding dramatically as he stretched himself in a long planter's chair with his legs propped up on the extended arms.

'You are really much too stout, Shudo,' said Proshanto disapprovingly. 'Kindly do something about it. Your cardiovascular system does not stand a chance in such a body.'

Shudhangshu stopped his irritable reply as a noisy covey of mini-buses rumbled by, sending up strong effluents of diesel. They were sitting out on the verandah, once the Sardar Bahadur's conservatory, in spite of the deafening roar and noxious air. 'A verandah is a verandah,' Proshanto always said. 'It is a great crime not to use it.' In his mind the sea and wind and waves roared in an idyllic memory reservoir as he floated away on the Chowringhee traffic waves. Over the years, the features of this traffic had altered. There were the double decker 'London' buses, the electric trams, successors to the horse-drawn tram-trains of the nineteenth century. When the electric trams were new they were shiny and sleek, 'the best trams in the world, better than anywhere else, Paris, London, Rome!' Proshanto was given to boastfully proclaiming. But the trams deteriorated as time overtook the scope of scant resources. Public transport was instead swelled with the addition of rashly driven mini-buses, their raunchy conductors banging the buses' battered sides in some bus code and adding to the cacophony. Proshanto didn't mention the trams any more, his boasts being reserved for Calcutta's recent raging pride, the underground Metro, though he had only been on one ride and had no need for the Metro anyway.

While waiting for the noise to subside, Shudhangshu felt his irritation swelling like the traffic. 'Wonderful Rajmahal!' he cursed. 'All that splendour to be surrounded by this pollution of air and noise. We have to sit out here where we have to shout and scream at each other as if we were deaf! Ridiculous Dada with his re-invention of events, which in his mind should exist and therefore *do* exist! I wouldn't be surprised if his rotten memory isn't due to this din. How can anyone think straight here?'

When Proshanto Mojumdar's memory played tricks, Shudhangshu at first protested. But later, with Proshanto's insistent re-inventions, he often had to shake himself out of an almost willing suspension of memory.

And here he was, so irritated by his brother's memory tricks, yet forgetting he had manipulated that very memory for his own ends. It was he, Shudhangshu, who had planted the worry in his brother's mind about his imaginary cardiac problems. The strange thing was that Shudhangshu sometimes caught himself out believing in his own inventions, and this increased his irritation with his innocent elder brother.

'No,' he would say, 'don't you remember? So and so wasn't there. Look. Here's the picture. Can you see him? He's not there. He couldn't come. Remember?' Proshanto would nod absent-mindedly. But soon, he would be re-inventing again, chortling at the typically amusing behaviour of the same so-and-so at the same event. And after a period of this, Shudhangshu would no longer trouble to take out the picture, but would almost remember so-and-so at the event himself. He would have to shake himself not to 'see' so-and-so in a particular position with a particular expression in the picture when he wasn't there at all! There would be an almost willing suspension of memory with Pro's insistent re-inventions.

Petrov's Diary: *Is forgetfulness invariable with old age? Today Proshanto Mojumdar spoke of the Metro again, the wonderful, incomparable Calcutta Metro! His brother Shudo complained that Proshanto was forgetful and had completely obliterated the years of torture to Calcutta's citizens while the Metro was being built. In fact, most Calcutta citizens have obliterated this memory of torture in their swollen-headed pride over the Metro! Memory can do many harmful acrobatics, denying an inconvenient fact which simply ceases, never was ... In this arena of memory and forgetting, truth and hallucination, people often cannot place themselves or identify their own roles. Taking the logic beyond its limit, one wonders if old age doesn't bring one's brain into the region of the absurd, to confuse invention with reality because it is made reality, because invention sublimates truth.*

Shudhangshu's relief at seeing his son's letter was short-lived. After a simple query to the shipping line, he discovered Rudrangshu was nothing but a steward, a waiter, on board the *QE II*. 'Mojumdar, Rudolph: Steward. Duties: Serving meals in first class dining hall,' was the terse reply.

'I didn't have a son for him to become a waiter! And exchange his name for a red-nosed reindeer!' he moaned. He couldn't accept that 'Rudolph' was unmitigatingly happy. Non-threatening and unthreatened in turn, he was in paradise. And it was only Rudrangshu's Mini-ma who could appreciate his success, his happiness, actually. When Mohini's ghost read the letter from over Shudhangshu's shoulder, she chuckled with joy.

Shudhangshu's reaction was the opposite. 'By Jove!' he declared. 'That boy is back to his lazy, tranquil self!' Shattered with the shame of the news, he felt a resurgent vicarious ambition for his offspring. Mohini's ghost was in a turmoil of speculation. 'I hope he's not on that track again!' she said.

That night, Shudhangshu went into a frenzy when he found the last crate of whisky innocent of bottles, the last bottle innocent of whisky. And all the shops closed. He shouted at the servants who had nothing to say, having themselves contributed unstintingly to the crisis. He foraged desperately and found a stock of gin. 'Inferior stuff compared to that noble drink,' he grumbled. 'But what choice do I have?'

The flat had been locked, the servants had left, and Proshanto was watching the late night news, a blind habit.

Shudhangshu came into the room. 'Dada,' he slurred, making an effort to keep a straight course. 'I've had enough nonsense from you! Now sign this!' He thrust a chequebook at Proshanto.

'No I will not!' said Proshanto with astonishing alacrity. 'I most certainly will not! I know what you are up to!'

Shudhangshu balked. 'But it's for Rudro!' he pleaded. 'Don't you want to do this for Rudro? He's like your own son!'

Proshanto smiled fondly and foolishly. 'Where is the dear boy? Rudro, Rudro!'

'Bloody hell!' shouted Shudhangshu. He tried to push a pen into Proshanto's hand, but there was no cooperation. The pen fell to the ground. The dog's growling could be heard from the next room.

'Damn, damn, damn …!' Shudhangshu lurched out of the room in a blurring trail of curses. Proshanto was lost in a vintage cowboy film when Shudhangshu came back, chortling to himself, with a gun in his hand. It was Proshanto's turn to balk.

Shudhangshu banged the chequebook down on the table next to Proshanto. 'Sign! On each and every cheque!' His gun was limp in a shaky hand. But Proshanto, without hearing, and reacting to the scene on the TV screen, was raising both his arms above his head. Shudhangshu backed away, and pointed the gun at his elder brother in a reversal of the cowboy sequence. 'Come on, you old skinflint! Sign!'

Proshanto's arms were paining, and he missed the rudeness. 'Can I put my arms down? Please. The pain is most intense.' His arms trembled like the Sardar Bahadur's when he had held the Guru Granth Sahib over his head.

'Who asked you to put them up in the first place?' said Shudhangshu without answering the question. He came closer, bumping into things. The enclosed room reeked with a distasteful odour.

'I cannot keep my arms up for such a long period. It is impossible!' insisted Proshanto.

'For god's sake put them down and sign!' The gun in Shudhangshu's hand was unsteady, he was rocking as he tried to keep standing. He put out a hand and lurched against a table. The table fell over and there was a crash of china.

'Ei! That is Mini's favourite piece! What are you doing?' said Proshanto, bringing down his arms at last. Shudhangshu's gun lay where it had fallen, in a heap of broken china.

'Mini, Mini! I remember the time when you and your Mini were fighting like cat and dog. Why this sudden devotion now that she's dead and gone!'

Shudhangshu bent down shakily to pick up his gun and dropped it again. 'It's this damn silencer! Too heavy!'

'Here,' Proshanto said kindly, getting up. 'Let me get it for you.'

'Fool!' Shudhangshu furiously grabbed the gun and whacked Proshanto on the shoulder with the butt end, falling on to him and knocking him over. 'Bloody fool!'

Mohini's ghost groaned. Shudhangshu pushed himself upright, gun in one hand, waving the chequebook with the other.

'Why are you doing this?' said Proshanto from the floor, just refraining from holding his nose. 'Have you gone mad? Have you forgotten my age?'

'Not at all, you old skinflint. I can hear your bones rattling. They should be rattling in heaven soon! Or better still, hell!'

The rudeness precipitated the dog's image. 'Bonzo, Bonzo!' called Proshanto from the floor. No sound and no dog. A thought tickled Proshanto's memory. Had he not heard a dog's short yelp, and an abrupt pop with it? Was it his imagination, or some other memory? 'Forgetfulness is the premier sign of age. Without memory one is nothing. And yet memory is the chief cause of all our misery!' he mused out loud.

'Shut up!'

'Bonzo, Bonzo!' he called again.

'Shut up!' screamed Shudhangshu, jumping up and down.

The city authorities, or an accident, activated a power failure at that very moment. There was a click and a total blackout just as the gun went off with a familiar pop. Mohini's ghost screamed unheard as the two men were thrown in opposite directions as if pulled by a puppeteer's strings. Proshanto, who had just got himself up from the floor, fell on to a chair, quite sure he was about to die. The procedure was surprisingly painless. 'I have been hit!' he thought, feeling a warm wet streak down his pyjama leg. Then realizing he was unharmed, he moaned with the belated shock and shame of having urinated in his pyjamas. The dog was utterly silent and it was steadfastly dark.

'Such a thing – at my age ...'

The violence and complete demonization of Shudhangshu had twisted up in Proshanto's mind in a tangle, a Gordian knot, a contortion of the brain. This was a burglar, no longer Shudo, his younger brother. In fact, where was Shudo? 'Where is he, where is that Shudo? Why are the lights off? Shudo, Shudo! Where are you?'

Shudhangshu was too astonished to react. And then, the full moon appeared behind the glassed verandah doors, and a beam lit up Shudhangshu's shoe. Proshanto started nervously. 'Perhaps hallucinations occur at full moon time, and lunacy ensues.' That frayed shoelace! Shudo! It was his own brother! That dreadful and well-known odour! Or was he himself, Proshanto Mojumdar, losing his mind? Can the identification of a criminal be based on a shoelace? And a hum? Is such evidence acceptable in a court of law? And then, that sharp yip and pop? Was it some other memory? Proshanto Mojumdar's mind strained. His head pounded. He blacked out just as the room lit up again with a click.

When Proshanto came around in a second and saw Shudhangshu he was relieved. 'Thank the good lord!' he said. 'Where were you when the lights went off? Absent when you are most needed! And where is the dear boy? Rudro, Rudro!' Shudhangshu walked up to him in a fury, whipped up a hand and knocked his brother's jaw right, left, whack, smack! Mohini's ghost exclaimed and hit out ineffectively at Shudhangshu. Proshanto slumped into his chair, and allowed the tears to roll down his cheeks. His thoughts careened crazily in his aching head. He started sobbing. When he could see again, he found Shudhangshu sitting on the opposite chair with a glass of water in his hands.

'Have some water, Dada. Come on. What is this? A grown man like you weeping. Are you a baby?'

Shudhangshu helped his trembling elder brother to sit up straight and put the glass into his hands, while Proshanto automatically held his breath and drank. He felt clearer in the head.

'It's Rudro. He has a problem,' said Shudhangshu.

'What is the problem?'

'You're so bloody tight-fisted,' shouted Shudhangshu irascibly again. 'How can you forget that I've asked you a thousand times already. Would you ever oblige me? "No, no, no" that's what you always say, without hesitation! "No, no, no" …?'

'But you said nothing about Rudro. Why did you not tell me about Rudro?'

'Dammit! How many times have I not told you? Have you forgotten how you insulted me, told me I couldn't fool you? Wouldn't do it for me, would you, you old skinflint!'

Proshanto's mouth snapped shut.

'Oh. Now you're sulking is it? And if you're so attached to your nephew why haven't you taken my hints yet? Did you try to help? Ever?' Shudhangshu fell into a brown study, equally hurt. 'However desperate I am on Rudro's behalf, how can I pull this off?'

He sat with the gun slack in his hands, moodily biting his lip while expletives revolved ceaselessly in his head.

Proshanto Mojumdar dozed off. His weighing scale of life had tilted decisively towards happiness after the swimming pool triumph and the revival of his libido, manifesting that very night with his hearty dream laughter. People at times weep or laugh in dreams, waking up expecting tears on their cheeks, or aching ribs, but with no such outward manifestation. They are unaroused after erotic dreams in spite of the power of the dream emotion. Others wake up to find the tears, the aching ribs and the arousal in reality. Proshanto Mojumdar was one of the latter. He usually laughed loud and long, a thick, phantasmagoric laughter, with a garbling of words. When Mohini was there, she would prod him and ask, 'What are you laughing about?' And Proshanto would wake up, his face wreathed in smiles, guffawing still, and say, 'Laughing? What do you mean?' And Mohini would say, 'But you were laughing and talking so loud! Look! You are still grinning all over your face!' But then Proshanto would get into an erotic mood, and Mohini would put aside her questions.

So here were Proshanto Mojumdar and his sibling on a nocturnal adventure, the one just about to begin a laughing dream, the other deeply lost in stressful thought.

'Quite a pair!' Mohini Mojumdar's ghost thought, watching excitedly over them.

Shudhangshu got out of his chair with an effort, overcome by exhaustion and emotion. He could sense the nasty atmosphere caused by his own nervous sweating. He walked over to the glassed doors with thoughts of opening them, looked out, and was shocked! The sky was bright, a tinge of pink instead of the grey-gold glow of city lights.

Frantically, he rushed to his brother. Proshanto's mouth had fallen open in a big, slack grin, with the spittle drooling from a corner. His white stubble gleamed in the lamplight, and he looked positively evil. Shudhangshu pushed the nozzle of his gun against Proshanto's cheek and almost fainted at the response, an unnaturally deep guffaw. It sounded to Shudhangshu like the mockery of the devil. Angrily, he prodded his old brother hard in the ribs, waking him up groaning and giggling at the same time.

'Don't tickle me like that,' said the devil incarnate, opening one eye. 'Oh, it's you, Shudo,' he said fondly, his face descending gradually as he slid off the chair. He shook with laughter like a drunk. 'What is this, a joke? Father! Father! I'll tell Father.' He fell asleep immediately on the carpet, still laughing away merrily.

Shudhangshu groaned and sat down with his head in his hands. What could he do, his wonderful and crazy and daring plan in ruins? Dada, the poor old senile thing, was unlikely to remember this long night. He was least worried about that. But it was back to the impasse. Rudro's failed life. His degrading, shameful occupation.

Shudhangshu went up to his collapsed chuckling brother, placed his arms under his shoulders, and half-carried half-dragged him to his bedroom. He manoeuvered him on to the bed, feeling like laughing and weeping at the same time. Poor old Dada! And shaking his head he switched on the fan and left Proshanto fast and noisily asleep, to the relief of Mohini's ghost.

Then Shudhangshu cleaned up the mess in the drawing room.

The pink of the dawn welled up and was reflected in the western sky. The cooing and flapping of pigeons mingled with the chirping of sparrows. Shudhangshu opened one of the large glass-paned doors and walked out on to the deep verandah over Chowringhee. He leaned over the balcony, breathing in the sulphurous Calcutta air mixed with the fresh scent of newly mown grass from the garden below. The traffic was already swelling, and an empty double-decker bus passed by crab-wise, listing dangerously as though the passengers already weighed down one side. Shudhangshu was aware also that the effects of the gin, which had earlier added to the dimensions of his odour, were wearing off, leaving a sour taste in his mouth. The light seeped across the sky like bloody treacle, resembling the blood coagulating around poor dead Rover whom the preoccupied Shudhangshu had quite forgotten. He had also forgotten the empty shells, one ejected after he had shot the creature, and the other after the accidental firing off at his brother.

Proshanto Mojumdar woke up in the morning, and found himself in great pain and in pyjamas smelling of urine. He pulled himself out of bed and righted his balance with difficulty. Not only did his body ache, but his hands and feet were chilly. 'My circulation's going,' he thought. He gave a tired yawn, snapping his fingers to save his jaw from locking, and went shakily through his ablutions. Warily, he removed his pyjamas, holding his breath and turning his mind away from the signs of incontinence. Was getting old really so dramatic? He remembered nothing and the puzzling pain about the jaws would stop him from shaving ever again.

Shudhangshu collected himself enough in the morning to rid the flat of Rover's body with help from the bemused servants. He himself would never recover from memories of that gin-drunk night and he gave up alcohol in contrition again, for twenty-four hours.

Circumstances now pushed Proshanto's lift campaign into its final stages. One day, the pulleys of the dumb waiter gave way and deposited the contraption, in which he was riding, with such a jarring impact on the lobby floor that he passed out for a second. There were many witnesses, most significantly, Junior, who was on the stairs.

'That does it!' he said. 'I've had enough! This contraption is going to be dismantled today itself!'

Proshanto, still struggling on the floor of the constricting dumb waiter, couldn't get his words together before Junior had stalked away. Junior saw to it that the dumb waiter was dismantled and all traces of it removed. Thus ended the last of Proshanto's aspirations …

More and more, as he lay in his bedroom, the *Hong Kong* salon's look-alike, he lived on board in his dreams, a way to bring back his prime and his wife in one go. Between decks he coasted vertically in the fancy lifts displayed in his brochures, emerging at each deck from a different model. He thought of death, though apart from a blood pressure problem and those few aches and pains, he felt quite well. The overwhelming will to live and enjoy his day made nonsense of these and other setbacks.

He didn't realize his failing memory had a part in this. Most senile forgetfulness, apart from obliterating the recent past, highlights stressful rather than pleasant memories of the distant past, reaching back to childhood. In Proshanto's case it was the opposite, only the happy past came up. Hence his laughing dreams. Mohini's ghost looked forward to the nights, because then she too could lull herself to sleep and imagine she was sharing Proshanto's bed.

The bevelled edges and glinting peacock tail-eyes of the room's finest glass caught the light, filling the air at sunset with golden sparklers and sprinkling the room at dawn with diamonds. To Proshanto the dawn was best. This was when he would wake up, in an interval in every dream, still with the promise of the rest of the dream to follow. The sun would rise over the back of the Rajmahal, and the south-westerly peacock windows would be pearly and opalescent, a playful Aurora-Ushas throwing streamers across to strike those cold jewels. Proshanto would savour the dream already passed and fall happily into it again. What were the memories embellishing that half world? What dolphins and mermaids disported themselves in the sparkling deep? What provoked him to this nightly rejuvenation of erotic laughter? Maybe it was something to do with the children of his lacking seed, sensual nights planting that seed, magically fertilized, and then awaiting the sequel in a state of timeless arousal. In and out of the spirit world, in and out of the looking glass of mortality drifted the couple in pleasant and expectant camaraderie. Never before in reality had they such harmony and peace as during those nights, one not in and not out of this world, the other in a dream.

But how long could such bliss last? Mohini's ghost was frantic on the night of Shudhangshu's madness. Unlike Proshanto, she was fond of the dog and sorry his ghost had appeared only briefly in great distress before vanishing, an indication of the deterioration setting in at the Rajmahal. 'Poor Proshanto's had enough,' she said. 'First, Shudo's installation in our flat. Then his unheard of violence.

Rudro and Rover's disappearance. And the Stracheys, our good friends in the end, into their graves together. Why did they have to take such a drastic step? Foolish ones! They didn't even show up in my world! Poor dear Proshanto! All he can do is call out and call out for the non-existent. Except for me. He can never forget I'm gone from his world. For good! Oh come soon dear, come soon to me! It's time.'

She grimly watched Proshanto, still dwelling on young girls, still devouring them with his eyes when he went swimming, a daily routine he kept up with tenacity. Still swirling the aquamarine water with his arms so that streams of translucent bubbles could connect him to the springing breasts and tight bottoms of those unattainable beauties. She could catch his thoughts. 'Where are the girls? The fresh girls with the utterly soft fingers and damp palms I once held so delicately while I taught them how to dance?' He would have to wait for the young ones, children, for that kind of beauty. Where did they come to the Rajmahal any more …? Where had the Mojumdars the joy of their own? 'It's time,' thought Mohini. 'There's only one worthwhile service left for him in this world, and that's to leave dear Rudro well-off. It's high time …'

Time it was that decided to cut short Mohini's vigil, and she was soon to receive the ghost of her Proshanto in her nebulous embrace. 'Cardiac arrest', the doctor's death certificate clearly stated, not doing that portentous event justice with this brusque brief. Proshanto was fortunate his death took place while he was in the middle of one of those laughing, happy dreams.

No sooner did Mohini's ghost scream with joy at her beloved Proshanto's still-dazed ghost joining her, than there was a whirling swirling agitation in the Rajmahal spirit world, and the Mojumdar couple vanished forever.

'Are they all going to leave like this without even bidding me farewell?' creaked the Rajmahal, its walls darkened permanently with loss. The remaining residents were slow to notice the growing gloom, but their spirits were affected, and they went about with grim faces for a while. The ghosts knew the end was near. 'The Mojumdars have got away in time,' they griped. 'Some are luckier than others.'

It was Rudrangshu who returned to perform the rituals of the eldest son at the burning ghat. Scattering scented powders on his uncle's spare en-flowered body, setting his soul free by smashing the earthen pot to the ground, putting to flame the nest of logs within which the body lay. As the flames crackled high Shudhangshu, who stood by his side, raised his shining eyes to his son, and sang to himself, 'At last! At last, my boy will get his chance!'

Other Rajmahalians who attended the cremation couldn't help but notice his widely stretched lips. For a moment they wondered if this denoted sorrow. Smiling and weeping are so similar.

Surjeet Shona looked away from the embarrassing spectacle. She avoided Shudhangshu and went up to Rudro. 'What are your plans, Rudro? Are you giving up your job?'

Before Rudrangshu could answer, Shudhangshu had come up to her, blooming, his moustache bristling with health. He laughed boisterously. 'The beautiful Shona, here in person! We are honoured!' Shudhangshu was making no attempt to hide his delight. 'Rudro must fulfil his destiny, Shona. Dada has made him his heir and there's no hindrance! Isn't God great?'

'Oh, Rudro's the heir,' she said. 'And, er, what about you ...?'

'It's all the same,' said Shudhangshu with uncontained joy. 'He's my son after all. He's the one who needs it most, not me!'

Surjeet Shona looked at the rich young inheritor, the son of this joyous father, and found something distasteful in his expression.

Later, when she visited the Mojumdar flat she would find Rudrangshu reclining on a chair, absent-mindedly pushing his fingers through his beautiful hair.

'Where's your father?'

'Oh I've sent him away!'

'Sent him away ...? Your own father ...?'

'So? He's an old rogue! Mini-ma and Uncle were more like my own parents.'

'But, where's he gone?'

'I don't know. Where he always went, I suppose? He doesn't need all this.' Rudrangshu gestured vaguely around him. 'I'm getting married, you know. And this is mine, all mine.' He hugged himself. 'All mine.'

This was the ruthless side of Rudrangshu again. The first sign of that ruthlessness had manifested when he had walked without warning out of his doting uncle and father's lives and gone to sea. Since then, the parameters of his ruthlessness had widened. With practice perhaps. And he had done something recognizably ruthless by disowning his devoted father.

4

The Book of Famine

In one of the second floor flats lived the Russian Anatoly Sergeivich Petrov. Firmly fixated on India and India studies, he fled the Bolsheviks, and was forced to take a tortuous and decade-long route to Calcutta via Tashkent and Europe. He reached when British Calcutta was descending from its imperial apogee with the shift of the capital to Delhi. But it was still commercially crucial, elegant, well lit by gaslight, and it could still reflect distant London to some and St Petersburg to others. Its flourishing port and riches still impressed.

Petrov belonged to a family connected to the Romanoffs, though not especially royalist in their leanings. His father, for one, was a dove towards his serfs, releasing them from bondage in imitation of his mentor Tolstoy. When he heard Tolstoy was helping the poor during the famine of 1891, he made plans to join him. But they never materialized, and his contact with the great man was restricted to a few letters. The obstacle was his obsession with his vast and orderly library, in direct contrast to the confusion in other aspects of his life. So he kept papers and cuttings on the famine neatly bound in numbered volumes, while his ideals struggled for translation into action.

From the time he could understand, Anatoly Sergeivich Petrov would hear his father's discourses on the subjects of Tolstoy, freedom and famine, and from his early teens, he had become familiar with all the newspaper cuttings that his father so sedulously kept in chronological order in his library, including records of Tolstoy's correspondence with Indian nationalists agonized by British rule. And by contrast, items on the ancient civilization and learning of India.

His father's aspirations re-appeared in Petrov at a remove. Where his father succeeded only in refined bibliolatry, Petrov longed to study and perhaps one day resolve a great metaphysical riddle – the existence side by side of 'civilization' and human degradation. Complicating this desire was a feeling of frustration at the impotence or lack of will of the 'civilized' state in fighting this degradation. He could identify some of this with the anti-royalist and Marxist fervour of his countrymen. But being elliptically inclined, he found himself veering towards the Indian situation and sympathizing with the Indian struggle against colonial rule. A fascination for philosophy gave the final push. India, he felt, would offer him the most dramatic theatre in which to witness the great riddle in action. And its philosophy, arcing like a rainbow over the collective mind of its people, would provide the answer.

Petrov joined the Institute of Oriental Studies in St Petersburg to familiarize himself with Sanskrit as well as Bengali, the languages he would need before going to India, specifically Calcutta. Thus his father's attitude to life and society and its effect on Petrov were to lead him on a philosophical mad quest, impossible of achievement.

Petrov knew it was only a matter of time before his fellow students denounced him with his imperial connections. He had two older brothers who were gearing up to flee to Germany, and Petrov, always dreaming of India, was left almost penniless when they disappeared westward.

Ali Sher, a co-student from Tashkent, kept Petrov revving with stories of a Bengali M. N. Roy, who had reached Tashkent with a train full of arms from Lenin. He heard of the sympathy for Indian nationalists, who sometimes used Tashkent as a nucleus. Of the prodigious scholars working from the last century turning out encyclopaedic histories of Central Asia with detailed references to India, and of Indian language courses developed and taught in Tashkent.

'Maybe I can study there for a start,' thought the young Petrov. 'It might be safer than St Petersburg!'

Ali Sher told him of the scholarship on the subject of British rule in India. Of Saeed Ali Khoja, who had travelled in India at the end of the nineteenth century, and written of the death of nineteen million people due to famine during just one decade. As compared to five million war-related deaths in the whole world in the hundred years enclosing that decade! He described the rulers' policies to retain and drain the fabled colony while the ruled lived degraded lives, bringing into focus once again the riddle that stirred Petrov's imagination. How could a power, great at the time, tolerate this burden of dehumanizing contrast, including famine, without a tremor, and yet claim civilizational superiority? How could its elite enjoy the flaky delicacy of a prima ballerina and denounce the heavenly hetaerae of Indian dance? He couldn't have forecast that he would witness at first hand the flesh and blood horrors of the Great Bengal Famine two and a half decades later in Calcutta, getting deeply involved in its ramifications and those of the tortured and wonderful metropolis.

He would play with the figures given to him by his friend – *'19 million dead people'* – and write it down on any scrap of paper that came to hand. *'19 million dead people equals ten years,'* he would write. *'That is, 1.9 million per year'* under the heading *'Famine in India'*. And next to it *'5 million dead people equals 100 years. That is, 5000 per year'*, under the heading *'War in the World'*. Another time he would write, *'5000 in war against 1.9 million due to famine of one-sixth of the world's population (India). Or 1 war death in the whole world against 380 deaths due to famine in India alone. Or 1 war death against the iniquity of 380 famine deaths multiplied by 6 equals 2280 ...'* And again, *'1 is to 380, 1 is to 380 x 6 ...' 'Which is justified, which is not? Why should that seeker put the two figures together? Is there greater consideration in and about war, consideration that only 1 person should be shot dead, the parts of his body strewn on a battlefield, when 380 (x 6 times the iniquity) are carelessly left to starve, strewn about the countryside in India? 5205 dead people in ONE DAY in India of famine! 13 or 14 dead people in one day from war ... Is the war machine less cruel than the manipulation or indifference which kills by starvation?'*

He would wrack his brain for a philosophical equation, the perfect formula, hardly aware that a famine was taking place in his own country right then, torturing, maiming and locking in its ratchet the customary countless faceless numbers. In the end all he could do was divert himself by practicing the lotus posture. 'That's the first step,' the eighteen year old would murmur. 'I must meditate. And before I can meditate I must be able to sit, for *hours*, in the correct manner. The answer will surely come ...' He learned to bend his unaccustomed legs, make them supple with yoga, and sat for hours in the lotus pose. But the answer didn't come. It never would.

Petrov went to Tashkent, assuming the cover name of Rahimbaeff. There he sought out the legendary M. N. Roy with the vague idea of enlisting his aid. Roy was busy rehabilitating a band of Indian Khilafatis on their way to Turkey with even vaguer ideas of rescuing the Caliph. Instead, they had got caught in the wilds of Central Asia, in need of a rescuer themselves. And Roy duly played this part. Failing to appreciate their desultory though romantic aim, Roy planned to transform them into rescuers of their own country, completing the reverse cycle of rescues. The plan was to smuggle them in from the mountains bordering India to mobilize and arm the local populace. Roy had organized a building, India House, and Petrov was allowed to stay there with the Khilafatis. But a sinister development finally winkled him out. Comrade Peter, vice-president of the Red Terror, part of the Cheka or Secret Police, arrived in Tashkent. The dreaded Cheka claimed the inheritance of Ivan the Terrible, now dubbed Ivan the Great, his example a part justification for its purges. Petrov was pushed into another room by Roy on a sudden visit by 'Bloody Peter' at the India House, and caught a glimpse of the tall thin man with a face as ugly as his deeds. Bloody Peter had found out about Petrov, but Roy, with his great influence, was just able to save him. Ever the pragmatist, the wise man advised him to leave for Europe. Poor Petrov left Tashkent despondent at getting further and further from his goal. The adventure deepened his fascination for India. Roy's plan may have been almost as impractical as the Khilafatis', but he loved big dreamers of such conviction. 'If there are others of that kind in Calcutta, its attractions could be legion,' he thought.

And he didn't allow *his* dream to vaporize. He fetched up in Europe, and stayed with his brothers. He tried academia in the 'Oriental' departments of European universities. But nothing could divert him from his attempts to access the original. Finally, when his brothers handed him his full share of the family wealth, the restless Petrov joyfully booked passage for Calcutta. The diversion had taken him almost a decade, during which he had had to battle the inertia of luxurious living in Europe, and pinch himself to believe his Tashkent adventure. So, in 1929, at the same age as the century, he finally reached Calcutta.

The British were suspicious of this exotic immigrant and watched him closely. In those days when spying was rampant all over the globe and particularly in Central Asia where British spies jostled with Russians, Turks, Afghans and Sindhis, this strange figure claiming to be from the Russian nobility but unfathomably hobnobbing with the natives, was automatically suspect. They were wary not only because of the age-old Anglo-Russian face-off in the region, the Great Game, but because of the complications of the Bolshevik Revolution, the activities of Indians looking for arms, and Lenin's sympathy for them. They became still more wary when Petrov admitted knowing the wanted revolutionary M. N. Roy, though his frankness was puzzling. He was prepared and trotted out his family credentials, hinting untruthfully that this underscored automatic royalist leanings and an antagonism towards anti-colonial activities. He had to flee the Bolsheviks, being from a noble family, he told them truthfully, and so the false name in his passport. And then, as a Christian and a European with an imperial legacy, how could he possibly be interested either in the caliphate in distant Turkey or in the freedom of India? He told them his aims were purely academic, to study Indian language and philosophy. His

British interlocutors couldn't get any more out of him but his friendship with local Bengalis continued to puzzle them. They confiscated his passport and kept him under surveillance. When M. N. Roy arrived in India in 1931, Petrov was taken in again for questioning. But no further connection could be found between the two, nor any active participation by Petrov in the communist or freedom movements in India. M. N. Roy, though he had broken from the Comintern, was still wanted by the British, and was arrested in Bombay and sentenced to a long imprisonment.

Petrov chewed over Roy's history in his quest to solve the riddle, the contradiction inherent in the 'legitimacy' of British rule in India. The British prided themselves on their 'rule of law', that they didn't allow summary executions and imprisonment like some despotic Oriental potentate, assumed to have no inkling of such practices as fair trial and due process of law. Yet, within this pattern of their own prideful claiming, even if just some trials were manipulated, or troublemakers confined without trial, what did that mean? And if the hardships all prisoners went through in jail often damaged their health irretrievably, as it did Roy's, what did that mean? There were the numbers executed, for instance, after the major uprising of 1857, for 'treasonous' or 'seditious acts', which pre-supposed a 'legitimate' ruler. The contradiction had already reached its full poignancy with the last Mughal emperor's exile to Burma and the assassination of his sons, their bodies displayed at the Khooni Darwaza, the bloody gateway, which still stands in the middle of a busy Delhi thoroughfare. Roy was allowed a say in court after his arrest, and his defence was trenchant. What crime was he guilty of in trying to unseat a government, illegitimate in the first place …? How could an illegitimate government presume to question an Indian's wish for self-government and call it 'illegal'?

In Calcutta, Petrov went straight to the university where he located a Sanskrit teacher. Soon, he found himself living with a Bengali family in an outlying section of Calcutta, among narrow lanes, straying animals, including an occasional hyena and jackal, swampland, insanitary open spaces and rural enclaves. This was the 'Black' or 'Native' town of the time, many leagues apart from Anglo-India, and to this day, though the rural atmosphere has been displaced, few non-Bengalis, let alone foreigners, are seen here.

The reactions of the Calcuttans were complicated by the 'Rahimbaeff' patronymic, which Petrov re-adopted in a burst of foolish orientalism.

'Is he a Russian or a Muslim?' they asked, assuming the two to be mutually exclusive.

'How can he be a Russian, Rahim is a Muslim name!'

'What about the rest of his name?'

'It *sounds* Russian.'

'And he has a white skin too.'

But the initial discomfort felt by the Bengalis at the presence of this foreigner was taken over by warmth because Petrov lacked condescension. It confused them, in any case, to think of a white person as Muslim. The only other whites they knew weren't Muslim, and the only Muslims they knew weren't white.

'Have you ever seen him in a mosque?'

'Or prostrating five times a day?'

'He doesn't act like a white skin either.'

'Yet he *is* white!'

'Most mysterious,' they added.

Petrov's knowledge of Bengali, his donning of the dhuti-Punjabi and his hunger for learning more about his adopted city and its culture won them over. In spite of his frequent incomprehension and peppery outbursts, his new friends went all out to locate tutors for him and help him settle down. When some of his Left-leaning friends learned that Petrov was not only from the home of the new politics but had known Indian revolutionaries, they felt more drawn to him. In their eagerness for his company they thoughtlessly violated his privacy, and Petrov had to control his swelling impulses of inhospitality.

'Can't they knock before coming in?' he fumed.

He locked his bedroom door, and soon gave up when the persistent banging became intolerable. But there were compensations, including dream sequences of singing by the women of the family. And the food. He relished the distinct flavour of each dish: the bitter starter, the savoury middle courses of vegetables, fish and mutton, the sour-sweet chutney-digestive and the sweets to follow. 'Bitter, salt, sour, sweet,' he said. 'The Bengalis have a genius for structuring their meals!' At first the bitter shuktoni was a nightmare, an artifice concocted to make anything else delectable by contrast. 'What a subtle test of the palate,' he sneered, grimacing over another dish of neem leaves and brinjal. 'Are they trying to punish me?' But by degrees he became an enthusiast then an aficionado, looking forward to the bitterness, followed by fish head and pungent mustard flavoured hilsa, and managing to manipulate hair thin fish bones like a true Bengali.

Very soon, putting his paranoia behind him, he admitted he was 'Petrov' and not at all 'Rahimbaeff', giving his Bengali friends the reason for the canard. The demystified white Russian was adopted with renewed ardour. Apart from the philosophy classes at the university, he had Sanskrit and Bengali private tutors. He was also taken frequently to the Bengali theatre, which helped speed up his learning of the language. It was now that his friends decided to nickname him 'Herassim', which was first reduced to 'Asseem', and then to its Bengali version, 'Osheem'.

Herassim Stefanovich Lebadeff was the adventurous Russian who had launched the first westernized Bengali theatre in 1795. Almost a century and a half later, Petrov was given Lebadeff's name because of the remarkably similar circumstances of their lives so far. Both were Russian, both were passionate Indophiles who had chosen to come to Calcutta and both had an interest in Bengali theatre. The slide of Petrov's name to 'Osheem' was a sign of his final acceptance.

Confusing the melodrama of the stage with real life, and still bemused by Calcutta, Petrov impulsively invested a small fortune in buying a theatre, a defunct auditorium, the Eros. He spent another fortune refurbishing and renovating the Eros, but it had the advantage of being strategically located in the theatre district of north Calcutta and was to turn into one of the leading drama centres of the city. And at last he came into direct contact with Bengali women who had begun to appear on the stage in place of adolescent boys.

The family he had lodged with till then, kept its women private, in contrast to the exposure he was forced into his own life. But he was sensitive to the new culture. That the women led lives somehow different from the veiled world of Turkestani women, though he wasn't sure how Hindus would react if he asked to meet girls from educated families. In the end his friends, realizing his predicament, encouraged him to leave their conservative home and shift to the Eurasian part of town. Impressed by their reading, and the delicate manner in which they had pushed him out, Petrov prepared for further adjustments.

He moved into a boarding house on Royd Street run by Eurasians, where he felt an immediate relief at being in westernized surroundings. But the relief didn't last when his privacy was violated just the same. This time he was swamped by the attentions of a group proud of showing off this desirable European at incessant parties and dances. This, together with his acquisition of the theatre, meant giving up his studies at the university. But the Bengali lessons continued and his tutor came to his lodgings. When his Eurasian friends discovered his interest in things 'native', including the theatre and the language, there was an outburst.

'Can you imagine! Sergie's bought a native theatre!'

'Sergie!'

'Don't you know ...?'

'What's the matter?'

'They're junglies, men! How can you put up plays in that half-baked lingo?'

'And he's learning it too ...!'

They insisted on taking him to the English theatre.

'Can't you see ...?'

'See what?'

'There's no comparison!'

Though Petrov couldn't be deflected so easily, he enjoyed this exposure to British Calcutta and the fashionable and better-lit areas of Chowringhee and Park Street. He gained access to the scholarly Jesuits associated with Calcutta from the nineteenth century through St Xavier's College. Life became even richer when he discovered a Russian couple who were to be involved in the launching of the *300*, a nightclub which served Russian food, followed by more international fare, and which would bring him into contact with the westernized Indian upper crust. His interests, talents and pursuits were following a familiar dispersal. Petrov was after all his father's son and Calcutta was layered like a rich cake.

While lodging in the boarding house on Royd Street he was distracted by the wild evenings spent with the landlord's gang, drinking and dancing, and mired in amours. Bars, nightclubs, flophouses and the opium dens of China Town were enough to fog his brain, already fog-bound by the women who attacked him ferociously for his pure white blood and money. Richie, his landlord, introduced him to Karaya Lane, the red-light district for Europeans, where the bungalows and gardens housed girls from Russia among others.

He watched cynically as his chaste Bengali tutor's eyes strayed towards the bared legs and bold looks of the women who lounged on the verandah of his boarding house, wearing shorts, smoking and carelessly flinging out glances and giggles. Whenever they sighted the socks held up with garters and exposing the reedy calf muscles of the Bengali tutor in his despised native dress, these giggles would reach a crescendo, and Petrov had to suppress his rage.

He was betrothed several times, tricked between his dreams and real life. It was during his third betrothal that he made a conscious effort to pull his life together.

'Richie,' he said to his landlord. 'A friend of mine wants your advice.'

'What's up, Sergie?'

'He has affianced himself for the third time without any desire for marriage …'

'So?'

'The first and second times were a mistake and he wiggled out. The third time is a mistake too …'

'So he wiggles out again …'

'How?'

'How do I know? Who's this fool?'

Petrov groaned. 'I,' he said. 'I am that fool. I have got engaged to Greta. After the first two! What can I do now?'

Richie was aghast. 'Greta! She's a beautiful girl, man, beautiful! I wanted to marry her myself. Bastard!'

'You know what it's like, Richie. All the time drinking and parties, parties, parties. I cannot at all remember asking her …'

'But you made a good choice Sergie. Imagine how she'll do in Europe …!'

'Europe! I plan to stay on here, in Calcutta. And how will she get away then, from this place full of Indians, Bengalis, what is it you call them? "Niggers", "blackies"? My best friends are Bengalis! I speak Bengali with them! I plan to run a Bengali theatre.'

'Bengali, Bengali, Bengali. And I suppose you plan to marry a Bengali nigger bitch, eh?'

Petrov sprang up, directing his arresting eyes at Richie, emanating a Tartar-Nijinsky personality, bulging uncompromising tights.

'If you say one more such word Richie, I will drag you by the hair to my friends to apologize! Come! Let me dare you!'

'Okay, okay, I'll talk to Greta. I hope she comes around. But y'all should really be less careless …' Richie edged out of the room.

Petrov flopped on to a chair, in his loose bush shirt and trousers, no resemblance to the imaginary tights. The melancholy pity of Richie shuffling away with stooped shoulders brought home to him the plight of the small Eurasian community.

'It will be wisest for them to displace themselves from this country of their origin. That will be easier than re-adjusting. For neither their countrymen nor the ruling foreigners will accept them with open arms. Not until the mutual disdain is forgotten by a new generation.'

Petrov was close to reality. Later, the children of those Eurasians, who would come to be known as 'Anglo-Indians', and who opted to stay on in India would put away the bitterness boomeranging from their earlier attitude. They would grow to take pride in their community's skills in education and other fields, and accept that calling this country their own was only logical.

In the end, he soothed the frustrated blonde with a generous gift. 'That absolves me of all guilt! I thank her silently! And my exposure to the Eurasians at close quarters will help me in my study of colonialism!' With this brave epitaph Petrov ended his association with Royd Street and moved into independent lodgings close to his Bengali friends.

During early days, Petrov occasionally visited the Rajmahal to meet Maninder Singh Ohri, a grandson of the owner, the Sardar Bahadur. From the time he first saw the house, then occupied in its entire magnificence of four floors by the extended Ohri family, he had nurtured a secret envy towards its inhabitants. His friend offered him a flat after the conversion, and when he was taken, as a concession to a prospective tenant, into the lobby for the first time, he felt as if he was in a cathedral, its inner spaces reaching celestial heights. The Rajmahal sensed his awe and a frisson went through it, generating a rainbow below the skylights.

Petrov was reminded of Russian settings, a combination of the stairway of his ancestral home and the melancholy village square flooded with pigeons. A white streak on his lapel didn't stop him from gazing upwards, when a flourish of heaven borne giggles came floating down, filling him with longing. He strained to locate the source, but his ears couldn't isolate it beyond the screen of pigeon coos. 'Being hit by bird shit is a sign of good luck, yaar,' Maninder assured him. They had a brief and hushed encounter with the great Sardar Bahadur in bed, hanging over himself in the ceiling mirror.

'I saw Tolstoy like this,' whispered Petrov to Maninder.

'What, in his death bed?' asked his cheerful Sikh friend. 'You knew Tolstoy?'

'No, I've never seen Tolstoy, dead or alive,' said Petrov. 'It was in a dream, and Tolstoy was exactly like this, exactly! His white beard spread out on a big bed with a mirror above, and surrounded by admirers.'

After this, Petrov became so covetous of the surroundings and the mysterious European ambience that he couldn't wait to move in. To continue his association with Calcutta yet live in such a place, the thought made his spirit soar like the staircase. In the growing atmosphere of mutual admiration, the house too longed for Petrov to inhabit it. When the tenancy papers were signed, there was rejoicing in the house, and the pigeons wheeled and plunged like planes in an aeronautical display.

Petrov had much earlier made the final capitulation to Calcutta by marrying a Bengali woman, Reema Devi. Reema Devi's family was Brahmo, but the Brahmos, like Surjeet Shona's Bengali side, were outside the normal conservative paradigms, and there was no great objection to this foreigner in the family.

The house and ghosts felt intensely proud of having Reema Devi at the Rajmahal.

'Imagine, it's Reema Devi! Aren't we lucky?'

'I watched her in her first season on the stage. She looked like a young boy! But her acting ...!' This was from a very culturally minded ghost.

'No one to match her ...'

'Yes, but why go and marry a mlechcha!' said the loud Swadeshi ghost again.

'Oh you and your mlechchas!' said the disgusted cultured ghost. 'Can't you forget all that rubbish for once?'

Now, in a sense, Petrov had the 'enemy within'. Reema Devi was fiercely protective of her autonomy and was as gregarious as most Bengalis. But in spite of the social surge, their bedroom stayed privileged and private. This sacred space was their enclosed world of carnality and any idea of subjugating strong-minded Reema was wildly exciting to Petrov. Another titillation was her powerful stage personality which seemed to vary her identity as often as her roles.

Reema Devi was a budding star when Petrov met her. 'A budding star with budding breasts,' Petrov always reminisced. He would never forget his first view of her on the stage. She was sixteen, so slight of frame she had to pad out her figure to play the heroine, an impersonation of a female by a female. An imitation of an adolescent male actor, common in those days when few women appeared on the stage. By the time they were married, the padding was forgotten and Reema Devi was a young woman in full bloom. She was now the centre of Petrov's life and a central figure in Calcutta's theatre world.

Petrov's decision to produce *Neel Dorpon*, the Indigo Mirror, was the result of his continuing obsession with famine, an examination of all the possible nuances of that terrible recurring phenomenon. Indigo was planted on precious rice paddy land at the behest of the planters, adding to the choiceless peasant's chronic hunger. Petrov imagined the peasants being forced to eat indigo in place of rice and turning blue before they died. No grotesquerie could beat the pictures imprinted on his gut.

1943, soon after his move to the Rajmahal, was the year of the Great Bengal Famine. Here he was, filled with the joy of his personal life, yet it was as if the world had entered the intrinsic darkness lying in the pit of humanity's stomach. He saw writhing before him the spilled and stinking intestines from that stomach's pit, defiling the pavements of his adopted city. 1943 plunged him into a well of cynicism, the deepest cynicism of which man is capable. It coincided with the other catastrophic cynicism across the oceans, Hitler's death and torture camps, which were shrouded in secrecy before hitting the world. Yet, and this to Petrov was the climactic point of that cynicism, the famine was out in the open, in full view in one of the largest cities of the world, but it would never be addressed by those who mattered at the critical time. It would never provoke the outrage and telling castigation that followed the end of the war in Germany. It would slink in slyly unheralded, and then like a whiplash, scourge, stun and destroy its mass victims. And there would be no rebuke, no redress.

It slunk up on Petrov with the same slyness, in spite of his watchfulness. Blaming himself for his insensitive antennae, he was drawn out, further and further, to probe painfully. He knew of the famines of his own country, Russia, one of which had taken place when he was a near adult. Yet he had never been able to visualize the reality. Humans foraging in dustbins, their sores infested with maggots. Live skeletons eating from drains, anything they could find. Children sacrificed by mothers. Little girls bartered to whore houses. Rice mixed with gravel, and a pitiless trade in gravel to augment that rice. At times he felt he was looking down the shit hole of some epochal slum where the unspeakable remnants of hundreds of years of shit festooned the squatting room, the walls, the floors and the clogged hole itself through which one could see the shit piled up below. He forced himself to examine it, look closely, face on, breathe in that stench, and it was so nauseating and tormenting that his defenses did their best to obliterate it. He had to fight this tendency, and then he would find himself grappling with another depthless frustration, the frustration of his complete helplessness, though he wandered the streets like a mad man with his car full of provisions, handing out gruel, bread, fruit, milk, water. The first to accept his offerings, an emaciated man lying next to his dead wife and children, oozing a glutinous jelly from his eyes, swallowed once, gurgled, and died, as if Petrov had fed him poison. He imagined the man's intestines, dehydrated, collapsed, with the walls sticking together, refusing the passage of food. That fatal swallow had ruptured the brittle noodles of his intestines and stopped his weak breath. The creatures, that is, what Petrov called them, so far removed were they from the human state, confused him with their reactions. Sometimes watching him listlessly with the desirelessness presaging death, at others mobbing his car and blindly hitting out in the scramble to grab and cram their mouths. At a friend's free kitchen, he saw a mother rushing in before the gates were closed, after thrusting her children out of the way. He saw his friends fighting with the mother to get the children in and feed them. And yet, he had already seen mothers dying while feeding their children before themselves … People were trying to help, one and two, twenty and thirty, perhaps a hundred starving humans brought back from the brink. Kitchens were opened in well-to-do homes for one, two hours. 'After all,' thought Petrov when he helped at these places, 'who would allow one's own plump wife or child to want, even for a grain? Would it not be shameful then to let others beat on the gates with skeletal fists, and refuse to fill out the stark ribs which have just slid down those gates, even with a little gruel?' So some gates were opened and the gentlefolk gave to the fortunate minority who stumbled against them. The very black marketeers who had fanned the famine, and were given indifference-based immunity by the authorities, also helped in this small effort, but with different motives. They did it to divert the wrath of the gods. And to buy legitimacy.

Petrov almost lost all feeling, but he could see that Reema Devi was incapable of accepting this abdication of human dignity. And he saw her abhorrence burst out one day when they came on a group of press photographers busy at work.

She went at the photographers like a tigress, snatching the nearest camera and dashing it to the ground. 'How dare you! Are they creatures in a zoo?' Petrov, struggling with the panting, resisting Reema Devi, waited for the photographers to strike back. But they were saying with awe, 'Look! It's Reema Devi. It's Reema Devi herself!'

Ignoring their awe, filling her lungs to the full and throwing out her voice from its base, Reema Devi's words attained a thrilling resonance. 'Pustules! Arrant swine! Is this the time for photography? Tell me! Have you no shame?' One of the photographers rashly raised his camera and clicked and Reema Devi furiously snatched it from his hold. Petrov was only just able to save it and hand it over before further damage was done. She breathed fire in Petrov's constricting grip and her voice rose to greater resonances, 'Oh so now it's me you want, is it? What a drama for you! What a scoop! Animals! Degraded, filthy animals!!' Trying to break from Petrov's hold, she kept crying, 'Let go, Petro! Let me go!'

The causes of this drama lay prone, their shrivelled wrinkled skin shining on their skeletons, their eyes oozing that mysterious white jelly. But their continuous moaning had reached a crescendo and become a euphony from hell, 'Ma, duto phan, duto phan dao – Mother, give me gruel, just a little gruel.'

'That's all they want after all,' thought Petrov, still grappling with Reema Devi. 'It's so simple. Just a little gruel after all!' And that chorus throbbed inside Petrov, throbbed through the city and filled it with despair. 'Ma, duto phan, duto phan dao.' Reema Devi had stopped ranting but her harsh sobs added to this euphony, to the power of her scene, and the photographers looked on with awe. Petrov let go of her and they went through the motions like automatons, handing out gruel and packets of food, helped by the contrite photographers. When Reema Devi turned to leave, staggering with emotion and supported by Petrov, the photographers at last dared to lift up their endangered cameras to click respectfully and guiltily when she was safely back in the car.

When Petrov picked up the next morning's papers, he saw the expected picture of Reema Devi on the front page, looking like Goddess Durga, and he thought, 'They, and I, understand completely why she behaved as she did. Each of us is as helpless as the best or the worst of us …' He knew there was no real will, no means, to combat the immensity of the famine.

The last time Petrov drove out with his supplies, he experienced the culmination of that surreal calamity. Young dying men were setting fire to the bodies of their wives, mothers, children, beating away the dogs and vultures. Then, as the flames grew fierce and engulfed the grotesque heaps, billowing out black smoke, he saw those very men gathering up their last strength to hang themselves from the drooping trees. He did nothing to stop them, just sat shuddering in his car, shuddering as much from despair as from the pervasive stench, with his arms on the steering wheel and his head in his arms.

Petrov's extreme slimness started from this time. Anorexia, an unrecognized condition for the age. He was able to eat only by acts of will power. Not eating was almost a compulsion which he had to fight with that will power. He watched in a state of detached depression as Reema Devi ate normally through her anguish, as if the availability of food to them had no connection to the famine. She, who was so passionately acting in plays about the famine and taking it on tours to other parts of the country. He didn't blame her or any of the others or himself for being able to sustain themselves, even through a conscious application of the will, against the prickings of conscience, while the millions starved just outside their doorstep.

Petrov's Diary: *How do politicians and controllers allow a tragedy like famine? What about the silent majority who simply stand and watch, steeped in inertia? And the rest, are they active or passive? Do they change anything? Let us categorize.*

Passive no-changers – Local inhabitants who either accept the disaster as the known pattern, the most common, or who are indifferent. Helpless, pained observers. A food minister who says there is no shortage of grain, a British governor who throws up his hands …

Active no-changers – Reporters, documentarists. Ineffective, disorganized conscience-salvers, handing out gruel from temporary kitchens. Organized humanitarians, desperately picking up, salvaging, saving.

Passive changers – Analysts, theorists.

Active changers – Doers, who may succeed, only against some categories of disaster, but after a prolonged struggle, sometimes posthumously. Like those fighting Apartheid in South Africa, or freedom fighters in India. But mass starvation does not allow for long-term solutions; it strikes too swiftly.

Or take the apparently noble motive of 'national interest'. In this case it was Britain's national interest, a lack of interest or concern for the other country. There are different priorities. There is an excuse to avoid facing an avoidable situation, a top priority excuse after all, a top-drawer war. There is no punishment for this negligence because the sufferers lack priority. The 'contempt' of His Majesty's Government is recorded by Viceroy Wavell and other observers of the time … 'I have found H.M.G.'s (His Majesty's Government) attitude to India negligent, hostile and contemptuous to a degree. I had not anticipated it, or I think I might have done more.' Poor Wavell. He tried to get Churchill to divert food to India, evoking a tardy response. But

Churchill's contempt for India and Indians had to be breached first! A real no-changer for the famine ...

Inertia of some kind applies to most people. The rare exceptions are driven by ideals, and work, sometimes passionately, for a cause. But this almost invariably leads to violence (not obviously but in spirit and content), as with some activists. Others, like those who assassinate British officials are more obviously violent than the moderate activists, or Gandhi's peace brigades.

In the Great Famine no one succeeded in averting or saving the situation. The failure was wholesale, massive, complete. All the great idealist fighters for freedom were mute and powerless in jail. It was violence of the highest, most inert, degree.

Man is really an extended animal. No better than other lower animals. He is never good, except self-consciously. Only an imbecile may, just may, be truly GOOD. The rest act on instincts and patterns. Instincts and patterns which are overwhelming, as with the lower animals.

Those who enquire, like myself, Petrov. Are we any better?

But, at last, the ones who try over a long period may succeed. Reforms take place. If so then is there also an instinctual goodness? The antithesis to the instincts of the lower animals for self-preservation, self-propagation and self-gratification? If the goodness is in name alone, then why is everyone paying lip service to it? Why frame checking laws to support the good, when most are so cynically uninterested in that good? What inspires this checking activity?

The group, government or society frames this checking activity. So, on the one hand, the group protects its members by creating checking activities for good. On the other hand it behaves in an evil (?) way, for the good of the group (?)? Look closer: the checks are created for the good and then if the group's self-interest is threatened, the checks are subverted, never mind who or what is harmed or damaged, while the lip-service continues...

Seeing all this, can one continue blindly, comfortably, passively acting for one's own interests? It seems, yes. Countries are always doing this. Such as 'good' States like Britain today. The unit is embraced by the collective. So the State is more important than the individual. So the colonial power's activities for its own gain are legitimate though colonial rule is obviously illegitimate.

So. An individual's suffering, whether from hunger, starvation, injustice, deprivation or poverty is unimportant. There is so much individual suffering. A close friend, a spouse, a son, can miss it completely, or be indifferent to it. You, an individual, are suffering deeply, just like a vast number of individuals, from loss, frustration, jealousy, sickness, failure, pain, sorrow, disgrace, ridicule, ugliness, old age, disease ... Or take the subject country rather than the ruling power. In the famine, individuals, a huge group of individuals, go through a huge range of sufferings. Hunger, deprivation, separation, helplessness, degradation, displacement, homelessness, shame ... No means are left even to shed tears. And if tears are shed, a child might lick those tears to slake its thirst. As in Steinbeck's Grapes of Wrath, *where a woman suckles a strange man to save him from starvation!*

Who is doing all this? Why is this being done? A tyrant, the colonial power, bad people? The 'Who' (the perpetrator of suffering) may be easier to answer in part. Or take a metaphor for the partial Who, a common example as a metaphor. A lover giving pleasure yet inflicting torture. Whose presence is intense delight and whose absence intense pain. Can the 'pain' be avoided?

The other part of the Who is unanswerable. For instance, who causes old age, senility? The 'Why' too is unanswerable. It always was and always will be. It is without even a part of an answer. What if science can work out equations and formulas? The metaphysical 'why' will always be without an answer. And all other human suffering? Nature? God? Or the Devil and God pulling from two ends in the danse macabre of vultures tearing at a carcass? Just as dogs and jackals fight over food?

India in modern times has had a conscious many-faceted struggle for reform. The fronts are endless, and the country's whole form is being chiselled, hacked, hammered, remoulded, sandpapered, to get it into shape. Re-formed. Formed again. Pick up any important Indian biography – it will tell you of a struggle for change, re-formers, fighters, Raja Ram Mohan Roys, Keshav Chandra Sens, Vidyasagars ... and after Independence all the new reform laws, against dowry, against untouchability, etc, etc thesis, metamorphosis, synthesis – a struggle which will never end till the country reaches the end of a trail. At least that trail which synthesizes human dignity ... Surely! Europe, the West, has reached the end of that trail. Its people have dignity accessible to them and have mostly taken it. Yet, they keep striving for more! In the never-ending spiralling circle they want more food, more thin people, more work, more leisure, more power, less aggression, fewer aged and longer lives. Reform is never complete. I have seen drunks and old decrepit men and women in Europe, today, foraging in dustbins! What hope then does this poor country, this India, have?

Bengal in India has had a particularly intense struggle. Its three quite recent great miseries, misery of violence and partition, misery of refugees, misery of famine, creating each time, a degraded mixed new identity. One generation has seen this and ages and dies without finding a synthesis-solution. Its dreams are gone, shattered!

A myriad freedom fighters died before their dreams came true. India became independent, but it showed tremendous cracks. India was a place to leave, escape. The thought of staying on filled many with frustration. So many from this very building, my children Boris and Meera, and an ocean of others emigrating to Canada, Australia, Great Britain, the Gulf, Germany, joining their cousins in East Africa, Hong Kong, Singapore, as if they couldn't bear the independence of their country, as if Valhalla was elsewhere after it had come to India.

The changes brought about by those three penultimate and ultimate colonial period cataclysms, the depletion and degradation, affected the countryside deeply, shattering generations of the future. Naturally they could envisage nothing but continued deprivation if they stayed back.

Yet, that day, the biggest headlines were of Independence, and what did Independence mean? How much did it change everyday lives? It had the emotional power to instantly put an end to the riots in Calcutta at least, the killing. Bas! To cause Hindus and Muslims to embrace in public. And for all to call 'Jai Hind', 'Victory to India!' with one voice, forgetting earlier quibbles.

But it had also caused the killings, because hand in hand with it went the cracking of the subcontinent into three. The mighty booming bang of the hammer of partition had become a necessity in the balance of negotiation, and the head of the hammer that had dealt that mighty booming bang was Independence! The map model of India cracked into three, and through those cracks came pouring out the flood of refugees, carrying violence, death, disease, destitution, hunger, adding to the State's deposit of misery. So, the headlines deserved their size. They contained all this and more. Following that violence and displacement. Justifying the replacement of subjection with Independence. Of course! And echoing in macrocosm the microcosm of millions of small, little battles, swirling like twisters across the surface of the land. Between ruler and ruled, between religions and castes and peoples, between illusion and reality. And forgetting all the way, the only end to it all, Old Age and Death.

❧

Reema Devi was now both middle aged and neurotic. The shoe-throwing incident at the English rendering of *Neel Dorpon* had upset her. Petrov was aware of this as they hurried out of the theatre and headed for Proshanto Mojumdar's insistent entertainment at the *300*.

'Imagine Petro!' said Reema Devi. 'Planter Rogue was concussed! Concussed!' Petrov watched Reema Devi, the marvel on the stage, trembling and upset after this violence to her fellow actor. In his anxiety he stepped in heavily. 'Martin's a mischievous one. And that little prissy miss, Gwendolyn … Maybe we should have seen some other play …?'

'You expect the Stracheys to sit through a *Bengali* play?'

Petrov laughed, diverted. Inhabiting different strata of society, he thought, was richer than sticking coyly to one's own. But was it truer? What did 'truer' mean, after all? debated the chronic philosopher. Did it mean traditional groupings were sacred and the Other profane? Or did it mean that encouraging differentness was untrue because it disturbed the comfortable certainty of the known? Couldn't it be truer that the conventional simply couldn't face the wider world? Did it mean they didn't want to discover the crackle of excitement in newness? Would he change his life so far? Reverse drive in time and space to Russia, get married to a penurious closet-aristocrat or a coarse borsch-slurper … Ah no! he thought, quickly re-reversing from the unbearable and unthinkable, life without Reema Devi and the Eros. Never! Petrov was a multi-dimensional participant, but he was an outsider and could, therefore, see from the outside. He could see his wife, the genius actress deeply rooted in her profession and culture, yet moving in other dimensions with pride and ease. He could see the Stracheys in their painful displacement yet peculiarly true to that displaced culture, more lost than the Anglo-Indians. Anglo-Indians like the Normans and Maudie Jessop, the Rajmahal's inhabitants, who too stayed, not 'behind', but just stayed without knowing if they belonged, jumping on a bed of pins and pain, for no real fault of their own. He could see the Mojumdars bumbling along in their eclectic kindliness, quite comfortable in the mixed arena of Calcutta yet displaced from the undiluted Bengal. The others. All located within the historicity of the Rajmahal. And could he, Petrov, who had fled from his homeland at a tender age, could he judge them?

They drove on without speaking, though Petrov looked frequently and anxiously at Reema Devi. He thought of her in her early days, eager for any part, confident and brilliant. Still young, she would take on the parts of old crones, gleefully disguising herself for those parts, secure in her youth. Now she desperately sought the youthful parts, refusing to allow the faintest mention of anything near her true age. The theatre world, most of all Petrov, knew where her nerves quivered and that the slightest stirring of air close to them could cause exquisite pain. Because they loved her and cherished the magnificent gift of herself to the stage, they would have applied the thumbscrews for her. But, one day, it would happen, and she would have to accept the fateful turn of the screw herself.

Menopause, what trouble that had caused her. Yet it had freed her finally from a phenomenon she had come to detest. 'I long for menopause, Petro,' she would moan. But the more she longed and moaned, the more the four-weekly metronome clicked away with painful regularity, till she was well past fifty. Reema Devi found the idea of menopause alluring not only because of the mess she found herself in during the dreaded days, but because of the effect on her acting. Menstruation weakened her to such an extent she could barely throw her voice, her most powerful attribute. 'What's the purpose of it all, Petro?' she said once. 'Creation, libidinous males, menstruating females? How can there be a God who creates such disorder? Left to nature we would be unacceptable, like animals. Can you call that order? I can assure you Petro, there is no God!'

Petrov listening keenly said, 'Suppose you try and imagine a disorderly God, mind you, just a supposition!'

'Oh no! That simply cannot be!'

'Why not? Think of it as a disorder, yet following natural laws, functioning inside an order.'

'The world was simply churned up from the ocean of milk. But you've got to leave out God!'

'Not the "Gods" eh? Without the Gods and the demons fighting, the ocean would have stayed unchurned and there would have been no nectar, no world!'

'Don't forget the poison, Petro. It wasn't just nectar that came up, but poison ...'

'Which Shiva swallowed!'

Reema Devi was silenced for a while, and then said, 'Can't you count him as one of the lesser Gods?'

'No!' said Petrov. 'Not at all! That I would call blasphemy!' and he would float away into a long-winded discourse on poison-nectar, good-evil, lesser and greater Gods, demons, order-disorder while Reema Devi forgot the original worry.

Petrov remembered constantly one of her renowned roles. Constantly her face in that role danced before him, filling him with a deep pleasure. That role was like a flower, a deep-wombed scented pink-and-saffron-coloured flower with a translucent tunnel, inside which the pistil of Reema Devi's magnificent gift, the gynaceum of the flower, seduced her audience. Just as he had been filled with longing when he had entered the Rajmahal the first time and heard the complex rill of laughter from above. He liked to believe that laughter had come from the very centre, the epicentre of his future home.

Reema Devi had turned the rear-view mirror on to herself and was frenziedly re-doing her face and hair. Petrov knew she was directing the upset of the evening from apocryphal triumph to failure. These negative impulses had gradually dominated her after their second child's death, a premature child too weak to withstand the world in infancy.

'You were wonderful, my Reema, utterly convincing in that overdone play!'

'Overdone! Naturally you would call it so with your, your Russian notions! Bengali theatre can't touch Chekhov, that's what you're saying!'

'Don't talk such nonsense, Reema. You made the evening! I wish you could have seen yourself! And the audience. It was all your fault!'

'Oh yes! Blame me …!'

'Come, dear. You know what I am trying to say, in my clumsy way. Don't you? Don't you know the audience was at your feet, ready to kill for you?'

'They threw a shoe, a shoe! Can you imagine …?'

'Yes, but they threw it at the rogue who was tormenting you, the utterly convincing victim of his lust! They were raging at him because of your perfect acting.'

'But you know the legend. It was the actor of the … "Planter Rogue" part, *his* acting, which drew the shoe. Not the poor girl, poor me!'

'If there is a shoe, "Planter Rogue" will always draw it. But today it was thrown at him for *you*, and *you* were the star! You have made a legend today, a new legend! Today's "Planter Rogue" couldn't even pronounce his English correctly!'

'We should never have done it in English! I knew it was a mistake, an unforgivable mistake …!'

'Reema, Reema! Stop it!'

Petrov was still under the spell of the famous and enigmatic smile which had transformed the whole play for him, and all the other plays, and his life. 'Fascinating,' he had heard someone murmur during the play. 'Most fascinating,' Petrov said to himself. Turning to her he said, 'Smile Reema. Smile at me dear.'

Reema Devi turned towards him, and Petrov found instead her cheeks shining with tears. He stopped the car and held her close. He could feel her trembling and thought, 'There are some people who should not be allowed to age. Reema should just pass away one evening, as she finishes the last words of the last scene of her last triumph!'

❧

The youthful Petrov had been slim and medium-tall with dark hair brushed back in two wavy wings on either side of a middle parting.

His face had a drawn look, with a long nose and shadowed grey eyes, though his figure was wiry and suggested a muscular elegance, as one would imagine the romantically sexy Nijinsky. This unarticulated quality had captivated Reema Devi the first time she saw him. He had been dressed in Bengali clothes, a white dhuti-Punjabi, while he sat next to the window at his desk. The light had fallen on his dark brown hair, striking golden notes, shining in his eyes and turning his skin and clothing a radiant white. Reema Devi was fascinated by the white skins of Europeans. They appeared to her sometimes like marble, sometimes like creamy yoghurt.

Now nearing ninety, Petrov's skin was more yellow than white, as if an infusion of saffron had blemished the yoghurt. The shine in his eyes was more like a pop-eyed gleam, he was skeletal rather than slim and his hair, shockingly, as with Nijinsky, had gone. He was eccentric, but then, as he himself said self-indulgently, some things should be allowed to him at this great age. His eccentricity could not, in any case, be compared to the eventual madness of Nijinsky.

Petrov walked along Chowringhee towards the Rajmahal. It was twilight, a time he favoured. To his right, the Maidaan glowed, a mess of crowds, vendors and the Ochterloney Monument, a needle probing the sky. At the old Firpos arcade, he paused in his peregrinations and leaning elegantly on his walking stick, gazed at the scenes around him. 'I'll have to stay on the street and risk being run over,' he murmured. He half knew he talked to himself aloud, but if he noticed people sniggering he was unaffected. Those who frequented this stretch, including the beggars, usually the most inclined to amusement, were used to him, and he to them. If he returned to the pavement he would step on to a carpeting of large, grey insects, an unknown species swarming and comfortably at home, ignored by the crowds and later the vagrants who slept right there among them, like larger versions of those same insects with their rugged and vulnerably thin sheet coverings. 'What insects are these?' wondered Petrov, shaking his head. 'Is it some new breed? They are so large and fearsome, and yet so easily eliminated.' He poked unsteadily with his stick at one of the fleshy creatures lying half-squashed and wriggling in its death throes, and put an end to its miseries. 'I wonder,' he thought, 'whether man has been created as an aberration, a ridiculously vulnerable aberration, unable totally to protect himself except by his wits. No mastodon might or muscular tonnage, yet lasting on, somewhat like these easily crushed insects. Humans and insects,' he continued, walking homeward on the pavement again at what was once a brisk pace and was now more hurried-looking than brisk, 'the two most vulnerable, and tenacious, of God's created species …' He looked up at the Firpos arcade, in its place a utilitarian store, and the habitual picture came before him of his neighbours, the Stracheys, skipping over the bodies of the victims of the deadliest famines of India, while inside Firpos, the nobs pranced and gorged under prisms of white light. As always, he imagined the Stracheys doing the fandango feverishly to forget the dehumanized images that had just passed before them. And now? Was he, Petrov, any different? He brushed off a small, dirty girl with outstretched palm and dropped a coin into the bowl of his friend with the withered legs, an echo of the legless beggars he associated with Russia through an Eisenstein film. A cheeky looking young man came too close. 'Girls, hashish, smack?' he sibilated and before Petrov could react, the young man was yanked up by the collar, slapped vigorously on both cheeks and dropped on to the pavement. 'Ei! Think you can harass anyone, eh, eh?' Petrov's sturdy protector, a pen-seller, yanked the offender up again and repeated the treatment. The moment he let go, the whimpering pimp vanished.

Petrov was bewildered and touched by this unexpected protection. Others were picking up the pens which had scattered on the pavement, and Petrov's endless monologue continued in his head. 'Why would he spring to my aid with such ferocity? He knows he will get nothing from me. I have never bought a pen from him in all these years, in spite of his daily wheedling. Is it from some deeply rooted servility implanted by colonial conditioning, that I, a white sahib, must at all costs be protected. Because I, the white sahib, am inherently the protector of all? Or is it just from a sense of kindliness …?'

'Dhonyobad,' he said again to the flushed and smiling young entrepreneur, and continued his walk.

As he progressed towards the Rajmahal, his eccentricity was to take final direction, inspired by a new beggar on the route.

Petrov was sitting on a cement protrusion, one of his usual resting places, waiting for the hoarding above him to light up. He was about to check his watch as it came on, when he noticed a figure lighted up in a recessed doorway. It was a beggar, sitting in the iconic lotus posture, his hair lifted into a knot, askew on top of his head, with a bleached spike standing out like a thorn. Apart from a loincloth he was naked. His eyes were open, but the lids were heavy and drugged. The combination of the hallucinatory lighting and the hallucinogenic gleam of the beggar's eyes inspired Petrov. He walked up to the illuminated figure. The red light of the hoarding intermittently exposed the bare body, which was smeared with ash and adorned with a string of rudraksha beads. Petrov's eyes were focused on the beggar's ribs which stood out starkly, barring his body in a fluctuating cage of shadows. In Petrov's mind was the Gandhara image of the Ascetic Buddha, and in this figure before him were all the weightlessness of space and all the weight of the Universe.

His internal bioscope showed him images from the Great Famine, the touchstone of his mental world. And at the same time an intellectual facet of his mind brought back his earlier readings, the fasts and penances of the great sages. It dawned on him that he must undertake such a penance, that at this stage of his life, such an action was required. The riddle remained unsolved, and before conceding it would remain eternally unsolved, was unsolvable, he would make this last effort.

So he determined to enter the state of the forest-dweller. Locating this 'forest' in the Rajmahal didn't seem contradictory, Petrov was too sophisticated. And deeply intuitive about Reema Devi, he was certain of her reactions.

'A statement of my intention will be understood by her in no time, in spite of her nervous condition ...'

He prized a coin out of his wallet with a shaking hand and threw it into the gourd rocking it on its round base.

'Take!' he said.

The mendicant-yogi came to life, picked up a pair of ringed iron tongs and clashed them forcefully and rhythmically, augmenting the beat with a hoarse tenor chant. A crowd collected.

Petrov turned too quickly and lost his balance. He was helped to steady himself by a passer-by, braced himself, and with the old man's forward slant, hurried home to the Rajmahal. He wanted feverishly to set out on his new course.

'Once I have solved the riddle the harmonious waves will calm all in my ambit,' he concluded. 'And, while I am at it, I shall become a vegetarian and undertake ever more frequent fasts in an orderly progression. Reema will accept that we are at the end of our quest. And Robi will be my comrade-in-arms ...'

Robi, who was rescued from the streets during the famine, was the Petrov's major-domo. He knew little of formal philosophy, but he was an expert in Hatha-yoga, learned while he worked in an ashram. Early in 1943, he had returned to his native village and had been trapped by the famine. His family, landless labourers existing on the margins of the economy, soon used up his salary and his widowed mother, who usually husked grain in times of need, couldn't find work. That year, in an atmosphere of war-related ordinances, inflation, uncertainty and indifferent governance, prices shot up and stocks dwindled. Buying grain became impossible with the unrecognizable new prices. Merchants turned overnight into hoarders, scaling an escalating spiral of greed. The phenomenon wasn't unfamiliar to the elders among the villagers. Robi thought of taking his mother back to the ashram which was in a far away State. But hunger forced them to trudge to Calcutta, the Mecca for millions of starving peasants. They arrived at the great metropolis in a fit state to join the corpses littering the streets. After two days of desperate foraging, they found themselves in a quiet upper class Bengali area where daily kitchens were opened in some houses. They were given hot freshly cooked khichuri with vegetables, and strong sweet tea in Player's Navy Cut cigarette tins. On the second day, the housewife called to Robi from the portico and after asking about him and looking at his ragged ashram papers, sent him and his mother to the servants' quarters to change into clean clothes, and then in a chauffeur-driven car to the Rajmahal. While Robi and his mother crouched in the car, they gazed about them at the gleaming shops and houses in this part of town, at the trams and buses and cars, and at each other, not daring to speak. Robi met with the Petrovs' approval and soon found himself employed at the Rajmahal, installed with his mother in a comfortable room on the roof. It took them time to acclimatize to their good fortune, that they had escaped death by starvation, and that Robi was now earning many times his old salary and working for patrons with a human face.

When he and his mother filled out again, sometimes a claustrophobic feeling would overcome Robi, a great sorrow engulf him. He would gaze out from the rooftop and see his village nestling in the clouds. When there was a lull in the traffic roar, the sound of a stray flute would create a fusion between his old habitat and this city and he would be filled with bliss.

⁂

After his walk along Chowringhee and his customary slow climb up the stairs to his flat, Petrov leaned back panting on his chair. Reema Devi looked at his white eyelashes and eyebrows, his yellow-white fringe of hair which could be taken for ash blonde, when he caught her gaze on him. A sudden gleam lit his eyes, and she felt her face grow hot, swelling as it did when she was excited, embarrassed or aroused. She was almost eighty, could she be any of these things? When did her face last swell that she straight away recognized the symptoms? There was a difference though. She put her hand up to her smoothly puffed out cheek. It was hurting, that was the difference, and she thought with amusement that it was hurting because the wrinkles had unglued themselves from their position of inward collapse and stretched. She smiled and caught Petrov's pale eyes again, sexy under the prominent white eyebrows and lashes, and she remembered a long ago reunion after a misunderstanding. How they had sprung together like two magnets. And in that powerfully tight clinch, Petrov had said, 'Did you think you could get away?' And she had disconnected herself from him, almost feeling a tearing of the flesh and heard him say, 'Don't you try to get away again.' And she had been far enough from him, before he pulled her back, to see that gleam in his eyes and realize that the misunderstanding still lay unresolved but didn't matter. She remembered how, at one time, she would have crushes on her leading men, especially with the heroic make-up and dissimulation under blinding arc lights. A period of fluttery, intoxicating runs as long as the plays ran. The stage nearness, suggestive touches, suppressed embraces taking on a deep significance. Then, with the rise to stardom, she would be impatient of too much respect. 'Come on,' she would say. 'We are on the stage. Act natural. Everyone is looking at us!' And sometimes she would tease, 'Make the best of this chance!' But by then Petrov had come into her life, and they were married, the ultimate theatre couple. She knew how captivated he was by her, and when she caught him gazing at her she would think, 'Petro, my dearest, you are embarrassing me! Everyone is looking at us!' The attentions of her real-life husband would embarrass her in public, but not of her stage lovers.

These memories came to her while she and Petrov looked at one another like that again, at this ridiculous age. They both smiled and got up and gently held hands to neutralize their tremors and walked slowly and straight to their bedroom. There they lay for a long time in an embrace. And then they went through the motions of love, softly, lovers at the summit of maturity. Subtly with the experience of age, stiffly because of their age, enjoyably in spite of their age, and without immediate carnality yet with the carnality of dense memories. Reema Devi wondered at this miracle, and Petrov remembered again that evening's usual walk along Chowringhee made unusual by the mendicant ascetic, and thought that what had just passed wasn't in contradiction to his resolve, but simply the signalling of an end. And he realized at last, that Reema Devi's beauty and love for him were not the only forces behind the powerful attraction she held for him, but that with her the love-making had been real, not a play. The others, not that many after all, were for the sex and the drama, they weren't real. He sighed. The mirror of the stage to sex and love-making. Why did he think of them as separate when they involved the same actions, the same cleaving and heaving? 'Cleaving and heaving!' he chuckled. Was the distinction imaginary, from the romantic imagination of a nonagenarian? He looked long and hard at Reema Devi, noticing again the ancientness of her face, happy and serene in repose. And while drifting off to sleep, he said goodbye to her. 'Goodbye my Reema, my beloved companion.' It was he who was getting away from her, against his own long-ago injunction. There was nothing further for him to do, and he was to leave her behind lost in the tremor of her nerves. He must now enter his transferred forest.

The shock to Reema Devi was intense. It took her time to realize her beloved Petro had removed himself from her life. The day-to-day exchanges were ended, all communication was ended. She swallowed her deep hurt, the final capping to a rich life full of triumph and pain. There was her Petro, stationed cross-legged on a low seat placed on the verandah, reduced in dress to a single loincloth, hardly eating, and uttering only a few monosyllables. The delicious secret of that last night was made bitter by this abandonment and sharpened the memory of her dead child. She had attained the ultimate maturity, and she would have to turn the hurt around, allow it to spread itself in her and strengthen her. She reasoned that Petrov's adoption of her culture, the Indian's last stage of life, as an ascetic forest-dweller, was an accolade to her country and therefore to her.

Surjeet Shona visited Reema Devi often, trying to fill in the cruel gap, amusing her with video cassettes of her plays, reading out reviews and notices which were available from orderly scrap albums, Petrov's inherited hobby. But Reema Devi couldn't hide her ebbing interest.

'Dear girl,' she confessed. 'In the end, it's Petro who remains my abiding concern. Not reliving my past career, or my glory. While he is still with me, yet not with me, I can't concentrate on any of this ...'

She preferred to settle into the cane armchair placed just behind Petrov out of the line of his sight, taking comfort in his presence and sending out waves of love to him. This was her only way to confront his transfixation.

❦

After a period of meditation, Petrov reached the last stages of hallucinatory malnutrition. The prolonged periods of sitting cross-legged impaired his muscles so he could no longer walk. He put behind him not only his dying wife, his dead son, his distant living children, his Eros which had turned lacklustre without the inspiration of the Petrovs, but his whole life. Robi, his tenaciously faithful servant, famine-precipitated, natural mystic, Hatha yogi, had to carry his master about in his arms.

And then one day Petrov said to Robi in his faint voice and chaste Bengali, 'I feel constricted by these walls, oh Robi. Only up on the roof, under the open sky, will it be good. Will you arrange for it?'

Reduced almost to the famine-induced state suffered by Robi during that tragic and remarkable period in Bengal, he intended to enter a state of bliss and gain the Universe.

Surjeet Shona was quick to repartée, 'But even Buddha sat under the shelter of the Bo tree. Can't the verandah be your Bo tree?'

But Petrov's will was unbendable. He refused to answer Surjeet Shona, or look at Reema Devi, who was sitting just behind him.

Robi, understanding his master would only sometimes visit the roof, was concerned with the logistics. The only access to the roof was by the servants' spiral stairway, made lacier than ever with worn away patches, impossibly narrow, precariously attached to the outer back of the mansion. The Rajmahal was in despair over it, sure that if just one of the iron clamps gave way, the spiral would snap from its moorings and sway out losing control and spilling its users from precipitous heights. 'We can take him up to Mallik Shaheb's and start from there,' said Surjeet Shona. 'It will make the distance very short, just one floor.'

'Are you not forgetting one thing, Shona baby …?'

Surjeet Shona knew the reference was to Junior Mallik. 'Come on,' she said firmly. 'Let's confront him!'

'You mean,' stuttered Junior irately, 'you mean you are going to drag old Petrov up to the roof in his condition?'

Surjeet Shona watched the tomato ruddiness of Junior's face turn to fire. 'I forbid you!' he flamed. 'I forbid you completely and totally! Do you bloody hear me! Do you ...,' he stopped an unprintable mouthful.

Surjeet Shona often felt pity bordering on affection for Junior, easily the most unpopular person inhabiting the Rajmahal, but this presumptuousness was too much.

'I would like you to know, Junior,' she said, icily cool, 'that Uncle Osheem is going up! And I would like to see you even so much as try to stop us!'

She signalled to Robi, who was grinning uneasily with hands folded in prayer, and marched out before Junior could untangle his face.

With the fretting Junior peering at them through a gap in a curtain, Anatoly Sergeivich 'Osheem' Petrov was gently carried up on to the roof by the devoted Robi from the Mallik kitchen on the vibrating spiral staircase. Reema Devi was on the landing to ceremonially witness her husband's ascension. She had steeled herself into a stoical, if tremulous, dignity and she kissed her dear Petro on each cheek. 'It's all right, Petro,' she said, trying not to react to the pathetic sight of her husband crumpled up in Robi's arms. 'I understand. I have always loved you ...' The couple raised weak hands in touching gestures of farewell. 'Goodbye Petro, my dearest. Goodbye ...,' whispered Reema Devi to her silent husband. 'It's all right, my friends,' she said to the grieving Robi and Surjeet Shona that very night, before giving them a benedictory look and suspiring to the last of her life's breath. With the tears streaming down their faces, the faithful twosome covered Reema Devi's body up to the neck after laying her on a groundsheet. Surjeet Shona took on the ordeal of phone calls, to the relations, to the press, to the theatre contacts. It was agreed that Reema Devi would be presented as she had liked it till the last, heavy pancake make-up, deep scarlet lipstick and a brightly coloured sari draped over the head to reveal a little of the still thick, dyed black hair, eyebrows darkened, while the closed eyes were kohled at the corners. Soon the photographers and lines of visitors were trudging up the stairs on their last visit to this doyenne of the Calcutta stage, whom they had lost sight of over the years. It was a mixed and colourful crowd which mourned the passing of the great actress, from wizened old stage prop handlers to screen painters and make-up men, from playwrights and directors to heroes and heroines both bygone and contemporary, from nephews and nieces to distant cousins. A representative from the Russian consulate, ordered to attend, having been told Mrs Petrov was Russian, wondered why she looked so Indian. Flowers filled the flat, gladioli, tuberose and marigold. Most of the visitors, not seeing Petrov, refrained delicately from asking for his whereabouts. 'He must be long gone …,' they whispered, not sure whom to ask.

Surjeet Shona and Robi waited for the Petrov children, Boris and Meera to arrive before taking the news up to Petrov. They found him at his post, as if he were a paper sculpture, the result of the siccative tendencies he had been showing for years. Meera wept to see her father. 'The slightest breeze will blow him away,' she whispered. Robi rustled him gently, calling him with endearments. 'Shaheb, dear Shaheb …' And Surjeet Shona thought, 'He knows.' Meera and Boris sat by their father, one on each side, with their arms around him, and saw two thick tears rolling from under his eyelids as if the last drops of fluid were being drained from his desiccated husk. He said nothing, but opening his eyes briefly, turned to each in turn and stroked their arms. There was no other sign from him, except that he didn't swallow his broth that evening. He resumed his 'normal' life the very next day. And his two children would wait uneasily for the end so they could sell their rights to the flat and the Eros and be done with their past.

Robi had done his best to prepare the roof, with the help and support of Surjeet Shona, before Petrov's ascent, having it cleaned, and one bathroom converted to the western style. The conditions were slummy. Even zealous Junior hadn't inspected the roof for years, and the repairmen often pocketed parts of the money paid by the landlord, while the roof was left to get discoloured, peel, crack and deteriorate. The Rajmahal had given up the fight and concentrated only on the water-proofing.

Petrov was fascinated to find the old riddle in another form. All his life he had been unable to reconcile the injustice of the rich to the poor, the exploitation of the colonized by the colonizer, the death by famine of thousands while the rich sauntered past to their repasts. Yet here, where the servants' quarters were located, was a reversal. It was the servants who were exploiting the trust of their rich masters. Too soon, he learnt of the servants' activities, gambling, drinking and whoring, of the perfidy of those who boasted of pilfering from their masters' flats, openly, to the hilarity of the rest, and the gossipy insouciance with which they disposed of the sexual depravity of Myrna Strachey, the nocturnal ravings of Proshanto Mojumdar, and, when they forgot the large ears of the ghostly figure on the divan, the Petrovs themselves. Here was a case study so close he had missed it altogether. Robi was partly responsible, such a hard working, emotionally predictable and honest servant, he had brainwashed Petrov into believing all servants, having been saved from destitution by their masters, were petrified in willing servitude till their deaths. Yet it was a complete reversal, an inexplicable, unanswerable question …

Petrov found it easy to adjust to the open air. When the resourceful Robi realized his master intended to stay up here permanently, he had a small portable canvas shelter built for times of excess rain and sun, and dewy nights. A utilitarian Bo tree. Leaving Petrov free to philosophize, meditate, allow his thoughts to meander, and to enjoy the open sky when weather permitted. And the weather was clement to a fault.

'But of course! I understand now! India is an outdoor country. It is not meant to have walls, roofs. This beautiful Rajmahal is a redundancy after all! Oh, what I have missed all these years …'

Petrov settled down to enjoy the open air while occupied in the self-absorbed pursuit of nirvana. Day after day he battled with the big questions in a knowingly unstructured manner, waiting for insights, the path to the answer. His mind ranged over anything that came to it. With the occasional blanks and time warps creating new patterns he delved this way and that, like the timeless interrogators recorded in the ancient scriptures. But he was unlike even the wondrous boys of the Upanishads, Nachiketas or Svetaketu, who asked the great questions about death and immortality, about life and God, or the questing wife, Gargi, warned by Yajnavalkya, 'Ask no more, oh Gargi, lest thy head fall off!'

Kali, the terrible black Goddess with blood-dripping tongue, garland of skulls and girdle of chopped-off arms, holds on one side the guns and knives of war and the decapitated head of the enemy, while on the other, her hands gesture gently to gratify and bless. The evil inherent in God is out in the open, balanced by the visible but temporarily subordinated good. Perhaps it is the vexing riddle of a supposedly ever-loving and benign God, in whom the existence of evil is unacceptable or never overtly acceptable in the Christian tradition, that baffled Petrov through the filter of his ancestral memory, a Christian memory. Yet mystics and philosophers such as Ramakrishna and Vivekenanda cheerfully accept the Goddess image and its evil aspect.

Does evil exist? Does good exist? Is either absolute? God-with-an-extra-O – good? Evil-with-a-D – the Devil? Is human nature immutable? Had he himself, Petrov, ever been evil? What would he have done if his father, or Reema's father or brother, had been one of those hoarders of grain during the famine? Why had he chosen to stay on in this country, almost immediately tying himself to it with a commitment to the theatre, racing off at a tangent from his aim, always elliptical? Was his aim really to examine the contradictions of country and society, ruler and ruled? What of his dubiously illustrious countryman, a century and a half ahead of him? Herassim Stefanovich Lebadeff. 1795. He too had come to Calcutta to study philosophy, language. And he too had involved himself in the theatre. He had been hounded out of Calcutta by the machinations of a rivalrous British theatre group thirsty for gain. That was a telling phrase. 'The gold glittering humours and silver glinting blood that runs in the veins of theatrical people thirsty for gain,' the wrathful Lebadeff had said. His theatre would be burnt down by his enemies, and the ruling power would see to it that the Russian 'infiltrator' would be made to run out of the capital of British India. They had been more concerned with keeping ahead in the Great Game than the fate of a crazy adventurer. Why had Lebadeff started a theatre in Calcutta, for Bengali drama, when no European would have any contact with Indians except for 'law courts, commerce, brothels and servants'? Why had he, Anatoly Petrov, set down roots before he knew about the old Lebadeff, along such dramatically parallel lines a century and a half later? British attitudes hadn't changed much after that century and a half, when he had arrived in India, still broadly restricted to the same four points of contact. But then, he, Petrov, in spite of being a white man, would find the life so rich, the strange and deep culture of the Bengalis, the indeterminate twilight tragedy of the Anglo-Indians, the Calcutta upper crust Joseph's-coat society. And so, instead of pursuing his aim, he had diverted himself with the theatre. And Reema Devi. And now, was he really fulfilling his destiny by going through to the last two of the four stages of life as ordained by the Hindus, of the apprentice, the householder, the forest-dweller and the ascetic?

Seated on his asan and looking out at the horizon through half open eyes he dreamed and had visions. He saw the flighted kites cresting the clouds, the black crows croaking and flapping below them. He watched the sun rising and setting in its myriad forms, cool mist-covered white, in and out of golden clouds, fireball.

He dwelt on his adopted language, Bengali, its beauty and expressiveness. On digonto – the imaginary line between sky and earth. Sheema – the limit, of which he was the opposite, Osheem – without end or limit. His Bengali friends had dubbed him 'without limit', in a semantic slide from the Russian Herassim. Did Herassim have a meaning, and did that meaning, through the bedrock of the Indo-European linguistic family, have any connection with Osheem? Would that lead to a clue in the great mystery, and would the confirmation of such a linguistic syllogism mean that he, originally Anatoly Sergeivich Petrov, was without limit? His mind moved playfully about the possibilities, soaring beyond semantics. He thought of Reema Devi. Did she age gracefully? Was he aging gracefully? Did those who kept as healthy and cheerful as possible without expectation, or those who wanted to be told how young they looked, or those who had face lifts, dyed hair and artificially removed fat, age gracefully? Wasn't there always a gap, a never-ideal situation?

So then, ultimately, the ideal can never be. The second that state is achieved it must end! The moment utopia is, in that split second, *it is not.* It follows, therefore, that the impetus for all being is conflict, contradiction. Though theories of the ideal state can be intellectually conceptualized and framed in constitutions and laws and safeguards by the good state, *it can never work*. There is no perfectly workable state of being. If there is, it must be the end, the imploding-exploding big-bang end! Perfection is an illusion. There will always be famine …

He sits and dozes, watching each morning and evening when the horizon, that imaginary line, digonto, appears and disappears in the changing light, and the globe and the dome merge, another illusion.

Why do the poor people on the streets of India laugh? Why do the beggars of India laugh? Do they laugh because they are happy? If one laughs, does it automatically mean one is happy? Do those whose intestines refuse to accept food ever laugh again, if they survive? Is old age its own exploitation? Where the fading faculties deprive the possessor of those very faculties, where that deprivation invites youth to exploit age? Does youth always exploit age? Why do children wish to discard parents after their use is over? He thinks of his children, Boris and Meera, Boris and Meera, he has to keep repeating their names like a mantra to recall their images, Boris and Meera, their eager distancing, of which he felt the currents even as they wept and held him. Didn't Rudrangshu discard his poor father in the end? Calcutta too is being discarded by many, those who find it old, aged. The aged interfere with the aspirations and fulfilment of youth, by holding up inheritance, by their very presence. And he thinks of Reema Devi who went long after the ending of her career, but just at the time when he, her husband, no longer needed her. Did he, Anatoly Sergeivich Petrov, exploit her? Is desertion exploitation, is indifference exploitation, the ultimate indifference of his children, is that exploitation? Are they waiting eagerly for him to die so they can get the flat, his treasures, his money? When Proshanto Mojumdar was cremated why did Shudhangshu look so happy? Did he gain from his brother's death? Did that gain make him happy? What about the Stracheys? Myrna the beauty, reduced to dithering old age, and Jack Strachey, dying together while holding hands? Who is exploiting whom? Is someone having a malevolent joke at the expense of their age? And old, whatever his name was, the titled sardarji who built the mansion, with the peasant face of Tolstoy, was he too exploited by his children in spite of his great power and wealth? In the time of famine, did children push aside their parents to snatch at the last morsels of food? But he had witnessed the opposite, hadn't he?

The mansion and its ghosts tremble and writhe. He is dealing with things that are sacred, turning them profane … Petrov's brain grows sharper, clearer.

'Dear Shaheb. Are you ready to come down to your own home? It is a void without beloved memshaheb. It behoves you to fill it with your presence to make up for that unimaginable loss.' Robi feels deeply hurt at Petrov's indifference to his great wife's passing.

The mansion wills Petrov to follow Robi's injunction, so that it will be allowed to nurture and soothe him till his end, instead of this unnatural exposure to the elements in its least propitious region. How it longs for him to come down so that it can manifest again through a rainbow, in memory of the first time.

'Dear Shaheb, have your broth,' says Robi. 'It is late and your body is weak.'

'Yes all right. Give me my broth Robi, oh faithful Robi.'

Hope flares, even excitement, when Petrov orders Robi to massage his body, the initial sensitivity gradually dissolving till greater vigour can be applied. Repeatedly Robi pleads with him to re-occupy his flat.

'Keep quiet, Robi!' Petrov scolds. 'How do you expect me to give up the free air for an enclosed space again?'

The Rajmahal groans each time it hears these words, and Robi sighs, while a tear trickles down his wide cheek. 'Hey Ma Kali, what can we do, what can we do after all?' In the meantime, he reinstructs Petrov in the simpler aspects of yoga. The earlier years of practice pay and one day Petrov is upright, able to take a few shaky steps and then walk, his knees huge between his fleshless shanks and shins. While the physical regeneration goes on, Petrov's brain is active. His mind relaxed, from all those vexing questions and in that state of rest, arrives at a culmination, the final full recognition of the non-existence of the secret. 'Why all these questions,' he asks himself, 'which of us can have the arrogance to claim we KNOW? How many of us are Buddhas and Christs or know if even they, the Buddhas and Christs, KNEW?' And his Christian grounding pulls at him. Cautiously, he takes his mind to his childhood. He thinks of the Christ, after this whole life spent in labyrinthine pleonasms. His early conditioning comes up to the surface. He now knows there is no-answer, no-secret. Only a simple rule. Of which his beloved Reema reminded him at the very end. Love. Love for the starving, love for him. The greatness of her acting was built on love, he knows that. He tries to remember the Sermon on the Mount, not abstract theories about good and evil and the existence of consciousness or the nature of the self, but a human state-of-being for those who will it or are blessed with it. Love. Ramakrishna, Jesus Christ ... He is combining his indelible conditioning – both pre- and post-Russia, the one inherited, the other acquired. He blows an imaginary balloon up into a vast, shimmering round with the breath of love and lets go the string. The balloon floats away and becomes invisible against the bright glare of the sky.

❧

The renewed Petrov commands Robi to call up Surjeet Shona from her ground floor flat.

Robi leaps up to obey, almost having an accident as he circles swiftly to the bottom of the stairs.

'Come, come, Shona baby. Shaheb is calling you.'

'What is it, Robi? Is he all right?'

'Yes, yes. Just come …'

They go up the broad inner stairway, sensing the house's unease, and access the winding staircase from the top floor Mallik kitchen. On the roof they find the ascetic teetering at the balustrade, the ancient mariner on the bridge of his ship, his age like the albatross, gripping him at the neck. Surjeet Shona joins him quietly, swallowing her emotions at seeing him exposed in his meagre loincloth.

'Uncle Osheem, I have come. Tell me. What is it?'

Petrov continues gazing out, but holds Surjeet Shona's elbow with one hand.

'Do you see it?' he points to the horizon. 'Look out there. Do you see the digonto, that non-existent and illusory line between there and here? We are all from that division, dear child, all of us, half here, half there. And there is the no-answer.' He puts up his hand to stop any interlocution. 'Now,' he says. 'Look down there, and tell me what you see.'

Surjeet Shona glances down. 'Oh no!' she says. 'Oh no!' She draws back jerkily, trying to pull Petrov with her, and Petrov directs his colourless eyes at her.

'Well?' he asks in his dry tone. 'Well?'

Surjeet Shona turns reluctantly to look down again at the ghoul in person, a vulture. It is perched on a ledge outside the far end of the verandah, but Surjeet Shona feels she can reach out and touch the bald head on the scrawny neck, comically emerging out of its large jacket of feathers. The bird hops clumsily away, one untidily hanging wing drooping out of alignment with its monstrous bird body so unlike other birds, whose wings fit sleekly along their curves, and who are so much *smaller*. She relaxes as the vulture flies away heavily, its powerful wings beating, to perch on the raintree. 'You're all for me,' it seems to say. 'In the end.'

Robi is frantically trying to drag his master back to his seat. But Petrov chuckles, 'What is it, oh Robi?' He soothes Surjeet Shona, stroking her trembling and hot arm.

'Why not some enjoyment now? Didn't Ramakrishna say that of his beloved Kali? Didn't he say, in answer to all those serious questions, that Kali visits us with such pain simply because it is great fun? Well then. What do you think I was doing, coming up here like this?'

Before either of his friends can respond Petrov starts heaving for breath.

Surjeet Shona swallows. She can't see the ghosts whooping at and shooing away the vultures, their efforts flagging, so tired are they with all the whooping and shooing at all the vultures which have been hovering in the vicinity for so long, more and more reluctant to leave as their bodies get heavier and heavier with dreams of carrion.

'What are you afraid of?' says Petrov gently, settling down cross-legged on his divan. 'Come on, dear. We all go into that unknown space. And even,' he smiles so very kindly that a halo seems to surround his beatifically pale head, like a modern-day Choitonyo. 'Even if our old friend Yama, with his noose and his net and his hook, the Lord of Death, finally gathers me to him followed by that beautiful and necessary bird, you will continue for the present ... I have nothing to teach you. You have had the solution always. And with that solution fear has no place.'

Surjeet Shona prepares herself for something momentous. It has to be momentous, with the sky gently glowing pale aqua among grey and white clouds, with the vultures draping the raintree in increasing numbers as they swish noisily and gracefully about their legitimate work.

After Petrov is helped to lie down, he says, 'I must sleep.'

Surjeet Shona speaks out strongly to Robi. 'Your shaheb has to go. Allow him! It is you who are holding him back!' She is angry. 'Let him go, Robi! He's old! Let go!'

'Tomorrow, Shona baby. Tomorrow itself, in the morning, I will see to the lowering of Osheem Shaheb to his proper abode, where he will end his life, its earned span, in dignity.'

Robi feels very strongly that exposure to the open sky lays one bare to birds and insects and naturally thrown up marauders. They stay at bay only if one is protected by four walls and a roof. The vulnerability of his early village years, where the air burnt and shimmered and spat at them, destroying their homes, their crops and taking away their livelihood could only be combated by well-being, wealth and the armour of a good house. He has made a connection between the extreme age of his shaheb and the outsized beak of the vulture and he is deadly afraid.

The Rajmahal too is disturbed by its emptying premises, flats imbued with the scent of stale incense and decayed flowers. It imagines the pillars of its verandahs cracking up and sprouting rooted weeds, providing no protection against the vultures, and it longs for the invulnerability of its youth here on the roof, where there are not even the fragile chiks of the lower verandahs.

Robi rolls the portable shelter over Osheem Shaheb and lies down next to him with a protective arm about him.

'No vulture,' he says to his wife who watches, shivering with superstitious fear from her room, as do other roof-dwellers, 'no vulture will be allowed to get near shaheb as long as he lives!'

Just as it is dawning, a piercing chorus of cries and moans from the roof, followed by a drumming sound above his head, wake Junior up.

'What the hell!' he curses. 'Tea, tea!' he calls as if any servant will be on duty at this hour.

Petrov has disappeared, vanished.

'That's it. He just vanished. Hey bhogobaan, oh God, Hori-bole, Hori-bole, Hori-bole …'

That drumming and chorus were caused by the servants calling and running back and forth, a frightened flock not knowing which way to turn, only some brave enough to peek over the balcony, certain of discovering the white, slight body of Petrov Shaheb lying smashed on the ground below. But Petrov is nowhere to be seen. Not even later and through the day. With Junior and the police swarming about, searching every room and cranny, the insides of the four water tanks hoisted on platforms at each corner of the roof, and in each and every flat of the Rajmahal, the garages, the garden, the godowns.

'I told you!' mutters a furious Junior to Robi, 'I told you something ghastly would happen.'

'Take it easy, Junior,' says Surjeet Shona. 'Don't excite yourself. Remember your blood pressure.'

But Junior isn't listening. Seeing Robi swaying back and forth on his haunches with his head in his hands he dances with fury, 'Bloody fucking idiot!' he shouts. And Robi sways even more frantically and beats at his forehead with his palms.

'Yes,' says Surjeet Shona clearly, looking out at the raintree, mysteriously divested of its vultures. 'What is the need for them any more? He's gone, the ephemerally light Uncle Osheem, a mere snack for them, returned to dust, to ether, to the elements ... Does it matter how?'

❧

The Rajmahal is getting lonely, one of its floors echoing emptily and its ghost population vanished. It isn't just the ghosts of the tenants who died after the lemming-rush begun by Myrna and Jack Strachey. Rover-the-dog, Mohini and Proshanto Mojumdar, and Reema Devi and Petrov. They are not the only ghost-deserters, as the mansion glooms. The other ghosts have left too, in a startling whoosh, with Anatoly Sergeivich 'Osheem' Petrov.

It had taken the brief time of abandonment by Robi, when he went on that automatic necessity of a call of nature, for Petrov's heart to stop beating. For the waiting vultures to swoop, unseen, silent in the dawn dimness, on his carcass. And as they carried on with their pecking and prizing open of his body with their fearsome beaks, squabbling and snatching at it, the body lifted up and down in its extreme feathery brittle lightness, tossed up and down between vulture rushes.

Jarred awake by the agitated Rajmahal, the sleeping ghosts were made to instantly manifest above the roof to start a spirited fight for Petrov's body.

'Why did Osheem become so harsh in the end?' the ghosts asked.

'These Westerners are like that,' the Swadeshi ghost shouted. 'Where do they have our tenderness? Did Reema Devi have a chance?'

'As if our men are kind to their wives …'

'Don't they take all the rights and powers to themselves …?'

'Yes, yes, that's enough,' one of the few sober ghosts said. 'Reema Devi had to leave, just as she had to die on the fateful day of Osheem's ascension!'

In the sudden vacuum caused by the ghosts' challenge, a wind swirled up and Petrov's carcass lifted higher and higher with the vultures' beaks and flapping wings. Astonished, the birds transferred to an air squabble over the remains, wafting up and up in swirls of warm air with the body till they reached impossible heights way above city lights. The ghosts swarmed with the vultures, and chasing and swooping, this macabre host raced above the Hooghly towards its confluence with the unending ocean. And there, where the many-headed Ganga lay dynamically sprawled, its mouths fanged with mangrove and crocodile, the vultures succumbed to their gibbering-prodding pursuers, and finally lost hold of their prize. So Petrov had the grandest end of all, with air and river and sea for his interment, the ghosts cushioning his fall, letting him gently down into the Goddess's multiple maw.

Having come so far and seen such wondrous expanses and the scope of the silver-gold glittering universe, who could hold those ghosts back? The fear of the unknown which had confined them to the Rajmahal and their pasts dissolved, and swift and eager at last they disappeared in currents of changing air.

5

The Book of Hope

When polo-widow Maudie Jessop moved in with her brother David Norman, the Rajmahal was neither pleased nor dismayed. Uneasy, it was uneasy about the widow who spent so much of her time prettifying herself yet with a clothes peg on her tongue. The house was sorry for her, recognizing the incipient weakness in her will, knowing in its bricks she would take to drink and be quickly seduced, both possible during one of the Normans' rumbustious parties. Too much drama around any inhabitant disturbed the house.

Maudie's husband Anthony Jessop was a member of the Indian Police. While on district postings, they visited the Rajmahal often. Maudie would then replenish her wardrobe at 'Right Away and Paid For', Whiteaway and Laidlaw's alias, or Hall and Anderson, or the New Market, and bask in the warmth of her brother's household and ready parties. Her arrival was an excuse for these parties. Maudie didn't unpeg her tongue to blossom into the belle of the ball but she relished dancing and picking out tunes on the piano. The traditional Anglo-Indian fare lasted as long as their generation. Meats, curries, wines, cakes and confectioneries, of which Maudie was a specialist in the rosy cocade, a rose-shaped sweet finished in a dip of boiling syrup. They belonged to the top echelons of Calcutta society, accepted by British as well as native circles. Most Anglo-Indians would be shocked to hear themselves branded by the pejorative 'native', but that, as recognized by an outstanding member of their community who led them well into independent India, was what they were. Even if the leader didn't use the despised word itself, he recognized his community as Indian, first and last, whatever their colour. Some of the community understood this, keener on adjusting to their difficult place in India than flaunting a superiority based on unreliable British patronage. Or claiming as their own an unknown, unseen country. The Jessops recognized this, and with Anthony's successes in the Indian Police, stayed on without question. The first body blow to Maudie's sense of a perfect life was her only child Eric's death, when he was barely an adult. Independence had come and receded and Anthony's climb in the police continued. But Eric hankered for the glamour of foreign lands. He, like many fellow students, and as expounded by Petrov in his diary passage on post-independent India, was sure Valhalla could exist nowhere but in the West. India held little immediate attraction. While some of his wealthy friends, mostly fully Indian, could afford a university education in England, the rest stayed back, giving vent to their frustration through verbal tirades. But they stabilized in a few years. Those who became leftists and held lasting convictions, and that wasn't just a pose but a solemn matter in Calcutta, entered into the violent politics of the State. The Jessops could afford to send Eric abroad too, but he couldn't pass the entrance exams. Stuck in Calcutta, he tingled with sensitivity at what he imagined was his friends' scorn towards Anglo-Indians. He decided to become a deck hand and head ostentatiously East, not West. This was his shallow defiance when all he wanted was to end up in Australia, the Eastern West. After exploring the non-Anglo-Saxon countries on the way, he planned to integrate with help from his cousins in Perth, whose address he surreptitiously copied from his parents' address book. He succeeded in the first part of his plan. But this time class became his enemy, and when the other ship hands discovered this sahib in their midst, they took to taunting him without mercy. He acquired a hard veneer and built up a reputation as a debauch in the exotic ports at which his ship docked, including Colombo, Rangoon, Chittagong, Arracan and Penang. Maudie and Anthony's worried attempts to keep contact through the ship's wireless, with letters waiting at the ports, and through the BISN Co. on whose ship, the *Clan McBride*, he was sailing, only fuelled his mates' taunts. Finally, at one of the ports, Eric, a handsome, strong boy with light colouring and honey blonde hair, got into a brawl with a sailor over a flattered prostitute, both were drunk, and Eric ended up with a knife in his heart. The knife reached all the way to Calcutta deep into Maudie and Anthony's hearts, and the ultimate knife-thrust for Maudie was Anthony's death.

Anthony was fascinated by cars. The morning of his death, he gave Maudie a driving lesson in 'Lover's Lane', the wide, quiet road skirting the racecourse and polo ground. They were using the Pram, an Austin 7 which Anthony cherished for its vintage value. Both knew Maudie would never be able to drive and the Pram was just a safe toy. Its playroom status had struck Anthony when, as a child, he sometimes saw another Calcutta Pram driving by with chauffeur and owner squeezed into the constricted front seat, two uniformed orderlies squeezed on the back seat, and a brace of mounted police toweringly clip-clopping alongside. This playroom-toy-soldier image went with the exaggerated trappings of the British Empire as it lost its sense of reality. It was also in direct contrast to the other Pram he had seen in the Bengali area of town. A pliable bamboo arched over the passengers, dangling a lantern in front in lieu of the broken headlights. Anthony's stable of cars, which included an Armstrong-Siddeley, a Humber and a Regal, names forgotten in the Calcutta of his last days, had been emptied, and the Pram was all that remained, apart from a Hindustan 14, the ancestor of the Ambassador. That day, the Pram nearly brought about Anthony's doom.

'Fate was after him. Look at the narrow shave he had just seconds before the polo game!' people said.

Maudie found herself grappling with a jammed steering wheel, and in her panic made the clichéd mistake of putting her foot down hard on the accelerator instead of the brake. Anthony's side of the

Pram crashed into a tree and a sharp broken branch just missed spearing his forehead.

'Oh there was no real danger. But the old Pram's done for,' he comforted the trembling and tearful Maudie. The police syces helped them out of the mangled wreck and Anthony patted it and instructed them to throw it in the junkyard. Maudie begged Anthony not to play polo that day, but he was already cantering away.

The polo players went thundering by while she became absorbed in the exchange of niceties with other onlookers. They were paying no attention to the players at the far end of the field when there was a collision of horses, and Anthony had a fatal fall. Maudie remembered little of events after this, except for the sight of a limp body as it was carried by on a stretcher. She could hear a whimpering sound which seemed to come from her, and feel her lips and cheeks stretching tight over her facial bones in an uncontrollable grimace.

After Anthony's death, Maudie was immediately taken to her brother David at the Rajmahal.

'Look at her. Just like a corpse, poor dear!'

'Let's keep her with us, Dore. She'll never be able to cope alone.'

David Norman and his wife Doreen were standing by Maudie, looking down at her lying in a drugged sleep, two hectic patches on her cheeks distinguishing her from the white sheets. Doreen agreed immediately, and Maudie recovered and became a part of the house. At times Doreen wondered if they had taken on too much with this uncomfortable guest who would continue to evoke bereaved attitudes with her sad, frail presence.

'You aren't like that!' exclaimed Doreen in exasperation to her husband. 'I wish your sister would stop behaving like a sleepwalker. Let's give a party this weekend, come on Davie! It's been such a long time ...'

David Norman grabbed Doreen and they jigged about, shouting and laughing. Maudie came in just then, and a smile, the first since her bereavement, showed on her face.

The party preparations went forward speedily, and the Normans took up their old exuberant existence, cheering Maudie along whenever they suspected a relapse.

Maudie stood waiting nervously in the sitting room when the first guest came in. It was the legendarily sexy Robert Rozario, in whose presence women found themselves breathing rapidly and anxiously.

'So you're up and about again, eh Maudie?' Rozario's eyes glinted under arched eyebrows, his Pavlovian way with women. He put out a hand and stroked Maudie's bare arm, raising goose bumps. She cringed, afraid her skin must feel rough. Rozario resembled a bronzed Anglo-Teuton of the Mountbatten variety. He had dark brown curly hair, cut and vaselined in the dated 'forties' style, bringing out the shapely bone structure of his head and showing off his muscular neck. A quick intuitive equation in Maudie's head killed her inhibitions and she threw herself into his arms, sobbing. Rozario, unsurprised, contented himself with stroking her honey blonde hair, the same as had been passed on to the tragic Eric.

'There, there. What's this, eh? Don't go crying like that, my girl.' He kissed the top of her head.

Rozario's silky soft voice and his 'my girl', an echo of Anthony, sent shudders through Maudie and she could feel the goose bumps again.

'It's so nice to see you Robby …' She smiled sadly as Rozario sat her down on a sofa and disappointingly distanced himself.

The party set the trend for Maudie's frustrated widowhood. Instilled with a Christian conscience, she felt guilty at experiencing that fleeting desire for another man so soon after Anthony's death. That evening, sitting at the piano, playing and singing the old familiar songs, *Irene Goodnight*, *My Bonny Lies over the Ocean*, and weakened by an extra glass of gin, she couldn't stop the nostalgic tears. Guilty hope awoke again when Robby came to her side, his pale-blue eyes sympathetic, and put his arm around her. '*Goodnight Irene, Goodnight Irene, I'll see you in my dreams* …,' he sang with Maudie, his pleasant baritone intimately mingling with her tremolo. And in that atmosphere of mild inebriation, the other singers jostled to hug Maudie, pat her back, and kiss her, including Rozario. 'He's waiting till a decent time passes,' thought Maudie, instantly quenching the thought as her conscience flared.

At another party not long after, Maudie was seduced while Proshanto Mojumdar did an exhibition cha-cha-cha for the guests. She was drunk and almost unconscious, and it was child's play for a notorious lecher, not Rozario, to inveigle her into her own bedroom. But the lecher was never to reappear, and this was the last time she would succumb. As for Rozario, he was a regular visitor at the Normans' but chillingly platonic. Occasionally, after decent gaps, Doreen and David Norman would raise the topic of Maudie remarrying.

'Come on now,' she would say, sadly shaking her head. 'Who'd want to marry old me?'

The morning after the seduction, she woke up with a hangover, and disturbing memories of the night. Was it a dream or reality? The dream she had woken from seeped back into her memory, but it was surprisingly devoid of carnality. Instead, it carried tantalizing glimpses from her wedding. A girlfriend living in a jute mill had been found dead on the riverbank, half-devoured by crocodiles. Maudie was among those who discovered the body as she walked in bridal attire towards the church. The dream recaptured in startling detail the elaborate decorations in the church, baskets of white chrysanthemum and maidenhair fern embellished with clusters of silver bells and horseshoes hung at the entrance to every pew, while more ferns and flowers decorated the walls. The bridesmaids, in pale orange dresses and hats, giggled and scattered rose petals as they followed the bride. Maudie herself wore a gown of soft white satin charmeuse with a trim of orange blossom and lover's knots and carried a bouquet of white orchids. Her hair, looped cunningly about her ears, was veiled with fine silk lace with the same trim. Her mother was particularly admirable, in emerald green satin with golden embroidery. But they were walking by the side of the river, and she had a train, dropped by the careless bridesmaids, which collected more and more mud and rose petals as it dragged behind her. When it became so heavy she could barely walk, the party came on Maudie's friend, lying at the water's edge. Without remark, they surrounded the mangled corpse and tried to pull it up. But the clay on the riverbank was slick, and while trying to save themselves from sliding into the water, they let go of the corpse, which slid away among bouquets and petals. Maudie woke up with a feeling of stickiness and dirt and doom, with the pall of the crocodile's menace hanging over her. She threw off her clothes and went into the bathroom for an endless purifying shower followed by a long soak in the tub. She wondered if she had actually been seduced, but was too scared to look closely for the signs. The ghosts who had turned away in shame could have enlightened her.

Her waking world was no better. She fantasized about Robby taking her in an irresistible impulse. Then one day she found his chin too large, his arms too thin and hairy. She imagined his legs to be as spindly as those disappointing arms, and then she imagined them densely covered with loathesome hair … But when he smiled she couldn't help responding, finding his smile warm and 'man-sweet', a word which came unannounced into her head.

'Tell me, Robby,' she pleaded in her fantasizing, 'why can't you tell me? Tell me it's me you want. Is there something stopping you?'

But it was she herself who was stopping men with her inner critical eye, her timidity and her fear of turning them off with her goose-pimpled rough ageing skin. And re-positioning herself to view Rozario from another angle, highlighting what she saw as his deformed jaw formation, she shored up her changed opinion. 'How could I ever have found him handsome?' she would reprimand herself yet flush with pleasure when she caught his eye and his 'man-sweet' smile. There was no redress for her timidity. Not only was she ageing, but her seduction, surely meriting at least raised eyebrows, was never discovered. Apart from the guilt, the reason for Maudie's reluctance to face the event was her ideal of a perfect marriage paired with sex. That night was too sordid to merit acknowledgement.

❧

Amit Dhar, a school friend Eric's and now a lawyer, kept steadfastly in touch with Maudie, and anticipating his company was her greatest pleasure. The Normans had never approved of Maudie's young friend, and were unimpressed by his mellifluous attentions. But what could they say? Maudie was safe, as long as she was with them. Over the years, their discomfort at Amit's presence increased. They squirmed when he was seen, one day, going into Maudie's room.

'Look at that,' whispered Doreen. 'What's he going in there for?'

'I don't know,' said David crossly, though equally surprised. 'She looks on him as her son. It's all right Dore. Stop worrying.'

After a while, Doreen walked boldly into Maudie's room to find Amit in the dressing room fidgeting with the objects on the dressing table.

'Hello!' she pretended surprise. 'What are you doing here, in the dressing room? And where's Maudie?'

'Hello Doreen-mashi,' said Amit coolly. 'Just dropped in to see Ma … She's getting ready.'

'"Ma"?' Doreen couldn't help exclaiming. 'You call her "Ma"?'

'So I do!' said Amit turning to face her with a charming smile. 'I must have slipped into it. Poor dear. I do regard her as such, you know, Doreen-mashi. She is Eric's mother after all. You don't mind, do you?'

'No, no, why should I? Why don't you let her get ready? Come on out and have a drink.'

'She asked me to wait for her here. I'm taking her to New Market. Thanks anyway.' Amit strolled out into the bedroom and picked up a magazine.

What was it, Doreen wondered, that had interested Amit so greatly? Cussedly, she walked over to the large Burma teak dressing table backed by Belgian bevelled and triple-panelled mirrors. Was it Maudie's splendid fitted hidecase, carefully preserved by her since her wedding? The open case graced the dressing table, carelessly spilling jewellery. Along the inner sides, lined with faded moiré silk, were silver-topped crystal bottles holding eau de cologne, unguents and toiletries, even tooth powder, and a silver push-up container for the rare solid English cologne, all held in place with silk-covered loops. The other objects on the dressing table were equally stylish. A silver powder box lying open with a puff billowing out of it, an ebony and silver hair brush, and enamelled crystal bottles. Doreen always appreciated Maudie's things. She had brought her own furniture for her room, and given the rest of her household's contents to the Normans. Doreen noted that Maudie's cocktail cabinet was, as usual, well-supplied. 'Just like a sitting room!' said Doreen brightly to Amit. 'All she needs is a canary and a piano!'

Amit looked up with a bored air and grunted, then turned rudely back to his magazine. Doreen left, glancing back worriedly at the dressing table covered with valuables. Amit didn't miss the glance. Smiling and humming, he went into the dressing room again and stood in front of the mirror, picked up Maudie's hairbrush and applied it to his already smoothly brushed and oiled hair, then walked casually to the cocktail cabinet and helped himself to a scotch.

When the tragic falling-out took place, Doreen was able to observe, 'It's that Amit Dhar. He's been at it for years and it's paying off at last!'

'Poor Maudie!' said David. 'Poor dear!'

Amit had turned Maudie against her protectors. She had caught him in her room one day with his ear pressed to the Normans' bedroom door and it was easy for him to turn his defence into mischief.

'They're up to something, I'm sure of it. Can't you sense it? Really Ma! You are too trusting!'

Maudie paused briefly to wonder what they could be 'up to' with their consistent kindness and concern, but a niggling doubt settled into her. 'What could they be up to, Amit?' she asked. 'What do you mean?'

The house and ghosts were urging her. 'Don't you believe a word he says! Scoundrel!'

'Oh really Ma!' Amit exclaimed again. He poured a gin for Maudie to distract her, pleased at stumbling on this stratagem.

Maudie began her practice of putting a wine glass to the Normans' bedroom door, imitating a film in her memory. And of course, when the Normans talked of leaving India for Canada, a debate lasting many years, Amit would look meaningfully at Maudie, and her attempts at overhearing their bedroom talk would become more vigorous. The debate finally ended years and years later, when David Norman retired and decided to join his children, who had overtaken him to Canada. The by now middle-aged Amit was able to say smugly, 'I told you so, Ma, didn't I?'

But Amit Dhar would disappear over long periods, his activities frustratingly mysterious to Maudie who had come to depend heavily on his company and his useful role as alcohol-procurer. If she bought alcohol for herself there were awkward encounters with David or Doreen, who would say, 'But I say Maudie, what's the need? Plenty of it here already!' This was no help with the different levels of refined hypocrisy which would then be activated. Maudie had to find alternatives, and the simplest was to use the services of the Rajmahal chowkidar. When Vir Singh Rawat was appointed to this post, he took on the chore readily, the tips and ways in which he could diddle the absent-minded memsahib giving him ample incentive. This was the second dubiously beautiful friendship which sprang up in Maudie Jessop's life.

The ghosts knew both friendships spelled trouble for their Maudie. And the house was afraid its premonitions would prove right.

'It would be something if she at least stopped drinking!' said dowager ghost.

'What do you expect …?' began the Swadeshi ghost, launching into its usual diatribe against Christians. But the house preempted any further discussion by dispersing the ghosts to distant corners of the premises.

⁂

Maudie was a Roman Catholic and went to mass every Sunday with the Normans. She looked forward to the cheerful congregation, including the nuns, her old teachers. But as the pattern changed from a predominance of dresses to saris and the Irish nuns gave way to Indians, mostly strangers, the cheeriness faded. The day came when Maudie broke out of her habit. She had entered the church, dipped her fingers in holy water, knelt in the aisle and made the sign of the cross. A wizened old man, whose embraces she had so far borne with stoicism, approached her with open arms. But that day, she shied away and hurried to her pew, leaving the old man scratching his head. The next Sunday she missed mass for the first time. Instead, she found herself growing curious about her environment, drawn towards the antithesis of her orthodox Roman Catholic conditioning, the idolatrous, pagan Hinduism and other 'native' religions.

Durga Puja was on at the time. Throughout her life spent entirely in Bengal, this important Hindu festival had passed her by without arousing her curiosity. She had registered the presence of the ten-armed Goddess, but though she was ignorant of the details, something of the mesmerizing sacredness of the occasion, the drumming with its frenzied climax when the processions of lorries converged on the river, the steely but smiling Goddess images with all their finery being tilted into the water, must have entered her consciousness. When Mohini Mojumdar, her Rajmahal neighbour, invited Maudie to the family Durga Puja, she promptly accepted.

'Ooh, I'd love to go! But I'm not a Hindu, you know, they won't chop off my head will they?'

'Of course they will,' said Mohini bitingly. 'Unclean, casteless Christian!'

Mohini had been Maudie's senior at school, and they both regressed to the girlish chatter which typified them as convent girls even at this mature age.

'I was just joking!' protested Maudie. 'But I haven't been to a puja, really!'

'You'll go to hell my dear. Better not take the risk.'

'Come on!' said Maudie, ready to defend her religion, heaven and hell against the usual mockery of her Hindu friends. 'What about y'all and your human sacrifices?'

'Ignorant woman!'

Maudie went to the puja dressed for the first time in her life in a sari, which thrilled the Bengali ghosts. She found herself riveted to the magic of the drummers' skill, their leaping, their muscular bare torsos and tightly tied dhuties, and the movement and rhythm they created out of the huge drums slung carelessly about their necks. The ringing in her ears intoxicated her.

'Look at Maudie,' whispered Mohini to her husband. 'She's never seen anything like it. And she's lived here all her life!'

'She must have Bengali blood in her,' Proshanto Mojumdar whispered back. 'Her ancestors are calling to her.'

Through the drumming Maudie was aware of the hypnotic quality of the central tableau, of Goddess Durga, her sons Kartik and Ganesh, her fellow goddesses, Sarasvati and Lakshmi, her rampaging lion-steed, her spear pinioning the dark demon, and the lolling head of the buffalo trampled under it all. In spite of the elaborate iconography of violence and gore, the Goddess and her cohorts were so celestially composed with their unfocused gazes and distant smiles that they seemed to Maudie to create a centre of utter grace and peace. She could have sat there forever, taking in the details, the colours, the frazzled hair of the demon, his blue chest bubbling with blood, the Goddess' raised leg in its powerful hold on her steed, the brocaded vestments. While Durga's acolytes performed mysterious rites, ringing bells, chanting, chipping little cymbals and tirelessly offering up their devotions. It was only when some devotees began an awkward jig in front of the Goddess, swinging incense censers, that she snapped out of the spell.

When Maudie was going through her dilemma about a renewed sex life, which to her meant a second marriage, the pulls and counter-pulls of her attraction to Robby Rozario were no different from her girlish crushes. She had accepted Anthony's proposal, because it had coincided with her current crush on him, and she anticipated a fairy tale ending. She had hardly changed, except that the sexual fantasies were more adult, experienced and explicit.

It occurred to her that 'hope' was a silly word. Looked at objectively, it had always been silly and should be banned from the dictionary. She became critical of some of the superstitions she had taken on from her mother and deliberately cut her nails at night. 'You'll never get married,' her mother had declared, 'if you cut your nails at night.' 'Who wants to get married again?' sighed Maudie, clipping away with uneasy defiance.

This signalled the banishment of Rozario from her hopes. Although no one else would fit her romantic ideal, it wasn't difficult to downgrade him. 'He's just an ordinary accountant! How can I compare him to Anthony and the police service!' And then, there was the matter of Rozario's physical drawbacks, his lantern jaw and skinny arms. 'Like Popeye the sailor without biceps!' Sometimes Maudie could indulge in mockery. But she couldn't fathom the depth and tenacity of 'hope', its rootedness in the mind without words. She thought she could be objective, understanding all, accepting all, making her own harmonious place in it all. But she couldn't stop 'hope' cropping up, like prickly heat, on the patina of her thoughts. The result, instead of exhilaration was a feeling of melancholy, signalling nothing but frustration. Was it because hope had 'gone'?

And what of sex? Could she, should she, have sex without love? Would Robby be interested? Poor confused Maudie, with all her introspections, losses and exploitations by those she longed to trust. Surjeet Shona felt her mind had finally snapped. But still, why the terrible end? Was it the tenacious 'hope' again, in the form of its deadly opposite 'despair'?

Maudie had inherited secure British stocks from her parents and had no financial problems as a widow. Even so, her brother refused payment when she entered his household. The Rajmahal sternly disapproved of her ingratitude when she put her ear to the Normans' bedroom door. At the mischievous Amit Dhar's prodding, her paranoia increased, and when David and Doreen finally decided to move to Canada, she categorically refused to let go of the flat. With lawyer Amit's connivance, she served notice that the flat was her home and she was staying on. The Rajmahal was flattered but it couldn't stop its feelings of disquiet. It felt Maudie could become uncontrollable without her brother and his wife. David Norman couldn't believe his docile sister could suddenly expose such a vicious side, in spite of their unstinting offer of a home with them in Canada!

'Where did we go wrong?'

'And after all these years. We took nothing from her, Dave!' Doreen wailed, deeply hurt.

They could scarcely afford the luxury of giving up the flat to Maudie, with the Malliks paying them the customary princely salaami for vacating, an essential ingredient of their emigration budget. All three parties, the Normans, the Malliks and Maudie, employed lawyers to represent their interests. Maudie of course had Amit to represent her. In the end, the situation was salvaged by compromise. One set, of bedroom, dressing room and bathroom, would be modified and retained by Maudie. The modifications would be paid for by David Norman and the rent by Maudie. As with most compromises, no one was satisfied. The Malliks didn't like the split flat and were nervous of a solitary and unpredictable Maudie. Maudie was sore she had been palmed off with a single room with ugly partitions in place of a fine palatial flat. And the Normans had lost a big chunk from their salaami.

'It's okay, Ma,' said Amit Dhar. 'At least you've got rid of them, and gained a nice little flat. Easier to look after, this size …'

'Yes, but …'

'And are you forgetting you have me?'

'Dear child! What would I do without you?'

Finally, after the labyrinth had been negotiated, observed fascinatedly by the ghosts and tentatively by the Rajmahal, new tenants moved into the major portion of the flat.

'No more ready-made rosy cocade, eh?' David said unhappily to Doreen. 'You'll have to make it yourself now, Dore.' While inside he thought, 'I wish she'd come away with us. She's doomed. My sister's doomed.'

Maudie's room was hurriedly partitioned by a seven-foot high wooden divider, which ruined the room, creating two disproportionately narrow areas. The dining and sitting areas were squeezed along one length, and the bedroom along the other. Although David insisted on leaving Maudie the grand piano, she soon lost interest in it, and all it did was shrink the space.

The room, not Maudie's original, had the worst location in the flat. There was no verandah overlooking Chowringhee, and no attraction in the wall-eyed windows set too close to the next door mansion and looking down on a servants' passageway. The kitchenette, unaesthetically jutting into the sitting room, was partitioned by another seven-foot wooden partition, allowing the free permeation of cooking sounds and emissions. The only luxury was a noble bathroom with an adjoining dressing room.

'I suppose the kitchen should have been sealed off to ceiling level,' admitted Amit. 'And there's no servant's entrance, they'll have to come through the sitting room.'

The Rajmahal and the ghosts tearfully bid the Normans farewell and braced themselves for an un-supervised and increasingly drunken Maudie. In Canada, the Normans occasionally heard news of Maudie, but she would always refuse to answer their letters. And she would put down the phone when they called.

But the paint was fresh and Maudie felt curiously sprightly at being on her own for the first time in her life. 'Just think, I'm all on my own at last!' she squealed. 'Wait and see what I won't get up to!'

'No mischief now, Ma,' cautioned Amit in the twee tone he adopted with her. 'I may not be able to rescue you this time!'

Maudie's sprightliness continued as she savoured her complete independence. She organized mahjong mornings, visited the club and toyed with the idea of keeping a dog and a canary, following Doreen's long-ago remark. But she was sixty-five, and the noisy and warm family of David Norman had disappeared, leaving an eerie silence in a claustrophobic space. There was no one to spy on and suspect, no one to laugh and joke with, and no one to share meals with. She managed to hold two mahjong sessions, after which there was an evaporation of socializing, along with the sprightliness. The dog was forgotten, and though the canary was acquired and hung in a fancy brass cage at the sitting room window, it soon came to grief. During Maudie's sprightly period it sang enchantingly, fluffing out its feathers and preening healthily, inspiring the aspidistra on the sill below to throw out one gorgeous bloom. But the creeping depression in the air, the house's non-cooperation, the dim light in the passage by the window with its stingy glimpses of the sky above affected both bird and flower. The canary grew silent, uttering only little cries when Maudie forgot to put out its seeds and water, the aspidistra withered. The canary's colour faded from the brilliant yellow it had been dyed in by the bird shop man at New Market to an unexciting pale lemon bordering on white. Maudie wondered if it was a canary at all, forgetting its earlier days of brilliant song. She woke up one morning to a half-dead aspidistra, and a canary cold and hard, feet up at the bottom of the cage.

Maudie's spirits plunged. Unused to independent social moves, she made no effort to befriend her new neighbours, the Gulianis, though out of habit she found herself listening at the entrance door for sounds of their comings and goings. When she put a wine glass to the flimsy plaster blocking the door between their rooms, she could make out voices. But the language wasn't English, it wasn't even Hindi or Bengali, and she could make no sense of it. The reason was simple, the Gulianis were Sindhi. Earlier, her social life had revolved around the Normans' circle, and the friends of her married days had disappeared. Now she was friendless. Where, before, she had been classy, a cheapness crept in. She frittered away the lugubrious time with beauty sessions and stood for hours before her dressing table mirror. She made herself up, tried on dated too-loose clothes, dyed and re-dyed her hair, patchily, killing its glow. And she chatted away to herself with her lips hardly moving, a dying trickle of a chatter. 'We'll try again tomorrow, my girl, oh yes, where's my drink, drinky, drinkies, why the hell waste time with this, no, no, tomorrow, yes, yes, tomorrow …' She was preoccupied with her darkening skin, the come uppance of her Indian blood. It was an incipient threat nursed from birth, which she combatted with 'snow', bleaching sessions and whitening make-up. 'Oh God! What the hell's wrong with my skin? What Mum told me to be so careful of, so I'm trying, no? Try my girl, try ...' But these attempts were intermittent, with long gaps caused by imagined ailments, when she would telephone her doctor and convince him she needed attention. His visits would be followed by a welter of pills, powders and potion, mostly harmless placebos. The Rajmahal watched, grim and sorrowful, and the other tenants, never too close to Maudie, kept their distance. Mrs Guliani was diffident in social matters, and felt no urge to access the friendship of the weird, over-painted pussycat of a firangi who scarcely greeted her. Mr Guliani was involved in a prurient quest for sex in the exciting city and hardly noticed Maudie. His quota of concern was expended on a genuinely invalid mother, whom he and his wife looked after with a respectful care, which filled Maudie with envy. She convinced herself her brother had shamefully deserted her, she was sure the Gulianis disliked her for occupying a part of their flat, and she knew Junior Mallik found her aberration of a one-roomer an insult to the beautiful structure over which he reigned. Maudie's paranoia mounted with pink gin after pink gin every evening, advancing gradually to the afternoon, then the morning, the whole day, breakfast, lunch, tea ... All her waking hours were passed in the bitter-spicy miasma of gin-angostura, her vision concentrated into that poisonously icy pink tumblerful, sip, slurp, swallow, pour, sip ... Her soliloquy trickle crescendoed from a discreet murmur to a loud gush, her health plummetted, intensified by the febrifuge qualities of the angostura. Her servant's slackness, his insolence and his persistent demands for loans, apart from his watering her gin bottle, caused her unending strain. Extracting work from him was hard. She developed a phobia against the smoke and curry smells of Indian cuisine, and restricted herself first to European meals, then to cold cuts and salads. Her family, prosperous general provision merchants, had supplied Calcutta's fastidious clientele with the finest selections of York cut hams, bacon in canvas, farm made cheese loaf cheddar and English brewed pilsner beer ... It took her time to realize those quality meats were no longer available. Such produce was made these days under dubious conditions, and her servant cheated her by using the cheapest outlets while charging her high-class rates. The family had in any case always been lovers of spicy food, indulging rarely in the merchandise they supplied to the Europeans. Maudie's spice-loving genes and the poor quality of the cold meats led to the near death of her appetite. But when she had fits, writhing on the ground and foaming at the mouth, she didn't realize her brain had been infiltrated by the worm hosted by badly cured pork. She would pick herself off the floor after these fits, murmuring to herself, 'Like dear Anthony used to say, "one too many, my girl",' little able to diagnose the true cause. And as she weakened with worm-ridden head, alcohol and poor nourishment, she exhorted herself bravely, 'As long as you don't get the D.T.s, my girl, there's no such thing as one too many, that's what dear Anthony always said.' She avoided confessing to her doctor, afraid she might be well on the road to the dreaded *delirium tremens*.

While Amit was a regular visitor, Maudie welcomed him as her son's replacement, the solace for his loss. For Amit, the visits were an escape from his wife's prohibitions, simple cocktail stops. The frequency of these visits increased as Maudie's vulnerability began to excite him. 'She's asking to be exploited,' he thought. 'It gives her a reason to exist!'

Maudie, who had so easily succumbed to suggested suspicions of her brother and his family, had a separate compartment for Amit Dhar. He was especially *hers*, *her* visitor, *her* friend. She let him take charge of her affairs and was easily persuaded to give him power of attorney over her finances even before the Normans left. 'But don't tell them,' Amit exhorted, adding to the haunting insecurity in Maudie. 'You never know what they'll get up to …' 'You never know,' he repeated to himself. 'Might come in handy one day.'

That day came soon after the Normans' departure. Amit found himself in difficulties, forced to resort to speculation with the funds most readily available, Maudie's funds. To do him justice, he had every intention of replacing the investment in full. After pocketing the profit. And without divulging the deviation. He was confident his brilliant manoeuvres would end with him rich, and then richer still as her heir. But Amit was no financial wizard. Gambling called irresistibly, he was soon trapped by the stock market, and one day, he and his family were gone, leaving not a trace. And not a rupee.

When Amit's phone number elicited electronic howls, Maudie knew her luck was about to run all out. This didn't stop her from addressing him endlessly in her soliloquies. 'Come in, dear boy, come in. Have a drink. As my Anthony always said ...' Her drinking increased dramatically.

Junior Mallik came down to see her two months into her rental defaulting. He could smell the gin, see the flat, suffer that one corner of the Rajmahal, however small, had been reduced to such a state.

'My, what a surprise!' said Maudie. She put a claw-like hand on his shoulder and drew him in. 'Come in dear. Come in.' Behind the alcoholic haze Maudie knew Junior had come about the rent. Her welcome, therefore, was masochistic. It was a vast pleasure, in any case, to have a visitor, any visitor. She moved old magazines and papers off a chair, dusted and smoothed the seat with bare hands, and invited Junior to sit down. Junior averted his eyes from her body, clothed in a translucent flowered dress which showed the outline of her nipples sloping over cascading breasts. There was a vestigial elegance in the uneven hemline which gave an impression of style, more because of her extreme skinniness than anything else. But her hair, cut in a ragged bob, her slipped face and eyes askew at the corners, the scarlet lipstick overflowing into the ribbing around her lips, denied this impression. Junior cleared his throat and sat down. He looked around him at the dust coagulated on surfaces, at a group of family portraits dominated by Maudie's handsome husband astride a horse.

'Would you like a drink?' Maudie asked in a slurred voice. It was past seven, the sun had set, and all right thinking people's thoughts veered in one direction, as dear Anthony always said. Junior declined stiffly while Maudie took habitually sure steps to her cocktail cabinet. The mirrors at the back reflected a number of empty decanters and a half bottle with a greenish liquid. She poured a generous amount into a glass cloudy with fingerprints and edged with a frill of red lip marks, poured in water, and shook the little black angostura bottle at it. The angostura curled in magenta whorls then spread into that delicious pale pink bitterness.

Junior looked away, 'Where's your servant, Maudie?'

'Don't know. Gone off somewhere. Haven't seen him for days. Three. Four days. Poor Charles.'

'Charles?'

'Canary. Charles was my canary. Left the day he died, the servant, Boy did. So yellow it used to be. "Nice yellow canary, Memsa'ab!" That's what the bird man said. "Sings like an angel," he said. Bright yellow it was at first. Though Boy, my servant you know, Boy said it was nothing but a cheap little munia, you know, one of those cheap little …,' Maudie trailed off nodding at her drink.

Junior shuddered. A canary! She had kept a canary in here. As if the pigeons weren't enough … He had always been against the incursion into the Rajmahal by the animal species. Proshanto Mojumdar had kept dogs, two of them, one after the other. Somehow this floor was accursed. He had been overjoyed when the last of the dogs had died. In the meantime, here he was, seeing death everywhere. The thought arose in Junior, spreading a macabre pleasure. 'And here I am wishing for more of it. For dogs and canaries! Old ladies too, why not?' Junior snickered and hurriedly sobered himself.

'Er. So he's on leave?' he asked.

'Who?' said Maudie tearfully. 'Who's on leave?'

'Your servant,' said Junior. 'How do you eat? Who cooks for you, Maudie?' he said in a louder voice. 'Are you, I mean, what are you eating nowadays, I don't see any signs of your servant. How do you …,' he stopped with a sick feeling. The stench had suddenly been identified, as of a dead mouse, dead and rotting. He looked reluctantly at the birdcage, swinging lightly at the window in a newly sprung-up breeze. Something black and crumbling lay at the bottom. Junior got up and saw the dead canary. 'I'll take this,' he said, controlling his nausea.

A rising hysteria gripped the house. With its own multifarious problems from its multifaceted tenants affecting it and its ghosts, time was taking its toll. It controlled a tremor starting down in its very foundation by a supreme effort of the will.

'Er, I'll be back,' said Junior. Tightly holding a shuddering breath, he plucked the cage off its hook and walked out. Releasing his breath he called to the guard down in the lobby, 'Ei! Come here! At once!'

The guard came rushing up the stairs two at a time, puffing, face to face with his grim master.

'Take this!' commanded Junior. 'Take this, clean it! Bring it back at once!'

Unburdened, he walked back into Maudie's room, dreading the remnants of poor Charles' stench. But it had been wafted away by the merciful breeze.

'Maudie?' he said. She didn't answer, and Junior grew aware of a continuous drone. Maudie was talking to herself, launched on her river, gazing moodily out of the grey oblong, its outline broken by the crazily wilted aspidistra.

A brainwave stopped Junior from expressing the harsh ultimatums said to issue from landlords in such situations. The old people's home run by the British Trust, that was it! As he quietly left, Maudie was sobbing to herself, the tears streaming down her cheeks and the gin down her chin. The house heaved a sigh of relief when Junior tiptoed out of the door, though it knew worse would surely follow. Junior stood a while on the balcony outside Maudie's room. He looked down into the lobby and, averting his gaze from the naked marble ladies, soothed himself with the sight of that harmonious space. The guard re-appeared with the cleaned cage. 'Take it inside!' he commanded. 'Hang it near the window!' He frowned as a pigeon drew his eyes to the head of one of the marble ladies, un-surprised but unhappy when it squirted her nose. Upstairs he broached the subject of Maudie's eviction to his father, carefully, because Ali Mallik was softly inclined towards his tenants and sensitive to his son's treatment of them.

Proshanto Mojumdar was Maudie's next caller on this unusually busy day. Sighting Junior leaving Maudie's flat, he was inspired to activate his lift campaign.

'May I come in?' He walked in.

Maudie was sprawled in her chair, pulling at her drink and talking, talking obsessively and sobbing. Proshanto confusedly assumed he had stumbled on to something extraordinary, an emergency, a catastrophe.

''ullo! And oo're you?' said Maudie, focusing with difficulty.

Proshanto was astonished. 'Maudie!' he exclaimed. 'What's the matter with you? Are you all right? Why are you weeping?'

Maudie wiped her face with a browned lace handkerchief, and sat up straight. 'Wha'shyourname?' she said plaintively. 'Jush, jush walkin' in'ere no name nothing!'

Proshanto spoke in a gentle, polite voice. 'I am Proshanto Mojumdar, Pro. Your neighbour, your old friend. Don't you remember us, Mini and Pro? Look!' He went to the door and pointed across to his verandah. Maudie got up, tottered, supported herself against the wall and came up behind him.

'Imagine!' she said. 'Sho you're the chap 'oo liv'zh there. Pro! 'Coursh! And wha'sh'ername, Minnie! Owdyoo shpeck' me to 'cegnizhe you? Looking all old and shcraggy! Never *ever* cumtosheeme! Werzh your dog? Love dogzh. Wanted a dog too. David shed nonono. Charles inshtead. Died, Charles did. Jush like that.'

'Quite,' said Proshanto, trying his best to be polite in spite of Maudie's rude remarks. 'Charles' he assumed was a dog he had somehow never seen.

'Canary,' clarified Maudie. 'Forgot 'is feed you shee.' Maudie looked at him dolefully out of her watery, bloodshot eyes.

'So sorry to hear that,' said the polite Proshanto Mojumdar. 'Well, I think I shall be leaving. I shall come and see you again though.' The shock of Maudie's condition had dislodged his memory and he had forgotten why he was here in the first place. And then he remembered in a brilliant flash. 'It is about the lift!' he cried triumphantly. 'Did I not tell you about the lift? I think we ought to have a lift here, Maudie.' His voice swelled. 'Do you not find it difficult to toil up the steps on your own legs?'

Maudie clapped. 'O what fun! A lif'! 'Ow nyshe, 'ow nyshe! Drink 'ave a drink! Le'sh talk 'bout it!'

Proshanto Mojumdar walked in purposefully, though he felt distressed when he caught the alcoholic whiffs. He couldn't remember how often he and Mohini had discussed Maudie, but something nagged him. He sat on the chair vacated by Junior Mallik and politely declined Maudie's offer of a drink.

'That boy, Junior Mallik ...,' he said. He paused, forcing his thoughts into order. 'Did he mention our endeavours regarding the lift?'

'Sh'rude,' said Maudie. 'Came 'bout d'rent. Jush imagine!' She sniffed. 'Shtill. I'm diff'rent. Well brought up, good, hiccup, mannerzh you shee. Offered 'im a drink. 'Nonono, 'e shed. You know,' she lowered her voice to a whisper. 'Ee'zh a M'ommedan, and M'ommedans you shee, M'ommedans don' drink!' She nodded significantly.

'Well,' said Proshanto Mojumdar. 'I may not be a Mohammedan, but I too have stopped drinking. At this age it is not good for one. My doctor has forbidden it!'

No response. Maudie had lapsed again into a catatonic silence. Proshanto soldiered on. 'And this is a building with four stories! Of course, you are a young lady compared to us old fogies! Perhaps you find toiling up the steps easy! Ha, ha, ha. I know a modern lift may not look nice in our lobby, but, unfortunately, it is most necessary. Ali Mallik is on our side, but it is that boy, Junior! He will not cooperate. What do you say, Maudie?'

Maudie's response was to fling her glass down, spilling her gin on to an already stained carpet. And as Proshanto gaped, she fell untidily and folded up on the floor. Her eyes rolled up under her eyelids, her limbs twitched, and a froth appeared at her working jaws.

'By Jove!' was all the poor octogenarian could say as he backed away towards the door.

His trembling legs carried him outside and, after some commotion, Maudie was taken to hospital.

Delighted his plan had thus involuntarily been put into action, Junior took on the responsibility of overseeing her treatment. His concern aroused the admiration of other Rajmahalians and he wasted no time getting in touch with the Society for the Aged. While Maudie was in hospital, the patron and Junior visited her and persuaded her to look over the Senior Citizens' Retreat. She was told about its big verandahs, the freedom to come and go, to eat either the food provided or one's own in the kitchen attached to each room.

When Surjeet Shona heard she got into a tussle with Junior.

'Come on Junior! Have a heart! Let her come back!'

'Mind your own business, Miss Busybody,' said Junior. 'It's the best place for her anyway. At least she'll get a couple of square meals a day ...'

'I can send her food Junior, it won't be a problem ... It's cruel to push her out ...'

But Junior was Junior.

Maudie recovered after prolonged treatment and moved into the retreat. She had no lawyer this time around, but Junior found it expedient to be fair. He paid her hospital bill, and granted her the expected salaami for her flat. This he invested for her, using the income to meet her expenses. The exit of Maudie was thus smoothened, and it was a welcome change to find Rajmahalians impressed by Junior's philanthropy. Maudie, sober and docile, with no other choice, accepted. She had been depleted of everything. Of her money by the rascally Amit Dhar, and, as was discovered, of her valuables by the absconding servant, Boy.

The flimsy plaster in the wall of the flatlet was broken down, the wooden partitions removed, with all traces of the kitchen, the room cleaned, repaired, repainted, repolished, and returned to its original state as an intrinsic part of the larger flat, for which the Gulianis agreed to an increase in rent. The Rajmahal was back to the way Junior wanted it.

While everyone was almost happily resettled, the Rajmahal had different feelings. For one, the Gulianis had long been causing it tremors by their strange ways, and the havoc caused by Maudie had shaken it to its innards. It could feel its strength being drained, a structural weakening every time it thought about Maudie. So its tendency was to forget about her, just as the other tenants did.

No one could put their finger on the moment of Maudie's return. Perhaps it was the lobby guard who first spotted her, wraith-like, drifting in and out of the sunbeams as she floated up the stairs and who ran up to stop her. He stammeringly addressed the collapsed, dead white face of Maudie Memsahib, salaaming her respectfully by habit, and then asking her where she thought she was going.

'I live here,' replied Maudie in her genteel fashion, 'and I am here on my own business. Please be so kind as to make way.'

She spoke in English, and the lobby guard was left scratching his head. Till he woke up and taking the stairs two at a time overtook her and rushed up to his master. Maudie stopped at the first floor and rang the Guliani doorbell. Her pancake make-up glowed in the gloom, 'just like a ghost', shuddered the guard who was peering down from above. The door was opened, according to him, by a servant who behaved in a disoriented manner at the sight of the apparition. Maudie disappeared into the flat, but not before Junior caught a glimpse of her. 'Maudie!' he whispered. He stood at the top of the stairs disbelievingly and before his astonished eyes Maudie re-emerged on to the landing. Guliani's mother was with her, smiling in spite of her bent spine, holding her maid's hand to keep from toppling over. Gravely, Maudie nodded to the old lady, turned, and climbed the stairs, watched by the guard and Junior.

Maudie strained and panted her way up to them, her shoes resounding loudly as she stepped from marble to wood. She entered the Mallik flat and sat down breathing hard. After a period of vacancy she said in her old sweet voice, 'I have taken up residence downstairs. I wonder if you noticed.' It turned out Maudie had 'taken up residence', not inside the Rajmahal, nor with the Gulianis, as Junior for a sick moment thought, but in the Rajmahal chowkidar's godown on a corner of the drive. The chowkidar, Rawat, had fortuitously shifted to new quarters a few days earlier. He had welcomed his old friend Maudie as occupier of the godown. The problem was the lack of a toilet. The servants' toilet, earlier used by Rawat and his family, was some distance from the room, and certainly unsuitable for a memsahib. So Maudie simply went up to her old room, taken over by the Gulianis, for the facilities.

The chowkidar, Rawat, faced Junior with equanimity.

'I naturally assumed it was with the sanction of your good self alone.' He defended himself unctuously to the foaming Junior.

'A likely story! Couldn't you at least check with me?'

'Who am I to question a one-time honourable tenant ...' He politely waited for Junior to calm himself before continuing. 'And it would in any case show a lack of charity and militate against the spirit of Pir Tasleem Ahmed and his sacred tomb ...' He referred to the tomb of a Muslim saint which lay just behind the godown.

Junior controlled himself, reserving judgement on Rawat's windy excuses. He knew the wily chowkidar was less than innocent. The Gulianis reacted with incredulity and anger when they heard their flat had been invaded by Maudie behind their backs, and Junior had a tangled situation on his hands.

If Junior had access to the Rajmahal's ghosts, he would have known they had mixed feelings about the Gulianis, for a time so much approved by him.

'Who are these Sindhis?' they objected.

'Shopkeepers! How did such people get in here?'

And other ghosts replied, 'It's that Junior! He is so befuddled by show!'

Great arguments followed as some of the ghosts defended Sindhis, who had such a long association with the city, providing not only wonderful shops full of rich merchandise in the New Market, but the best book shops in central Calcutta.

'After all, if they can give the city books they can't be all that bad!' they said.

'But those are the Calcutta Sindhis!' shouted the Swadeshi ghost. 'These are upstarts! I wish the Normans would come back, even if they are Christians! Look at the Gulianis' flat!'

'Oh I love it!' breathed another elderly ghost. 'It's so gay. Do you remember our village fair? Once there was a fat lady with yellow hair. From America. And she was dressed just like the plaster-of-paris-lady-with-the-lamp at the Gulianis. We had to pay two pice to see her. Inside a hut.'

'What about Mrs Guliani? Have you seen the way she dresses?'

'At least she looks after her mother-in-law.'

'And what a mother-in-law! Only sixty-nine and all bent up!' said the dowager ghost. 'I lived till eighty and I was straight as a rod!'

'But she's kind to our Maudie,' butted in another. 'And what about Bhanushree! All bent up when she was a mere child!'

'She was born like that!'

'Don't quibble!' And they were distracted by the wails of the insulted ghost of Bhanushree.

The house intervened at this stage, as the shouting Swadeshi ghost was setting up an awful clamour, giving rise to an atmosphere of whirling agitation which affected mortals if they were too near. It spirited them out of the way to the isolated centre of the roof. But it sympathized, because it had been in agony over the Gulianis for a long time.

Guliani had acquired most of the Normans' furniture when he took over the flat, though for the present, he had stored it away, unquestioningly accepting his wife's taste for fancier fare. When Maudie was sent to the Senior Citizens' Retreat taking only some of her furniture, he snapped up the rest including the piano. Junior deeply regretted the move when the Guliani daughters were heard crashing on the keys, sending the Rajmahal tenants half mad and bringing down a mass of complaints on his head.

'Wait, wait,' he said. 'I hear they are getting a piano teacher. It's possible they'll improve.'

But the tone-deaf Guliani daughters showed no promise. When they continued the painful playing after the piano went out of tune, Junior decided to pay a call. He had never been inside the Gulianis' flat and his visit dismayed him. The sofas were in the shape of white swans, the upholstery was garish and Junior shuddered as he looked around him at other evidence of the unspeakable. Was this the home of the same soft-spoken Guliani, the Guliani who had spent five years studying engineering in Germany, his current favourite? He reluctantly reminded himself of their initial lapse, when they had hung out mounds of washing from their verandahs, and the Rajmahal taboo had to be conveyed to them before they stopped. But with the harmony generated by Guliani's demeanour and no regression into public clothes drying, Junior had obliterated this memory. Nor had he ever set eyes on their belongings.

'This can't go on,' Junior complained, averting his eyes from the skirted plaster lady holding a lamp, so exciting to the elderly ghost.

'Certainly,' said Guliani readily. 'Of course. I am very little at home and I didn't realize … Have a drink, Mr Mallik. What can I offer you?'

'I don't drink,' said Junior curtly.

'Something soft?'

'No!' And abandoning tact Junior added, 'I must tell you that we don't retain tenants in the Rajmahal who cannot observe the minimum, er …'

His anger whipped up at the sighting of pencil squiggles on a wall. He was convinced the kitchen and bathrooms swarmed with cockroaches.

'I must press you to look for alternative accommodation!'

'Mr Mallik, Mr Mallik! Such a small thing … And as you know I am mostly out and my wife is, heh, heh, a little lenient with the girls … But I quite understand. The only solution is to sell the piano! There! My mind is made up!'

Guliani knew it wasn't simply the noise that had provoked Junior's reaction. He had guarded his seclusion precisely because he recognized his family's limitations. Not interfering with his wife's territory was the quid pro quo for his pursuit of pleasure in this thrilling city. At the same time, having the Rajmahal address on his card was a plus for him in Calcutta's snobbish commercial circuit, and even if he couldn't entertain at home there were enough clubs and restaurants for all that. But as Junior spoke it was clear Guliani had a problem on hand.

'What about Maudie Jessop!'

'Pardon?'

'It was you who encouraged her by offering her your facilities! She should never have been allowed back into the Rajmahal!'

'If you remember,' said Guliani softly, 'she came here unasked. My mother may have been "guilty" of being hospitable, but she is an old lady who was brought up traditionally. It is impossible for her to refuse a friend.'

'Friend! Your mother never set eyes on the old cow before!'

Guliani's sensibilities quivered at this onslaught and the almost visible thread connecting his sacred mother to cows. He little realized that Junior's use of the rude phrase was linked to his subterranean contempt of Hindu cow veneration and all that went with it.

He took a deep breath. 'So you think we enjoy having her visit us five times a day for this, this indelicate purpose?' he said, standing up to hide his agitation.

Junior took this as a signal. 'Goodbye,' he said abruptly, and marched out.

'A piano!' thought Guliani with disgust. 'A piano has to lose me my flat!'

With the determination that had brought him this far from his modest background, he planned his manoeuvers. He unhesitatingly sold the piano and arranged to bring in the Normans' furniture. 'I will ask that friendly Surjeet Shona for advice. She has generations of good taste behind her … Let it be done in a finger-snap, so that next time that Muslim fellow will think he was having a bad dream.' It was essential to avoid further humiliation.

'Listen to him!' exclaimed the ghosts, when Guliani approached Surjeet Shona. 'He's trying to change!'

'It's no good,' riposted the sceptics. 'A tiger can't change its stripes.'

And others said, 'How can you compare a Sindhi shopkeeper to that noblest of animals, the Royal Bengal Tiger!'

But it was too late to avert the desertion of the mansion by some of the older ghosts.

'It's time,' they muttered. 'This is just the thin end of the wedge!'

Not long after, when they were all to vanish after Petrov's death, the Rajmahal would both rejoice to be rid of them, and lament at the clear signal given by this desertion.

While these events and ghostly non-events precipitated by her piano were going on, Maudie was settling into her godown on the driveway, the repository of sacred accessories for the saint's tomb. There was nothing much there. A small cupboard with a few boxes of incense, matches and candles, along with a tin trunk with a variety of colourful grave cloths. Maudie had her remaining furniture brought back to the Rajmahal and installed in this room with the help of Rawat, her old alcohol-procurer. He cleaned up the room and surreptitiously shifted the tomb's accessories to his quarters.

Maudie happily and hazily felt, at the end of the operation, that this wasn't such a bad place. She lay down for her first night's sleep in her own bed, relieved at the ease with which she could order her drink through her old ally. And the location on the ground floor was of endless interest. The view along the row of magnificent palms progressing down the drive, the Chowringhee traffic as it trundled by the distant gate, the activity on the Rajmahal drive. Even her visits to the Gulianis' didn't wear her out, though she could only communicate in sign language with the bent-up lady who greeted her so graciously, and who was so hospitable with her offers of tea. Maudie had no idea that her cup was kept in the separate kitchen meant for people of indeterminate or undesirable caste.

The respectful care given to Guliani's old mother was paralleled by the house's attitude to all its older inhabitants. The Stracheys death had caused it great upset, but it was also relieved they were out of their misery. Maudie created a sentimental stirring in its bricks with her return, and it felt remorseful at its earlier carelessness. It was chuffed that she so longed to return to its embrace, even if it was to that aberration on the driveway. Her heavy boozing and the chowkidar's complicity were of some concern though, and it wondered how Hindu middle-class morality, the Islamic taboo and Junior's zealous eye could be juggled with her weakness. 'This will be interesting,' thought the Rajmahal. 'Which side should I take in a confrontation?'

The matron and doctor at the retreat had come down heavily on Maudie's addiction, and this had forced her to take flight. When she left, bag and furniture, they advised her against the move, to blunt the indecent haste with which they actually helped arrange for her departure. Dipsomaniacs were a constant threat to their routine and sanity and this was an old folks' home, not a prison. They did their duty by informing Junior and the committee and then kept very quiet.

Maudie led pleasantly unrestricted days as she eased her way back into her twenty-four-hour alcoholic haze. When Junior asked her, in his rough way, if she wouldn't be better off at the retreat, her skin tautened over her cheekbones giving her the skeletal look that overtook her in a crisis, as if about to snap apart into bony fragments. Junior gave up the direct approach. He would have to think of other stratagems.

'He can easily have me carried off,' confided Maudie tremblingly to Rawat. 'What's to stop him?'

'Who can dare to do such a thing when I am here!' the chowkidar growled, puffing out his burly chest. He wanted Maudie here, pleased at the prospect of bleeding her of some of her precious riches. He would have lost his cheer if he had known Maudie's 'riches' extended only to the small residue of money released to her by the retreat's matron. After all, how much do a few bottles of gin cost? The chowkidar was the only one who truly wanted Maudie, and that too under mistaken assumptions.

The experienced Rawat recognized the familiar glazed look on Maudie's face. Pre-empting her he said, 'Here, Memsahib. I have put everything out here, the gin-sharaab, the water, the lemon. I go now? Okay?'

Maudie's diminishing world was exemplified by her ever-diminishing room space. From a grand flat with her grand private bedroom to just that bedroom split into a multi-purpose flat to this godown. Here, Maudie's dressing table, cupboard and bed left cramped space for two chairs and a table.

She took to strolling about the narrow strip skirting the drive, between the row of palms and the peripheral wall, the area highlighted by Pir Tasleem Ahmed's tomb. Junior had especially planned this corridor, and with the care of the gardeners it had turned paradisial. A secret garden with an illusory spaciousness, its green carpeting made mysterious with inlets and recesses. Negotiating a cunning maze of hedges the visitor would come suddenly on the open space holding the tomb. A small pavilion had been built over it, with columns holding up a curving Bengal-style roof and it was kept pristine with white-washing. Every day, after supervising the cleaning, Rawat would spread a fresh grave cloth over the tombstone and light the lamps in the niche behind it. Maudie looked forward to the varying brightly-coloured and glittering raiment, the fresh flower petals strewn on the tomb each morning, the flaming lamps. She spent time here, lost in day dreaming under the trees and surrounded by the green of hedges and creepers. A semul tree had burst into waxy red flowers brilliant against bare branches, attracting squirrels which nibbled at the huge buds held in their minute hands. She most loved watching the sun birds, shimmering blue-black and pale yellow-green, weightless enough to sit on the petals without bending them and dipping their needle-beaks into the cups of the flowers. So tiny and perfect were these birds, that they appeared like normal-sized birds diminished by great distance, yet another illusion of space. Hoopoes knocked at the row of perfectly matched palms marching down the drive, tok-tok, riddling them with holes and highlighting the vista. Crows, flocks of parrots, doves, pigeons, bulbuls, mynahs, sparrows, seven sisters whirled and skirled, scolding and singing around Maudie who had found a perch on a ledge. Here she would sit leaning against the wall, her face tilted up in the sun, sometimes to be distracted by the devotees who came by to salute the tomb or light a candle. They would greet the strange white apparition in a dress and have small chats with her, about the weather, her health, and the grace of God. Most of them were the servants of the Rajmahal but there were many outsiders who had attached their sentiments to Pir Tasleem Ahmed's sacred remains.

Surjeet Shona came on Maudie soon after her arrival, strolling about by the enchanted shrine with a drink in her hand, as if she were at a garden party.

'Aunty Maudie,' Surjeet Shona gently chided. 'What are you doing here?'

'Oh I love all religions, SS. God is one, no?' she said with simple sincerity.

'But, Aunty Maudie. You know, you can't do this.'

'Do what?' the alarmed Maudie asked, fearful her independence was being questioned again.

Surjeet Shona hesitantly explained the obvious. Drinking alcohol would offend all at this location, not only the spirit of the Pir, but his devotees and the Rajmahal.

'You should cover your head here, Aunty Maudie. The same as in a Catholic church. Do you understand?'

'Watchman never said anything before,' sniffed Maudie. 'I don't remember covering my head.' And she added suspiciously, 'You aren't a Mohammedan are you?'

'Of course not!' laughed Surjeet Shona. 'You know that, Aunty Maudie! But I'd definitely advise you against drinking here.'

So Maudie's slide into her incoherence of alcohol-induced states of euphoria or despair was stopped short by this distraction. She circumspectly wore her little Catholic veil when she visited the tomb and cut down on her drink. The house was rigid with uncertain hope. Had Maudie's break from the known performed the miracle? 'Is the Pir at work?' it wondered.

Left unsaid was the fear of Junior Mallik, the one person Maudie needed to propitiate. And Junior Mallik was observing the issue with keen anxiety.

'What's the old cow up to?' he fretted. 'Come on, oh Pir,' he pleaded. 'Surely you can't condone her getting away with such blasphemy. And what about my devotion to you all these decades? Does it count for nothing?'

But the Pir's ghost, though his vibrations emanated ceaselessly, was inactive. If Junior could read his thoughts he would have suffered a shock.

'I was old too,' the Pir's emanation vibrated. 'Oh yes. I was old too. And though I was never called an "old cow", I was called many other things for my great age! What sin is there, in being old, and helpless, and weak after all? Is that not what all humans encounter, or dread? Why does it invite ridicule? Is Allah be-fooling us? Did I have to wait for the uncovering of my tomb to regain my respect?' And here he sighed a great sigh, which drained the spirit of the tenants for a second. 'And the little lady shows me respect with the covering of her head, does she not? And she refrains from drinking in my space. How then can you, in spite of all your service to my remains, please my emanation?' he said to a deaf Junior.

This same deaf Junior was obsessed with the ouster of Maudie Jessop. Once the obstacle of her squatting was removed he longed to leap at the obstructive godown with iron staves.

'Even if I can't get rid of that shifty Hindu chowkidar, there's the godown,' he thought. Junior had always been anti-Rawat, but his father's self-conscious secularity was a block. Ali came on so strong at any hint of prejudice that Junior was completely frustrated.

When Surjeet Shona offered Maudie alternate toilet facilities at her flat, Junior's thoughts became unprintable. 'That mindless do-gooding bitch doesn't realize what a disservice she's doing Aunty Maudie. And me.'

'Listen,' he said to her with extreme constraint. 'That's a great service you're doing for Maudie. But don't you think it's demeaning for her to live among the servants? That place was the chowkidar's godown, for god's sake!'

'You listen to me, Junior,' said Surjeet Shona firmly. 'I know you want Aunty Maudie out of here. But the godown's been here forever, and it was empty. Why can't you let her spend a few happy years?'

'Oh, you think I'm running a charity do you? A repository for dipsomanic inmates of old people's homes, eh?'

'What nonsense, Junior!' said Surjeet Shona. 'Can't you be kind to her for a change?'

'Kind? Why don't you try being kind instead of lecturing others?'

'She's using my loo isn't she, and I feed her, don't I?'

'Who do you think bloody looked after her when she was ill, who do you think …?'

'All right, all right, you did a lot for her. But then, she hated the home! And what about her happiness?'

'Happiness! All happiness means to her is drinking. Day in, day out, that's all she wants. And what about the Pir's tomb? I suppose you don't care if there's no sanctity there and drunken old biddies rollicking about …'

'Don't exaggerate!' said Surjeet Shona, shortly. 'Haven't you seen how she venerates the tomb? She only drinks in her room. And haven't you noticed that she covers her head and …'

'The poor Pir must be doing somersaults in his grave!'

'Now who's being disrespectful!'

But Junior didn't let these circular arguments get in the way of his resolve. Maudie must go.

She did, but in a way not quite expected.

❦

Maudie's earlier hospital stay, enforced circumspection at the retreat, and the new distraction of the tomb garden had drained her system of alcohol and restored some of her balance. Her anxiety only sharpened when she grappled with her life and the continuous confrontation with Junior. The dead white paint no longer adorned her face.

'If I'm old and dark, that's how God wants it,' she reasoned with herself. 'Why fight Him?'

For the first time since her illness, she looked over her bedraggled body in the mirror, and straightened her shoulders. 'Mum always told me to stand straight,' she said out aloud. 'That's better. Much better, my girl.' The 'my girl' reminded her of both her husband and handsome Robby Rozario, who were merged into one in her mind. 'He never got 'round to asking me,' she sniffed when she noticed two little raw patches in the corners of her lips. 'It's some vitamin deficiency,' she said, forgetting Rozario. 'That's what Anthony always said about Mum. Funny how she had the same thing … Doc, I'll have to call doc …' She leaned closer to peer at her lips and caught the reflection of a dark metallic object in her open almirah. It was a gun, once her husband's.

'My,' she said. 'I'd forgotten about that!' She admired it, examined the bullet chamber.

'It's some protection at least!' she thought.

Junior, acting as if a black angel had descended on him, was going about breathing mushroom clouds while he ruthlessly targeted the widow.

'I'm stopping your money, Maudie!' Junior pronounced, preparing for the final push. 'I'm not obliged to do anything, am I, with you cluttering up this place uninvited?'

'Oh my,' whispered Maudie.

'And you'd better follow my conditions or I'll have you thrown out!'

'What, what conditions?' asked Maudie, too nervous to argue.

'One. You have to give up drinking completely, because you are living in sacred precincts. Two. You are forbidden from entering the domain of the Pir's tomb. And three. You are forbidden from entering the main Rajmahal building, except for Surjeet Shona's flat on the ground floor, which you may access only by the garden! That is all!'

Junior quickly marched away before Maudie's face could take on the stretched skeletal look again.

The ultimatum had sent a door crashing shut in her face, fracturing her will. She badly needed to drink again, but the source of her money had dried up. She sat wringing her hands, too afraid of the chowkidar's reaction if she told him of her penury. She knew that friendly though he was, there was always that little greedy gleam in his eyes. 'He'll chuck me to the wolves!' she said, and softly keening, swayed with her hands over her face. That was how Surjeet Shona came on her.

'Aunty Maudie,' she said. 'What is it?'

'That Junior Mallik,' she sobbed. 'That Junior Mallik's so wicked! He says I can't go to the tomb any more, or into your flat except by the garden … And no more money, and no more … no more … you know!'

'How can anyone have the heart to do this to her?' thought Surjeet Shona.

'How much do you want, Aunty Maudie?' she asked tentatively, knowing her kindness could destroy the old lady.

❦

So Surjeet Shona lent Maudie the small sums she needed for her deadly addiction. And her kindness was the end of Maudie. For drink was her devil, not Junior. She grew weaker and weaker, hardly eating the tempting food Surjeet Shona set out for her each day. She forgot the Pir, the birds and flowers, the trees and woodpeckers.

'Goodbye Maudie,' said the Rajmahal sadly. 'Goodbye dear, gracious, sad lady.' And it mimicked what the Swadeshi ghost would have said if it had not vanished by then along with all the other ghosts, 'Ah, why do these Christians do this? It is men who are said to be addicted to such weakening substances.'

❦

One night, Maudie went ricocheting between the walls of the hedge-maze, scratching herself till she bled. She reached the Pir's tomb, lovingly took her place on the ledge, and re-positioning her little Catholic veil, tilted her head at the familiar angle. The moon shone perfectly round on three of its quarters with the fourth quarter smokily unfinished. It swam swiftly upwards in a sky of great luminosity against clouds shining from within, yet edged with blackest density, the unfinished moon swimming, swimming swiftly comet-like with its smoky tail, yet staying within the ambit of her upturned eye. Then a golden star, just one star, gleamed at her from an opening.

'It's not twinkling, it's a planet,' said Maudie. And it reminded her of her lost star-stud golden earrings. 'They stole them all. My jewels. My money.' And then, as drunk as she had ever been in her life, she looked again at the mesmerizing bright silver moon riding so triumphant over the evilly circled clouds, and thought, 'It's a sign. Look! So bright, the silvery moon!' And then, as her tongue darted to the sour little sores at the corners of her lips, the moon diminished, slowly grew smaller and smaller, and vanished. And the sky was cast over with deepest black mourning. Against the remaining light in the sky, the semul tree stood out, bare, not a flower to be seen. And then she saw that not only the flowers and the moon, but the golden star, the reminder of her losses, had vanished. A chilling drop of water fell on her cheek. She felt it as the tear of the world, telling her, 'Go Maudie. Do what you have to do.'

Maudie went weaving back to her room, crushing the bulky semul flowers on the ground with her feet, and staining her white sandals. In her room she picked up the gun, as she had been doing for many nights. Then she raised it to her temple with a trembling hand.

'Do something!' the Rajmahal exclaimed impotently. 'Oh God!'

Urged by her black cloud of despair, her opposite-of-hope, Maudie was about to pull the trigger, when the door opened to Junior, furious at hearing she had violated the tomb ban. Her desperation and resolve funnelled sharply towards him, such a wicked man, and she turned the gun on him and fired. Junior registered the flash and a scalding streak along the side of his head. And the chowkidar, who was approaching outside felt the buzzing of an extra-strong bee as it whizzed by on a suicide mission and thudded into the pained Rajmahal wall. Maudie's hand recoiled with the shot and the gun splintered into the bevelled glass of her splendid triple-mirrored dressing table and dropped from her hand. 'Seven years bad luck,' said Maudie, passing out in a dead faint.

PART 2

6

Surjeet Shona Moves In

For a time after the Sardar Bahadur's momentous departure, the ground floor Rajmahal flat acted as a curtailed visiting pad for the Ohris, till Surjeet Shona moved in. Much to its delight, for it longed for one of the blooded Ohris to honour its insides permanently. Surjeet Shona was the daughter of the same favourite great grand son, Satinder, who had dared to question the Sardar Bahadur's last wishes. Surjeet Shona Kaur, daughter of Satinder Singh Ohri, son of Maninder Singh Ohri, son of Rupinder Singh Ohri, son of Sardar Bahadur Surjeet Singh Ohri. So the 'Surjeet' was after the progenitor on the Sikh side, and the 'Shona' after an illustrious Bengali ancestress. The redeeming feature, of course, was that she was from the aristocratic family of Raja Sheetanath himself.

'See here, ji,' the Sardar Bahadur's wife had protested. 'How are you sitting quietly and saying nothing at this shameful thing?'

'It had to happen someday, didn't it? I expected worse when we sent the boy out of the country to study. Aren't you thankful he hasn't come back with a mem and the girl is from a Raja's family, connected to us by this house? And haven't we lived so happily in this house, in Calcutta, a Bengali city?'

'I told you even then!' said Inderjeet Kaur as if he hadn't spoken. 'I told you something terrible would happen. And what about Satinder's children? They will become soft with eating rice and fish! They will not even be proper Punjabis, let alone Sikhs! The line will die away and they will speak that gole matole rasgulla language!' She rocked back and forth and slapped her forehead.

'Arrey "I-Say", they will be Ohris, and they will be brought up as Sikhs! That has been made clear. And they will speak Punjabi, even if they know a little Bengali. Don't I know Bengali!' he thundered. 'Are you saying I am any less a Sikh?'

'I know how you learned Bengali, "Rupinder's father",' mumbled Inderjeet Kaur. 'Oh yes, I know very well!' The reference was to Sardar Bahadur's ladies, who had acted as sleep-in language primers to him, so he didn't answer.

The Rajmahal, on the other hand, found the double pedigree of the Sheetanath-Ohri conjunction most auspicious and a cause for rejoicing.

Surjeet Shona, the firstborn of that upsetting, breakaway marriage, was able, in the end, to absorb both Punjabi and Bengali currents and speak both languages, neither well. She was aware of the xenophobia of both sides and would often discuss the problem with the Rajmahal's resident philosopher, Petrov. At the end of one of his discourses, Surjeet Shona forced the issue back to her personal self. 'And in any case, what should I, as a hybrid, then do?'

'Nothing, dear child, nothing. You are an important manifestation of what will inevitably happen after a hundred years, when every Indian is a hybrid like you and all the cultures fade out, and the not-this-not-that hybrid shines out like an arc lamp!'

'God forbid!' shuddered Surjeet Shona. 'What a deep loss that will be to us. Even I, a hybrid, feel this! Just a hundred years, you say?'

'Even if it were after a thousand years, you would still say, "God forbid", would you not?'

But all Petrov could do was to inscribe this discourse in his diary, which Surjeet Shona often dipped into in idle moments, or when she drifted up to talk to the old man. If she had known her great great grandmother she might have understood her fears about her parents' marriage, because Surjeet Shona herself was gripped by confusion, sometimes overcome with loss at her split heritage, at others with elation at the unimaginable richness of that heritage.

'Fifth rung' Surjeet Shona had been taken away by her parents to Delhi soon after her birth, coinciding with the change of hands of the mansion. When she moved back into the Ohri flat, therefore, she had never met any of the Rajmahal tenants nor returned to her city of birth till now.

Entering the Rajmahal as an adult, she felt the warm embrace of her ancestors' abode. The Rajmahal, having got back this Ohri-cum-Sheetanath as a resident, was beside itself with emotion. If it could it would have shed sentimental tears when the tall strapping beauty, whom it had last seen twenty-six years ago as a newborn baby, walked in. The ghosts murmured approvingly. 'This is an auspicious day for us, after a long long time, our own young one has come back to us!' And poor helpless disembodied spirits, they would have shed sentimental tears too, if they could. The time had passed when the Bengali ghosts thought a 'Punjabi contractor' acquiring the property such a disgrace. The grandeur and glamour of the 'contractor' with his titles and riches had soon obscured such prejudices.

Surjeet Shona had just lost her husband. She was reeling from the suddenness of her widowhood, the unfathomable cruelty of her Delhi landlord, who had evicted her with such short shrift, and her in-laws' rapacity as they tried to close in on her wealth. Torn from Delhi, where she had spent most of her life till then, and transplanted to Calcutta, she hated the city before seeing it. The warm feeling spread by the house, therefore, was reluctantly, then gratefully received, and she sank on to a regal and dusty armchair to survey her surroundings. Unwittingly, the Bhaiji repeated the words of the ghosts, 'Oh this is an auspicious day, Bi'ji, an auspicious day. I myself heard the order to the goldsmith for making the fifth rung the very day of your blessed birth. Wahey Guruji!' Surjeet Shona invited this protectiveness with her vulnerability, though she wore no widow's weeds. The charm of the room gradually impressed itself upon her. The chandeliers and lights were ablaze against the dark interior and she asked her new servants to pull up the bamboo chiks lined with blue markeen, which screened out the hot sun along the verandah. She followed them into the sub-aquatic length of the verandah's blue gloom, with the flash of brass representing fish and the palm fronds brushing her face like undersea vegetation. One by one the chiks were drawn up, dispelling this vision, and revealing the long verandah frontage of pillars. Shallow stairs went down on to a lawn ending at a high wall trapped by twirls of barbed wire. These formidable fortifications against the incursions of Chowringhee were offset by sunlit creepers and grass and by a magnificent raintree standing in a corner and spreading the perfume of its pink, silk-panicled flowers. Her lifting spirits were helped along by the joyous whisperings of the ghosts leaning over an upstairs balcony and gazing down fondly at her and her mother, who had joined her out in the sun. Encouraged by the house and the sight of the young widow and her mother, they forgot all about their frustrated tearfulness and watched with detached tolerance as the two women were led into the Guru Granth Sahib room.

'I never thought to see our girls doing all this Sikh thing,' said Raja Sheetanath's mother's ghost.

'But then, Tha'ma,' said a daughter's ghost. 'You always told us the wife must jump into the same well with the husband …'

And Raja Sheetanath's wife's ghost put in quickly and cattily, 'I know. Ma said it at least ten times a day. "A good wife will jump in blindfolded after her husband …"' The ghosts' laughter trilled and the dowager ghost had to keep mum, especially as one of the Ohri ghosts drifted in just then.

The musicians burst into song while Surjeet Shona and her mother veiled their heads before the Holy Granth Sahib, the old Ohri book, open in all its splendour. The Bhaiji proudly read from its pages through the worship that followed. Surjeet Shona's mother came from a Brahmo Samaj branch of the Sheetanath family, and since her marriage to a Sikh, at which it had been more startled than dismayed, the Brahmo branch had included a Sikh reading at every religious function. Surjeet Shona, like her parents, was religious by inertia. She automatically welcomed the ready-made setup in the Rajmahal flat, enjoying the pleasant cadences of the singing and warmed by feelings of loyalty to her father and late husband.

The Rajmahal tenants, at this time middle-aged and still active, welcomed the newcomer and Surjeet Shona, so much younger than them and of such a kind-hearted disposition, would find herself eventually the nursemaid-cum-caretaker of this motley group. It would strain her and lead her to latter day lapses, till when the group approached the geriatric stage and the deaths started, she would remark, 'I have to get out of this houseful of near-skeletons. And look at the Rajmahal! It's falling apart like a dehydrated skeleton itself!' The walls would creak then, registering the house's distress, and Surjeet Shona, herself well into middle age and familiar with the house's moods, would stroke the verandah pillar against which she stood, and lean her cheek on it.

That was a long time away. For the present, she was surprised by the mix of tenants. She had expected chiefly Bengalis, having little idea of the heterogeneity of this part of Calcutta, the one-time capital of colonized India, a global village before the phrase was invented. Yet here were not only British, Russian and Anglo-Indian tenants, but the Mojumdars and Malliks who were far removed from the image she had of Bengalis. She was struck by their style and their households, and her initial surprise soon gave way to pleasure.

But Surjeet Shona still had to cope with the loss of her lover, her husband. She had been too thrilled with her marriage to see Gurdeep as anything but a lover, with herself as the desired one, the mistress. And her mind was taken up with the tearing away and loss of that delicious relationship. So, her melancholy pastime was to dwell on the bitter parting, the fascination for one another transforming a minor tiff into an impetuous motorcycle ride to death.

Guru, short for Gurdeep, kept his hair uncut as a conforming Sikh. When they made love his turban came off and it was a joke with them as their limbs were enmeshed in the coils of their equally long hair, that Guru's was the more lustrous of the two.

'Oh you lovely boy,' Surjeet Shona would murmur, 'Such gorgeous tresses!' And she would stroke his head erotically as if he were the female aspect.

'Ai Kurriyay, bat mat kar!' Guru would say crudely to exemplify his masculinity and his lust. That earthiness copyrighted by his language lent itself perfectly to the situation. And Guru's body was unmistakably male, darkened over with hair while Surjeet Shona's was as smooth as alabaster. This ideal femininity would drive Guru crazy with desire, the contagion of his ardour spreading rapidly to Surjeet Shona. 'Diabolical woman!' Guru would snarl. 'Diabolical, perfect woman!' Their youth and grace took them on perilous rides on Guru's new motorbike which aroused them as much as their embraces, so that when they roared back they would barely be able to shut the door behind them before hurling themselves at each other. Surjeet Shona knew the tiff which had sent Guru off on the machine would bring him back feverish with desire, and it would end in such wild passion there would be no time for reproach. While anticipating this, she had begun heating up and melting, putting out of her mind, and then forgetting completely the cause of their tiff. But death had replaced that fantasy. Death had always been close on those rides, yet the pair had felt immortal, protected by their lust. The logic, which was invented at such times allowed no interference with its consummation. When the knock came and the incoherent condolences, Surjeet Shona ran into her bedroom, locked herself in, and while others banged on the door and called anxiously, she ranted and screamed at her husband for the unimportant cause of their tiff and this end. Looking back on it, Surjeet Shona felt she may have temporarily lost her mind.

The tragedy filled her chest and abdomen physically with pain, pushing tears into her eyes, which overflowed when her introspections continued uninterrupted. At other times, it made her frustrated with yearning and when Guru was conjured up through fantasizing, the pain would intensify and bathe her in the overwhelming heat of desire. The Rajmahal's tenants formed a bizarre chiaroscuro about her self-absorption, impinging on her only when she stepped out. There, with someone's gleaming eye usually on her, she would straighten her shoulders and carry on with a determined sniffle.

Surjeet Shona remembered the robust life of sex, sport and socializing she and Guru had led. For her, at least one aspect of her old life with Guru was reviving. Their favourite pastime had been horse riding and though she couldn't ride, being in the middle stages of pregnancy, she drove out early in the morning to the Maidaan by the race course and polo ground. With polo came the races, and Surjeet Shona was soon part of a group where, if not for her swollen abdomen, she would have been vigorously courted. The pain was temporarily anaesthetized when she met others, or thought of her coming child, or realized she would recover and marry again. But Guru was sharply present, still the core of her pain.

She was with Maudie Jessop and Arny Aratoon, an elderly Armenian, at the polo ground when Maudie's husband fell to his death. Anthony's body looked so much like Guru's after his accident that Surjeet Shona felt a bizarre retraction in time. She looked at the blurred images, the ultra-pale Maudie, the running figures, and heard the chattering distortion of fear. From that day, the eminently normal, courageous, sexy, and healthy Surjeet Shona would be haunted by the fear of death. This reminder of the implacable nature of death's sickeningly selective power would not allow the fear to leave her. The pain of Guru's death seemed abruptly gone, and she felt a hysterical panic that she was ageing, ageing too fast, prematurely, precipitated by Death. She was heading for that very Thing, waiting like a ghoul to snatch her to its bosom and crush her into a mass of broken bones and dead flesh and then to discard her, leaving in her place an enveloping miasma of fear. She was gripping a chair and retching when she heard a call, it was Arny Aratoon with another white man, stooping over her and trying to revive her. She could smell Arny's cigars and leather, and saw the other man, in polo player's gear, with a shaving cream and sweat smell, a combination she would for a time associate with her fear. In that swoon she realized the other man was Martin Strachey, who kept appearing and disappearing from his parents' flat on the second floor of the Rajmahal. But the concern of the two men was peripheral to that dread. This carbon copy death of her husband had driven it into her, the young fast-ageing widow, obliged to witness Maudie's widowing within six brief months of her own. Later that day, when the same Maudie came to stay one floor above her, it was a hurtful reminder.

Surjeet Shona knew some traditions in her country demanded that widows, often young like herself, must abdicate life, a greater sacrifice surely than an emperor abdicating his throne. That embrace and abdication called for skulking guilt, a shaved head, vegetarianism, an artificially shrivelled sex drive and servitude. The widow's punishment for having, by her negative emanations, caused her husband's death. So, was this terrible fear Surjeet Shona's punishment for Guru's death?

❦

Surjeet Shona's fear grew every time she thought of Martin Strachey or Arny Aratoon. But it was towards the younger man that it added a devastating thrust to the attraction she felt growing for him as she went through her pregnancy.

Martin was large, as large as Guru had been, but he was white, with fine blonde hair, a direct contrast to Guru's darkness and bristling black hair. Martin was also stockier in build, with thicker limbs. But his mischievous blue eyes held an inherent sexiness.

Did Surjeet Shona know what she wanted from Martin? At the moment, the far from frail young widow was ready to enter the classical situation of a stormy love affair full of passion, without calculation. Her body craved a replacement for the precipitately and permanently withdrawn Guru. Martin had also observed Surjeet Shona going through her pregnancy and emerging unscathed with a baby at the end of it. He found the tiny appendage added touching overtones to her already touching image. They flirted with their eyes and a few teasing words whenever they met, till three months after the birth of the other Gurdeep, (what else could Surjeet Shona have called her firstborn?), the inevitable happened. Martin's bumping into her on the drive was far from circumstantial, he had been watching for such an opportunity. In his caressingly light voice, he asked her to join him at Firpos for an ice. His mispronunciation of Surjeet Shona's name sent shivers down her spine. 'Sur-jeet,' she corrected as she unhesitatingly accepted. 'Not Sir-jeet!'

'Soorjeet! Soorjeet! Soorjeet Sona!' chimed Martin, mockingly in time with the evening bells of St Paul's.

'Shona, not SSSSona. Look, it's easy, SSsurjeet Shshona! Go on! Try it!'

'Sona, the golden, Soorjeet, Conqueror of the Gods, Conqueror of the Sun! How does such a very feminine girl have such a manly name, Conqueror of the Gods, the Sun?'

'Sikhs do that,' said Surjeet Shona. 'Sikh women are as brave as men! But go on, say it together … SSsurjeet Shshona …'

'Shshsh, SSSSs,' tried Martin valiantly. 'Ess Ess. That's what I'll call you,' he said firmly. 'SS. Much simpler …' Thus it was Martin who set the trend for Surjeet Shona's name form among Rajmahalians, the grandiloquent words shortened to a repeated letter of the Roman alphabet.

In the heat of the car and in the midst of their laughter, Surjeet Shona could smell her fear again, and in the unbearable edge of excitement emanating from that fear, she put a hand on Martin's shoulder, the spontaneous outcome of their shared laughter, and felt him grip it and press it so hard to his chest she thought her fingers would snap. 'This isn't the way to Firpos,' she managed to say. The car rolled to a stop on an isolated road on the Maidaan and the answer never came, because Surjeet Shona responded without reserve, and mad with lust, she and Martin clung to each other, kissing and tearing at each other's clothes. Every time Martin uttered the incoherent words of love, he sounded to Surjeet Shona so very romantically British, like her favourite film stars, James Mason, Peter O'Toole, that they sent more shivers through her. For Martin too, this was his first time with an Indian woman, and he would live consciously within the pages of the *Kama Sutra*, which he had read in college. Restarting the engine frenziedly he swerved the car back on to the road.

'Where to?' choked Surjeet Shona, trembling and holding herself together.

'Somewhere,' said Martin, continuing to caress her through her clothes with his free arm. 'Not Firpos.'

Eventually, with the car skidding to each embrace as if they were in an obstacle-strewn tunnel of love, they drove through an open gate. It was almost dark and, stumbling out, Martin pulled Surjeet Shona into an old musty smelling house through a door which opened magically to a key produced by him. Behind the closed door and in that semi-darkness, just as Surjeet Shona had done with Guru countless times, she and Martin fell on each other hungrily till every shred of clothing was off and they were wildly copulating.

Martin's excitement mounted when he realized the shamelessness of this Indian girl. Had he not been told again and again, both that Indian women were overwhelmingly prudish and that one must at all times be circumspect with them?

Surjeet Shona could sense Martin's astonishment. She felt again the fear, which had receded temporarily in the heat of their encounter. Inside her, it was spreading its poison and she knew her frank submission would in some way turn him away. She was sure his excitement was mainly due to new lust.

They writhed their way into a large room and on to a dustcloth covered sofa. Martin struck a match revealing a romantically translucent curtain of cobwebs and looked his full at Surjeet Shona, caressing her, making her shiver in the heat and arousing her again. He was convinced this was the belle of the *Kama Sutra* come alive for him. She lay there in front of him, naked, the exotic, oriental, female principal representing the primal yoni, with him the primal lingam ever the lord of universal desire. While he went through the rites of passion his academic mind waited to find out if Surjeet Shona was not the type of the highly accomplished *Kama Sutra* courtesan. With this trysting place available to them, the two continued their meetings but Martin kept doubly busy checking back on classical references, visiting the treasure trove of the Asiatic Society on the corner of Park Street, or the National Library at the old Viceregal Palace, trying to ferret out paintings, poetics and ideals of erotic Indian womanhood. 'Was their supposed prudery merely a thin veneer covering a depthless erotic fervour?' he excitedly ferreted. And ever a reductionist *ad absurdum*, he sought out the red-light area. But when he drove through the narrow lanes of Shonagachi, 'Shona again,' he thought, 'ah delicious gold!' he found himself retreating from the beckoning pimps and painted prostitutes, fearful of a repugnant lack of hygiene. 'Karaya Lane wouldn't have been like this,' he thought as he cruised along. 'Surely not!' he had read of the gardens and bungalows of the now vanished Karaya Lane and its ladies who had come from Singapore, Hong Kong, French Indochina, 'and add Russia,' Petrov could have told him. Here, in Shonagachi, Martin was certain the local ladies would pass on the very worst types of venereal diseases, little realizing that, decades earlier, Petrov had contracted an infection passed on by a Russian 'aristocrat' from a superior Karaya Lane establishment, and had to undertake a humiliating cure.

In the meantime, this was a crazed period Surjeet Shona and Martin went through, with all the signs of a great love affair, yet fatally marred by Surjeet Shona's fear. And she wondered briefly for the first time at the bizarre fact that Martin's scent was already there on the dust cover of the sofa on which they lay. The next time, and later, she would forget this fact, thus cancelling the cautionary effect it might have had, yet underlining her fear.

The Rajmahal knew of these goings-on, easily given away when Martin's hand wandered over Surjeet Shona at brief meetings, or when they whispered about the next tryst, or when others, including the servants, gossiped about them. It allowed the ghosts some inklings too, trying to inure them, to allow Surjeet Shona her freedom without interfering emanations. It was not this which troubled the house, but the sensing of a rival. Where were the lovers trysting, within the walls of what house? It heard sometimes the whisperings between them about 'the house on Ronaldshay Road'. But where was Ronaldshay Road, and what other house could be worthy of this conjunction of the Rajmahal's pedigreed inhabitants? It wasn't to know the house on Ronaldshay Road belonged simply to friends who had left the keys with the Stracheys, and Martin had used it before for the same purpose.

Nothing could stop the blinding affair between Jack and Myrna Strachey's son Martin, and Surjeet Shona, direct descendant of the Sardar Bahadur and Raja Sheetanath. Their frenzy would reach new heights each time they betrayed the Rajmahal by using the Ronaldshay Road house. And forgetting the original, Martin and Surjeet Shona invented their own *Kama Sutra*, sometimes twisting an ankle and pulling a hamstring, as they knotted themselves into intricate configurations. It was magic for them, any thought of any moment of which would make Surjeet Shona's breasts overflow, so that little Gurdeep never wanted for his mother's milk and would grow into a buxom lad with no pretensions to spirituality. They were completely unaware that from the very first night, the gardener and his entire family, who lived in the outhouses of the Ronaldshay Road house and guarded it, would desperately batten on the windows, peering into the gloom and trying to figure out the activities of Martin and his latest paramour. Surjeet Shona knew she was inviting outrage by her scandalous behaviour, but she didn't waste time agonizing over it. Even when her mother threatened to come back after hearing rumours.

There was controversy over the affair between the Rajmahal and its ghosts. The Rajmahal favoured an unconditional happiness for its inhabitants, without too much interference by tradition. Most of the ghosts, on the other hand, belonged to the most hidebound vintage of that tradition.

'It's shocking, a disgrace!' they whispered. 'She's not observing the smallest of the requirements, just look at her!'

'It's the Sikh business, the crossing with Sikh blood,' sniffed Raja Sheetanath's mother's ghost. 'Didn't I tell you?'

Though they recognized that Surjeet Shona was half Sikh and therefore not expected to rise to *full* Bengali refinements, they expected at least some circumspection in her situation. But they shut up when they felt the constricting disapproval of the Rajmahal. 'Hushshsh!' the Rajmahal seemed to scold. 'How can you be so prudish when she has gone through such pain?'

When the Sardar Bahadur's wife, Inderjeet Kaur's ghost sometimes drifted over from Amritsar to see how 'fifth rung' was doing, the house ghosts would simmer down. The Sardar Bahadur was too remote an ancestor to try to understand a modern woman, but Inderjeet Kaur's ghost urged Surjeet Shona to be happy and live her life without reservation. The late widow couldn't forgive herself for her useless fidelity to the Sardar Bahadur.

It was a middle-aged man, Proshanto Mojumdar, who precipitated the dousing of the fire of that lust. The Mojumdars, who lived just above her flat, had known Surjeet Shona from her childhood, when they had voyaged aboard the same liner to Europe. Surjeet Shona was struck by a feeling of recall when she saw the mirrored bedroom of the Mojumdars' flat. 'It looks so familiar,' she said. 'I think I saw something like it in a film, or …'

'It was the *Hong Kong*, my dear,' said Mohini Mojumdar. 'The lounge of the *Hong Kong*. Don't you remember? That's why we chose this flat, wasn't it Pro?'

Proshanto Mojumdar remembered perfectly their honeymoon on board the *Hong Kong*. But at the moment, he didn't want to dwell on unpromising marital mementos in front of the young beauty. His face had taken on the bright yet foolish expression easily recognized by his wife. Proshanto's idea, 'Brilliant only to himself,' thought Mohini, was to invite all the younger generation of the Rajmahal to a lengthy entertainment lasting the whole day. 'Everyone's here,' he said. 'All the young people are visiting the Rajmahal. They must be bored.'

But as Surjeet Shona grew more engrossed in herself and her biological processes, Proshanto Mojumdar fell out of infatuation with her. After her delivery, the temporary loosening of her figure and the imagined aroma of milk militated against his sensibilities, the opposite reaction to Martin's. The outing was shelved. But Proshanto was soon feverishly involved in organizing a river picnic. 'There's that English girl. A fetching girl, most fetching. She must be bored …' He was referring to Antonia, the current girlfriend of the landlord's middle son, Mumtaz Mallik.

'He's off again,' thought Mohini Mojumdar.

Proshanto had stylish invitation cards engraved. 'Mr and Mrs Proshanto Kumar Mojumdar have the pleasure of inviting x to a riverine excursion and lunch on board the *Brahmaputra*, followed by dinner and dancing at the *300* Club. 10.30 a.m. at Prinsep Ghat, Sunday …'

The guests showed a concerted social zealotry in the outing. While caviar on thin rounds of buttered bread was served on silver platters, Arny Aratoon mixed genteel Pim's Number one, its pale amber lightened with lemonade and decorated with delectable slices of orange and mint leaves, pastel colours bobbing with ice and elegance. As the *Brahmaputra*, a big steam launch, moved on to the broader stretches of the Hooghly, Antonia was seen with Martin, kissing behind a capstan. It was a kiss which achieved an undeserved resonance, because the *Brahmaputra* couldn't provide it privacy. Surjeet Shona stumbled on them while evading the especially tipsy Arny Aratoon, with Proshanto Mojumdar in bleeding Madras shorts bringing up the rear. She felt stabs of a nightmare at being forced to view so closely that sensual betrayal, and the triumphant gleam of Antonia's green eyes framed in satanic red hair. This was followed by confusion when she faced Martin's shrugs and innocent wide-eyed look. Mumtaz, up on the bridge, would have had the clearest view of his girlfriend's brazenness. He watched the romantic-erotic group breaking up to disperse on the main deck, while Martin's mother, Myrna Strachey, lay blissfully at peace, in scanty white shorts and pink halter top, sunning herself on a deck chair. And then they watched a passing barge piled high with bales of jute with its men standing up tall to get a better view of the naked 'mem'. Mumtaz came down and joined Surjeet Shona, both tight faced. But Antonia was made of stern stuff, her giggling and flirting creating a frivolous whirlwind around the permissive Martin. The saving moment came at the end as they were steaming back, and the sun was about to set. The party was assembled on the main deck, and Mohini and Proshanto Mojumdar spontaneously began to sing. They sang an asexual Robindro Shongeet about sentiments deeply embedded in Bengal's country and river life.

Proshanto was looking at Mohini's glowing face with such admiration, and both were singing in such mellifluous cadences as if they were always meant to sing together, that the earlier farcical happenings seemed inconceivable.

Ah at last the sweet flood's come
To swell the sad river
Cast off, cast off and call
Victory oh Mother

Hey boatman, boatman
Where are you boatman
Call out now
With all your soul

Hey open up and hoist the sail
Open up and hoist the sail
Hey open up and hoist the sail
Open up and hoist the sail
Loosen all the strings and ropes …

Oh friend day after day
Your debt has grown
No buying no selling
Not a cowry in hand

Day after day went by
Tied to the ghat
How will you even
Show your face

Come all together take the oars
All together take the oars
Life or death what must be must be

Ah at last the sweet flood's come …

Most couldn't understand the words but the folk tune and lilt were catchy and sad at the same time. Tears came to Maudie Jessop, then a willowy wispy forty-five, Myrna Strachey stopped adjusting her halter neck, Petrov was composed in the lotus posture with his eyes closed, and the others were humming and tapping their feet. Arny Aratoon, wearing his riding gear out of sheer force of habit, leaned forward over his jodhpured knees to hide his emotions, though everyone could see his bald head turning red in sharp contrast to his very white fringe of hair.

Surjeet Shona couldn't distance herself from Martin, and after an initial struggle found herself tightly clasping and unclasping hands with him under the table. She snatched her hand away when Antonia pulled a chair up close on the other side of Martin and placed her sandalled foot against his leg. Feeling hot and cold at the same time, Surjeet Shona was jolted when she caught Mumtaz Mallik's eyes looking directly into hers. She wondered if the song had lifted him from his misery.

The launch had cut its engines and by their sides drifted the evening tide of the brown river, dealing watery slaps to the hull, shades of sand and mud eddying and making whorly patterns just below the surface. On the far bank tiny-looking palm trees and buildings were sharply etched, black on the paling twilight sky. A country boat, with its big hooded thatch, showed barely visible in the gloom, its boatman effortlessly swaying and swinging his rudder-oar in the silted-up shallowing river. His melodic tenor voice floated to them across the river, as sharp and clear as the etched palm trees, rising above and below and around Mohini and Proshanto Mojumdar's song and weaving itself in like a master craftsman's jamdaani sari. Both melodies were in the same raag and the boatman's song was of the river too. It was a blessed passage.

7

Surjeet Shona Moves On

Surjeet Shona took the break with Martin staunchly. It passed her by and left her calm. She felt the demented but therapeutic interim after Gurdeep's death must have been provided by God, in whom she simply believed. And she carried on with her interrupted mourning in the Guru Granth Sahib room. There she sat, with the Bhaiji softly reciting, the tears bathing her cheeks and her little son on her lap, crooning him to sleep, often falling asleep herself on the cushioned ground. Absorbed in consolidating herself and her child, she stayed away from others. With time Surjeet Shona normalized, taking to riding again. Later, she accepted a job offered by Jack Strachey. The work was undemanding and involved administering a small section at Sharp's, but it filled up Surjeet Shona's time.

And then Martin brought his bride, Gwendolyn, to the Rajmahal. Surjeet Shona caught a glimpse of her in the lobby. 'She's not at all as I expected,' was her first thought. She wondered at Martin's choice of this scholarly looking woman, with the blonde plait haloing her head, the Madonna likeness spoiled by a pair of gold-rimmed glasses. Gwendolyn's petite rounded figure was such a contrast to herself, big-boned, tall, large-breasted and to the disrupter of her brief bliss, Antonia, a medium-sized redhead, that it seemed much in this world was inexplicable. When she recalled the passion of her affair with Martin she was pleased at feeling little emotion. But the small hairs at the back of her neck stood on end at the very thought of Martin's particular persona of shaving cream and sweat, and she felt vulnerable and reluctant to meet him. Arny Aratoon, the other instigator of her dread, had packed up and left, to bemuse the populace of his new home in rural England with his dated Rolls, his shooting stick and his stable of horses.

When Martin and Gwendolyn neared the end of their long visit, Surjeet Shona forced herself into a joint outing. 'I must do this,' she thought. 'I can't keep hiding.' As Petrov's acolyte she often went visiting with him and this time it was to introduce Martin to Professor Shanto Bose, Petrov's Bengali 'brother'. Surjeet Shona found herself in a state of uneasy anticipation at the challenge of meeting the young Stracheys, but Martin came alone. 'After *Neel Dorpon* all Gwen wants is to get away from this country and everyone in it …,' Martin apologized. 'I've tried clubs, parties, plays, palaces … But nothing moves her. So, no more Calcutta for her.'

'Back to the known …,' said Petrov.

Face-to-face at last with Martin, Surjeet Shona hid her uneasiness. 'It's almost as if he's forgotten,' she thought noting his lack of embarrassment. 'Oh it's definitely over …'

She was right. Promiscuous as he had been so far, Martin's current lover took up his complete attention, surgically cauterizing the past. To him it was perfectly legitimate, a sexual encounter should lay the base for a platonic and warm future friendship. His disinterest in Surjeet Shona didn't occupy him for an instant.

'What a careless boy he is,' thought Petrov, as always keenly observant.

Martin's object was to penetrate this Calcutta, a Calcutta non-existent to his parents. It would help him gain insight for his specialized researches into colonial Bengal. 'He would become like my Russian guru if he stayed on,' thought Surjeet Shona.

❦

The Bose drawing room, comfortably familiar to Surjeet Shona, had a musty-sweet aroma from the books lining its walls and mounting to the ceiling. Martin's sensitive nose quivered in response to the pests and moulds infesting them and he exploded in a sneeze.

'Sorry,' he apologized. 'I must be allergic to something!'

'Like your wife is to us,' thought Surjeet Shona.

Another sneeze set him rocking on his seat and Petrov and the professor burst into childish laughter. Martin discovered his seat was an unstable stack of king-sized books disguised with a coverlet.

'Good God,' he said, worriedly looking around at the mottled books. 'Why did you let me sit on these? And what are they? I've missed so much!' He changed his seat.

'Oh, you shouldn't worry,' said Petrov. 'There's too much. And these books are mostly in Bengali. Do you know Bengali?'

'Er, ektu ektu,' said Martin in such a heavy accent that his claim was instantly thrown into doubt. Surjeet Shona giggled.

'Your Bengali isn't too good either,' said Martin, and sneezed again.

'And the relevant books may not suit your conclusions,' added the professor dryly.

'Come come,' said Martin. 'You a professor and making assumptions about my "conclusions"!'

'I apologize,' beamed the professor. 'You must enlighten me of course.'

'I'd rather listen to you!'

'Sergie-da is the expert.'

'I know, I know. I've wasted my time here. Too much dancing at Prince's.'

Surjeet Shona saw Petrov flinching and glancing at the professor.

'Intellectual snobbery,' she thought. She understood very well that such haunts were irrelevant to the professor. He belonged away from and *above* that world.

'How is old Prince's, eh?' said the professor suddenly. He looked blandly at Petrov. And Petrov stared hard back at him. Surjeet Shona suppressed another giggle.

'Oh super!' exclaimed Martin, noticing nothing of these exchanges. 'That's the only part my wife likes in Calcutta.'

'So you will come back, but without your wife?'

'My parents are here, my interests …,' and in a burst of empathy, 'Gwen simply can't take any of it. The city, the people and my parents. My mother *can* be a bit trying you know.'

'They quarrel, your wife and mother?' Petrov persisted.

'They don't quarrel, but there's this awful chilliness when they're together. Gwen can't stand Mother's rudeness to the servants. She hates it when they don't answer her back.'

'But they mind,' Surjeet Shona couldn't help saying.

'You were brutal in your time, you British,' said Petrov. 'Beating up employees, showering vile abuse, flogging them and kicking them …'

'Are we any better?' the professor interrupted. 'Our servants dress poorly and sleep in any corner of the house, on a piece of cloth, cardboard, anything, and they work from dawn to midnight, or as long as we require them. And the housewife, a truly thrifty Indian housewife, will give them minimum food to keep body and soul together. So. Perhaps there is not much difference?'

The diplomacy of the professor's interjection hadn't escaped the others.

A servant, a mere boy in shabby shorts and vest, came in to clear away the glasses. 'Oh, oh,' thought Surjeet Shona.

Martin, as diplomatic as the professor, quickly turned away from the boy. Surjeet Shona noticed and reprimanded herself, 'There I go! Still sensitive to Martin!'

And then, Surjeet Shona completely lost her bearings. She could never remember exactly what happened next, except that her eyes were snared by the penetrating gaze of a complete stranger, who had just walked in. 'Neel Banerjea', she heard over the roaring in her ears. And then, 'Come, come, sit down. Neel is an anthropologist,' the words filtered through to her, 'single-minded about exposing the exploitation and erosion of adivasi culture! We are lucky to catch a glimpse of him. Otherwise, he is always wandering away to the interior. Which tribe is it now Neel? Oraons or Bheels?'

'You are poking fun at me as always, Shanto-da.' Neel spoke with the long vowels of the refined Bengali in a quiet husky voice.

'Nice voice,' thought Surjeet Shona. She had caught his incredulous look when he had first sighted her before her reactions overwhelmed her. Neel Banerjea was fiercely good-looking, with a rangy figure, dark, his receding hair emphasizing his arresting eyes and small eagle nose. Surjeet Shona recognized the same mischief that reigned in Martin's eyes, and warning bells rang. She felt an overwhelming desire to run away.

'I just remembered I have to ...'

'Am I driving you away?' the voice was interrupting her.

'Where are you going, dear? We've just come ... Sit down!' ordered Petrov.

Surjeet Shona obeyed, almost afraid to raise her eyes. All her efforts were directed to breathing normally, and she didn't realize her hands were tightly gripped together. That quiet husky voice speaking articulately and at length completely absorbed her, though the words made no headway to her brain. She would remember nothing of the details of the evening after this point.

8

The Landlord's Family

When Ali Mallik bought the the major part of the Rajmahal in 1942, he had chosen the top floor flat for himself because he didn't want tenants trampling all over him and preferred this distancing from up on high. The Malliks furnished their flat luxuriously. Apart from the fixtures on the walls and the plumbing, most of the original furniture had gone out with the Ohris. So the flat had no pretensions to regal splendour. But it had the approval of the Malliks' many Europeanized friends.

Ali Mallik favoured sharkskin for dress occasions, and cut a dash in his tailored evening suits usually sharpened by a bow-tie and scarlet cummerbund. His tailors were Barkat Ali's, hard to surpass anywhere in the world. Ali was slim and handsome in a skeletal way and his circle often teased him of starving to look like Mohammad Ali Jinnah, a family friend. Ali denied this, citing his pencil-thin moustache as evidence, a contrast to the clean-shaven Jinnah. Mrs Mallik, Saira, was tall and statuesque with shoulder length blondish hair, a nose stone, and claimed her ancestors were royalty, Moghuls from Samarkand. Where exactly this was and whether Samarkandis were blonde or not, no one was quite sure, but the mystery made her doubly glamorous. By middle age she had reddened her hair with henna and tended to have unhealthy-looking pouches under her eyes. But she was still handsome and her height added to the patrician effect. She wore chiffon saris and chain-smoked cigarettes in a long jet holder, aggravating her chronic asthma and suffering doubly on the long trudge up the stairs. She also liked to tipple occasionally, when she became harmlessly drunk, her favourite drink being a lethal dry martini of which only the *300* knew the subtleties.

Ali Mallik didn't connect his wife's immodest behaviour, smoking and drinking, or his own taste for whisky, as against Islam, considering all this as merely peripheral. He was a highly successful barrister, one of the richest in Calcutta, and Gandhiji had asked him to give up barristering to join the freedom struggle. But Ali had seen colleagues fritter away their lives in jail, and he also did not want to enter the uncertain arena of Hindu-Muslim politics. He knew that ever since Lord Curzon's abortive partitioning of the old magnum Bengal in 1905, this politics had got murkier and murkier. But it was the big one, the riots and the final Partition itself, which had left an incipiently painful scar. He refused to consider moving back to his home town, Dacca, simply because he was a Muslim, just as he refused to accept the need for Partition. Secretly he longed for the Muslims to be the majority group in the new India, so he could take over the smug and snug feeling of his Hindu friends, and lay claim to India with the same arrogant proprietorship. It never occurred to him to long to be a Hindu because he was a Muslim through and through. He was sensitive to the fact that Hindus and Muslims were inextricably linked in a terrible and seductive symbiotic relationship on the Indian subcontinent which would have a long and unhappy history. But he was also convinced this must end in eventual synthesis and harmony. He felt he wouldn't mind if one of his sons married a Hindu so this synthesis could be attempted right under his nose. But never did he voice this wish nor show any reaction, other than mild acquiescence, when one of his sons did just that. Nor, for the present, would he concede that the synthesis would never be complete. Like a primitive mixer for hot and cold water, which scalds one side of the hands and chills the other.

❦

Junior, the Mallik firstborn, with the proper name of Riyaz, though an endearing child with feudal airs, turned out severe. The tendencies of his youth were exaggerated into a dogmatism exemplified by his unquiet watch over the Rajmahal, his refusal to install a lift and his zeal over Pir Tasleem Ahmed's tomb.

In his younger days, Junior had stumbled on the neglected tomb near the boundary wall and decided to restore it. He had it cleared and cleaned, patched up with plaster and painted.

'Why does Junior have to be so aggressive about it?' said Ali.

'Yes. And so sanctimonious,' agreed Saira.

They worried about the trouble-stirring potential of the tomb, and their fears were borne out almost immediately.

The tomb was partly camouflaged and partly straddled by the Rajmahal wall. When Junior had the wall breached and extended into the next compound to clear space for it he made no reference to the neighbour who grew hot under the collar and demanded an explanation. Junior was slow to respond and the neighbouring landlord, a Hindu, erupted.

'These Muslim fellows are all the same! Are they still ruling the roost or what?'

Though he was out of the hearing of the house, the more conservative ghosts also made similar observations.

The neighbour gathered up his resources to stall this takeover of his property, just four square feet, and exhorted his supporters to knock down the extension. There was a confrontation and a skirmish, and Ali had to call in the police. The local magistrate persuaded the neighbour to allow the extension if a written request was made, eschewing legal ownership of that all-important four square feet and undertaking not to encroach further. Ali drafted the document himself, putting it on stamped paper and swearing it as an affidavit in a court of law. The merchant could hardly reject his venerable neighbour's circumspect gesture, and kept seethingly silent.

The tomb was identified with 'Tasleem Ahmed', the name decipherable in a faint inscription on the headstone. The 'pir' was added as an inspired afterthought. 'Pir' Tasleem Ahmed was endowed with a skeletal history after some stories were spread by locals, and Junior appointed the chowkidar of the Rajmahal as ex-officio tomb guardian. A brick godown, not far from the tomb, was put up at the corner of the drive for his dwelling.

Ali and Saira usually stayed away from the feast days invented by Junior for the Pir, citing the problem of the stairs. Junior would tighten his lips but keep his peace. His main objective was to highlight the little shrine and thus pre-empt the neighbour or his progeny in case they started getting ideas.

❧

The Mallik's middle son Mumtaz, Antonia's other victim, had come back to India permanently and joined one of the big companies. His new girlfriend, Lalitha, appeared on the scene, her deep lilting voice and bubbling laughter sending happy waves through the Rajmahal. The ghosts on the other hand were dismayed at this rank outsider becoming a part of the now prime family.

'First a Muslim landlord …,' said a narrow-minded ghost.

'And what's wrong with him?' interposed a more modern ghost.

'Nothing, nothing,' said the first narrow-minded ghost hastily. 'It's just that Junior of course!'

'But Ali Mallik is not Junior, is he?'

There was a pause, as by now, all the ghosts had become admirers of Ali's.

'Then Russian, British, and Anglo-Indian, and now a South Indian,' continued the narrow-minded ghost.

'I'm tired of discussing the same thing again and again. And if you object to Lalitha's darkness, half of Raja Sheetanath's family is …'

The conversation came to an abrupt halt as the ghost of Raja Sheetanath's mother came in, her inquisitive nose quivering expectantly.

When Mumtaz decided to marry Lalitha, a Hindu, and that too from the South, there was also a general turmoil within the Mallik breasts. Ali Mallik wondered why Mumtaz hadn't veered towards Surjeet Shona after his break with the satanic red-haired Antonia. What was wrong with this beauty from the other corner of India, this fair-skinned, straight-haired, long-nosed, Northern-eastern version as against the dusky, curly-haired, large-eyed southern one? Would he, Ali, have preferred that? But Surjeet Shona wasn't Muslim either, was she? One wasn't quite sure what she was! The contrast was highlighted when Lalitha became friendly with Surjeet Shona and they were often seen together. Why had Mumtaz switched from white Antonia to this other extreme when he could have fallen back, right here outside his front door, for the charms of someone more intermediate? He came to the same conclusion as Surjeet Shona about the inexplicable nature of attraction and desire.

Junior Mallik, the only one to express himself, had endless squabbles not only with his father, but bitterly with Mumtaz, the 'misguided' bridegroom-to-be. He tended to act as if Lalitha didn't exist. Can't you at least *greet* 'Litha?' said Mumtaz bluntly. 'It's uncivilized!'

The situation was made more poignant by the fact that this Lalitha was stunning, her sultry charms enhanced by the red bindi between her eyebrows and the flowers nestling in her mane of hair. She wore no make-up but her enormous black eyes and clear lips needed no artifice. Mumtaz burnt with a feverish lust at the very thought of her. Religion, thanks to his parents' vagueness, hardly impinged on his thoughts and actions, except remotely at Eid, when he joined the family celebrations.

'Tell me,' Mumtaz repeated. 'Go on. Why can't you greet 'Litha?'

'You know bloody well why not!' said Junior vehemently.

'No. I bloody well don't!' said Mumtaz as vehemently.

'How can you marry a kaafir, a Hindu and of all things, a South Indian?'

'Kaafir!' raged Mumtaz. 'What the hell sort of word is that? Does one actually use such words?'

'Well, can't she, is she going to become a Muslim, change her name? Why doesn't she do that, then there won't be such a problem.'

'And what exactly is the problem? Besides, if she changes her religion or her name, she'll still be a South Indian won't she, Keralite to be exact!'

'Bas, bas,' said Ali Mallik, looking up from the newspaper he hadn't been reading. 'There's no need to argue. Listen Junior. Mumtaz has decided to marry Lalitha. It's his choice just as Nadira was yours, and she is a perfectly civilized, decent girl, and I have no objection. So let's leave it at that!'

'But the *family* proposed Nadira for me!' protested Junior. 'I followed the custom by marrying her!'

'It was *your* choice,' insisted Ali Mallik. '*You* wanted to follow the custom, didn't you? We didn't force you …'

'And have you forgotten how many Hindu friends we have, and Christian friends and Parsi friends, and Brahmo and Sikh … all "kaafirs", including SS, hello SS, who's right here in the room with us!' burst out Mumtaz. Surjeet Shona had just walked in.

'Dad. Tell me,' said Junior heatedly, completely ignoring Surjeet Shona. 'Has any Mallik ever married a Hindu?'

'No. But Khalid married a French woman. You know that.'

'That's different,' said Junior.

'Oh really?' sneered Mumtaz. 'That's different is it? Why? Because she's white? Because she isn't a dark-skinned beauty from the South of your own country but an ugly pink Medusa from the styx of outer Paris?'

Surjeet Shona was trying to greet everyone normally in this storm, when Saira Mallik came in through the front door.

'Hello SS. What's the fight about, darlings? Don't you know everyone can hear you, right down to the ground floor?' she exaggerated.

'But she became a Muslim!' said Junior, ignoring his mother as well. 'I wouldn't have minded if you'd married Antonia … She had class!'

Everyone flinched.

'Unbelievable,' thought Ali, catching Saira's eye. 'Junior is unbelievable!'

Surjeet Shona was intently examining a book and Ali kept quiet remembering his relief when Mumtaz had broken off with Antonia. Mumtaz, though as sensitive to the crass reference, was more inflamed by the transferred insult to Lalitha. 'Class! Well let me tell you … 'Litha doesn't have a pink face. But by God, she has class compared to anyone … And, and, if Antonia isn't a, what did you call it, "kaafir", who the hell is?'

'She would have converted like a shot!' said Junior with a wild surmise.

Mumtaz glanced at Surjeet Shona, aware that everyone in the room except Junior was feeling embarrassed.

'I'll come again,' she murmured. 'I have to …'

'Don't be silly, SS,' said Saira. 'You're supposed to have lunch with us. And I don't know why Lalitha's so late …' She looked pointedly at Junior who had finally woken up to his faux pas. In his abrupt way he wheeled and left the room, just as Lalitha walked in perkily saying, 'Hello everyone! Sorry I'm late!' Junior brushed by her muttering 'Hello!' for a change.

Mumtaz smiled delightedly, as he always did when Lalitha was there, and his attention unreservedly locked on his fiancée.

Saira was distressed. Deep inside her she was unhappy that Mumtaz had decided to marry a South Indian girl. The Hindu part was peripheral, almost to be expected. But she didn't tell any of this to Ali. Saira was aware of the dichotomy and knew they would have to put a lid on it. Both were unfamiliar with Keralites, and had to force themselves to see Lalitha's beauty through the screen of her dark skin. But both were also truly eclectic, and their minds made them surmount the vestigial conditioning. To get out of the rut of marrying cousins gave the whole thing an air of novelty, they consoled themselves. Ali converted his distaste at having to face his harder line relatives into a challenging confrontation.

Saira adored all three of her sons. 'You'll live in the Rajmahal, won't you?' she said hopefully to Mumtaz.

Mumtaz was silent. He didn't fancy living so close to his parents with the foul Junior breathing down his neck and criticizing Lalitha for every misperceived difference. Industry was subsiding in West Bengal and his company had transferred its head offices to Delhi. Most conservatives saw this as the deterioration, the beginning of the end of Calcutta.

Mumtaz married his Keralite Lalitha at a simple civil ceremony thinly attended by members of both families, and the pair went away to Madras. From Madras Mumtaz was transferred to Bombay and later Delhi, but never to Calcutta. There were no tangible problems to the immediate family from this marriage. Ali Mallik found Lalitha's parents courteous and he was grateful they were distant. Junior managed to keep the minimum decorum in their presence though he was never able to look Lalitha in the eye, and rumblings from the rest of the clan were ignored.

Politically, there was a series of coalition experiments in other States, a lean majority for the Congress at the Centre, and a shifting and settling movement in the body politic of the country which would take place with greater frequency as colonial rule receded behind two decades of semi-euphoric socialism and the passing of two idealistic prime ministers. This would affect not only the country as a whole, but many individuals, families and societies, not least the Malliks. Their Muslim and Indian identities would come under scrutiny and they would continue to be affected by the Hindu-Muslim relationship. And they would see painful bloodshed as if some inexplicably vengeful satyr was sitting on their shoulders saying, 'So! You thought you could ignore all this, did you?'

The satyr was at work when Ali Mallik looked out of his chamber window one ordinary day and saw, as in a dream, a man running down the centre of the deserted street with a knife in his back. Ali shivered as he watched the man being picked up by a passing police van. But for the life of him, he couldn't remember whether the man wore lungi and skull-cap and was bearded or whether he wore dhuti-Punjabi, or whether he wore a neutral shirt and trousers. All he could see in his mind was that knife handle jutting brutally out of the screaming man's back and not a drop of blood. Where had the blood gone? Had it spread down the skin of the man's back, slowly staining his clothes from within, or was he haemorrhaging internally? Did he die in the end? Did the police help him or harass him? Each time Ali remembered, he cursed his friend Jinnah, for he very simply believed he was the sole cause for the break-up of the country and the deeper rift within India between the two communities. Almost till the end of his life, Ali Mallik convinced himself there would be a reconciliation. Though Pakistan may never rejoin India, there would surely be a stop to the hostilities between Hindus and Muslims, Pakistan and India. An atrocity against oneself or one's family, surely, should not in the end affect rationality for all eternity. He hadn't deduced, from the break-up of Pakistan and the creation of Bangladesh, that there was scant hope when even the so-called natural unity of subcontinental Muslims was so misperceived. But nor had he ever contemplated going over to Pakistan, though Jinnah had offered him high office. The two broke off their connection for the short remnant of Jinnah's life. And Ali had his law practice which rarely brought him face-to-face with these other, could they be called larger? issues. That almost forgotten routine of a Hindu-Muslim disturbance, a blip, confused and saddened Ali Mallik. Such things had diminished in West Bengal, seeming to justify the claim of some that the divisive hype was manipulated rather than being a true hatred of man for man. Whether this claim was correct or not would be forever without answer, leaving poor well-meaning Ali Mallik forever confused. The leftist predominance in West Bengal politics ushered in more a period of conflict between left, extreme left, idealism, capitalism, intellectualism and revolt than between traditionally clashing communities. But the blip happened and became a tattoo beating in Ali Mallik's head, like a tinnitus of the ear. Man-with-knife-in-back, no blood, picked up by police van, whisked off to unknown terrors, tortures, or revival and freedom, who knew? Why was Ali so sure, instinctively, that it was a Hindu-Muslim matter? He would never find out, no one he talked to knew anything of it. Ali's newspaper, *The Statesman*, a respected paper in impeccable English, said nothing. If Ali had thought to ask his clerks, he might have been shown a small paragraph on page four of a Bengali newspaper, thus clarifying for himself it had been a reality, and the result of a Hindu-Muslim clash, that the man with the knife in his back had been a Muslim, that the police had taken him to hospital, where he had soon died. What the paper neither reported later, and what Ali Mallik never would have learned, was that there was propaganda about the incident across the border in East Pakistan which whipped up little twisters of violence. A retaliatory Hindu killing in Jessore, counter-retaliation in Agartala, and if tracked further more and more retaliations till the original little incident was obliterated, the immediate cause changed each time, and the twisters, if they had been combined, would have formed a whiplashing tornado of untold destructive capacity. Greedily such particles are swallowed for nourishment as the twisters grow, criss-crossing swiftly, furtively and fragmented about the land, an unpredictable concourse of whiplashes. Till one day, they combine to cause one of the cataclysms that milestone history.

❧

There was a Hindi play, *Who Am I?* Petrov had said to Martin Strachey once. He was trying to explain the days before Partition, when the theatre world was carrying out its job of mirroring the times. 'A man is attacked and wounded in the riots and cannot remember thereafter whether he is a Hindu or a Muslim … So the protagonist is taken in by a Hindu family and his wounds are tended to. When he gets well, he remembers who, or rather, what, he is, but he will not tell.'

'What about Ali Mallik's story?' said Jack Strachey. 'He saw a man with a knife in his back once, running down the street. He can't remember if the man was a Hindu or a Muslim …'

'But his dress would have shown …'

'Yes, but Ali cannot remember!'

'Maybe he doesn't want to remember …'

'The name Mallik is as ambiguous. It could be either Hindu or Muslim!'

Ali's man with the knife would always trouble him. Visions haemorrhaged inside him, spreading poisons. 'Be exorcised!' he commanded, desperately. But the man would taunt him forever, sartorially indeterminate, sometimes even naked, white and veinless, with the knife handle sticking out neatly between his shoulder blades and not a drop of blood. It wasn't that Ali's imagination couldn't stand the notion of blood. During early days, he had practiced as a criminal lawyer, and seen enough when he was involved with clients at the sordid end of life. But this bloodlessness was closely associated with the latent poison of prejudice, haemorrhaging, finally to kill, sprouting a knife out of the back.

❧

Fayyaz, the youngest Mallik son, was disinclined to take up a normal career. From his college days spent in India, rather than abroad like his brothers, he had been drawn to the Communist movement with which the city was identified. This had been partly inspired by Petrov who lived a floor below. Petrov's stories had lain dormant in Fayyaz till he reached his teens and gone to university, where he had again been thrilled to hear and read of the Revolution. Convinced it was the most glorious happening known to humankind, he idealized and eulogized everything about it, like his comrade-students, and joined the Communist Union. By the time the party had come into its own, he had become a cadre member. As a result of his dedication he didn't marry, though there were some fiery young girls in the movement with him. He had liaisons, self-conscious attempts at revolutionary behaviour. But in the end, he righted himself to an extent and lived with a plain girl from a lower class background. Poor Saira had to recognize that her youngest was way out of reach, though she kept on hoping. She eagerly offered him one of the flats when it was vacated. But Fayyaz preferred to head for the Mecca of communists, Moscow, and when that love story ended, to a tenement in the old Black Town. Saira and Ali were blessed with wealth and status strengthened by Ali's eminence as a barrister and an ideally happy marriage.

'It must be the rough justice of fate that they should suffer through their children,' thought the Rajmahal.

9

Surjeet Shona Goes on a Journey

The Raj Mahal was to witness another marriage soon. Neel Banerjea, who had caused Surjeet Shona so much confusion at their first meeting, was to become a regular visitor. And she would go shining-eyed, and paradoxically, blindly, into her next love affair, putting aside all her fears. She would spend a blissful period during which she would pledge her life to Neel, and she would marry him unhesitatingly within a year in spite of her little son's truculent behaviour.

'Hate Neel Uncle!' Gurdeep, not yet four, spat out once, surprisingly forceful for his size. Surjeet Shona put her hand over his mouth to shush him. Neel was at the door and could have heard.

The wedding was quiet, soon after and similar to Mumtaz Mallik's, but Surjeet Shona felt she was the luckiest and happiest of women. Such a man to make her life whole. She was echoed in this by some of the Bengali ghosts who were relieved to at last have the approved Bengali caste represented in their midst. But others, including the mansion, refrained from hoping for too much.

The first current between the two newly marrieds had transformed itself into an electrical eroticism. At night, the contrast in colour between them was sharpened, when dark bodies became darker and light skins caught whatever little sparkles remained in the air. So Neel's muscled body, with a fusion of hair nestling in his chest, became mysteriously black and Surjeet Shona's glowed like a moonbeam. After the magic of their incoherent love-making, she would lie with her body aligned to his and adore this play of shadow and light. Then she would gaze at Neel's profile in the dimness of the night, at the lashes lying on his cheeks, his lips, his sharp nose, as it moved slightly with his sleeping breath.

The indulgence was mutual and whenever Neel looked at Surjeet Shona his heart would almost stop. In the morning he would hungrily take in her unconscious form, sprawled, abandoned on the bed, the proportions perfect whatever the angle, the hair and face ravishing whatever the state. He would lightly trace his fingers along the body and wait for Surjeet Shona's slow awakening, the response in her eyes.

Completely absorbed in her husband, Surjeet Shona gave up her job at Sharp's to devote herself to Neel's work with adivasis. Neel fooled himself he could 'make up' for the loss in her income. But Surjeet Shona was financially independent, the job was irrelevant and Neel's habit of pushing himself away from organized employment, carrying on with intermittent patronage from the government and others, kept him forever short of funds. Surjeet Shona, who could easily afford any extravagance, quickly learned to be circumspect, though she was the one who paid the bills. She was sensitive to Neel's feeling of inadequacy as 'the man', but the contradiction of his intelligence and this attitude baffled her. To her, their beautifully interwoven lives made nonsense of formality and she rejected Neel's bad-natured outbursts.

'Everything of mine is yours,' she said, with such utter and innocent conviction that Neel was disarmed. The situation galled him though, and he would never try to rationalize his reactions.

In the meantime, Surjeet Shona accompanied Neel on his field trips eagerly, putting up with the discomfort of living in minimal camps and dak bungalows, too awed by the elemental beauty and pathos of the setting and its denizens, and the early attentions of her intensely romantic lover-husband.

But the tally of contradictions increased. At the very start, Surjeet Shona strongly resisted shifting to Neel's small flat near the Lakes.

'You've always complained about your flat. It makes no sense to stay on! There's so much space here. And I've had shelves made for your books.'

'But I like living near the Lakes. All my friends are there!'

'You can make friends here too. There are the Mojumdars and Malliks. And how can you forget the Petrovs!'

'Petrov is a white man!'

'A white man! He's hardly a "white man" in that sense.'

'Maybe! But the others are! White or brown they are all sahibs!'

Surjeet Shona refused to be hurt and burst into peals of laughter. 'I'll make you into one yet,' she joked. 'Wait and see.'

Neel muttered to himself. 'Don't grumble!' murmured Surjeet Shona, fondling her husband in her sweet besotted way. 'Do you know, you're the most sophisticated person in the Rajmahal!' Her reactions were similar each time the subject came up. How could Neel counter such persuasion?

He moved into the Rajmahal, embarrassed by his shabby suitcases and possessions, reluctantly transferring his precious books to the new bookshelves. And Surjeet Shona went into a frenzy, arranging his study and lovingly unpacking his few clothes into one of the big empty cupboards.

But at bottom, both knew Neel was more at home with his own, his professors and his adivasis, though he mingled peripherally and reluctantly with the cocktail crowd. In time, the fading culture of the Rajmahal and all that went with it, the wealth, the style became slights to his innermost self. And Surjeet Shona was well aware of the constriction he must feel after his earlier free and close-to-wild life. When the 'husband' swamped the 'lover', she wondered if this would have happened with Guru, if his death hadn't spared them. Other terrifying possibilities stemmed from Neel's open admiration for the adivasis, primarily the women, with their sensuous freedoms. She sensed this had everything to do with his work fixation.

A turning point was a trip into the neighbouring State of Bihar, to Neterhat, a small hill station in Chota Nagpur. Neel had a decrepit jeep which Surjeet Shona distrusted though by now she knew better than to say anything.

The Grand Trunk Road was a high point of the tour, and Surjeet Shona was lost for a time observing the life along the celebrated route. At the crossing over the Barakar River, which marked the Bihar-Bengal border, a cluster of elegant temple spires flashed by, rising from the dry river bed

'Neel, look! Let's stop. Please Neel!'

'Not now. We'll stop on the way back. Let's get on now!'

'They've been excavated from the river!' exclaimed Surjeet Shona, craning her neck to look back at the temples. But Neel didn't reply and, hurt at the snub, she stopped chattering.

Transferring her attention back to the window, she saw that the people looked different from the Bengalis they had left behind; the style of clothing, the language, it was almost like another country. The geography had changed too, from brilliant green fields arabesqued with white paddy birds to low tabletop hills and Sal forest. The common factor on both sides of the border was the blot of untidy industrialization, with collieries and factories grinding out smoke and other effluents. Neel had planned a stop for the night at Topchanchi, a lake and forest not far from the Grand Trunk Road. When they passed Parasvanath Hill with its white Jain temples shining on the summit, Neel put off another eager request from Surjeet Shona, promising they would climb up on the way back. At Topchanchi they drove into a romantic dak bungalow surrounded by hilly terrain, so close and yet so unconnected to the industrial wasteland. Thin scrub led into dense forest-covered hills, and the silence was pierced by the plaintive call of peacocks and distant roars. Surjeet Shona's senses tingled. This was tiger country! Driving around the lake in the late evening, she was imbued with a feeling of desolation sparked by a magical beatitude. But she didn't question the mysterious contradiction or its link to the remote quality of the place. Dusk followed by dark came too soon for them to sight a tiger, though they eagerly scanned the glowing green and yellow eyes shining in their headlights, sometimes halfway up a tree, sometimes deep inside the forest. The night buzzed with the sawing of crickets and they slept cradled together, in the light of glow-worms on a shrub outside their window. At dawn they went out to the lake again. The deer grazed peacefully, ignoring the low grumble of the jeep as it passed by, a group of wild boar rushed aslant into the trees and a sambar stared at them before belling loudly and turning away.

'A tiger, a tiger, Neel,' whispered Surjeet Shona. 'That's what I want to see. All this is so tame by comparison.'

'You'll see one today, Shona, I feel it in my bones,' Neel had barely whispered back when Surjeet Shona's heart lurched. In a pool of sunlight barely twenty yards in front of them, lay a huge tigress with two cubs tumbling around her.

Neel braked abruptly and the jeep stopped short with a squeak. The tigress blinked indifferently at them and once Surjeet Shona's breathing normalized, she cautiously raised her camera and kept clicking. They stayed half an hour while the cubs tumbled, licked occasionally by the powerful tongue of their mother. Then the great beast yawned releasing a fearful sound, stretched and shepherded her awkwardly new cubs to the water's edge, and as suddenly as a dream, they melted into the wall of the forest. Surjeet Shona, stiff and baked in the heat and filled with bliss, hugged Neel exuberantly.

They left Topchanchi early on the long journey to Neterhat, through dry scrubland, the burnt grass covering giving it a charcoal tinge and scrunching underfoot when they walked out to ease themselves. The pristine silence of the countryside was only disturbed by the liquid ringing of wooden cow bells, a sound that became irresistible to Surjeet Shona. Craving to access it at will, she called to a boy ambling along with a herd, 'Come here! I want one of those bells!' She could feel Neel stiffening next to her, but her bliss gave her a sense of power. The herd flowed around them in a honeyed river of sound punctuated by bucolic mooing.

'A bell?' said the astonished boy. 'But this is for the cow. Why do you want it?'

Surjeet Shona's laughter mingled pleasantly with the bell-river. 'Oh but I have a cow too,' she said. 'And she has no bell. Come now. Give me one! I will pay you for it!'

The boy, in loincloth and torn vest, a ragged cloth around his head, with a bamboo flute tucked into it, obeyed Surjeet Shona. He took the money from her, his eyes popping at the ten rupee notes and after tying them carefully into the top of his loincloth, sleep-walked to a cow, untied its bell and handed it to Surjeet Shona. 'Take this for your cow,' he said. 'It is my best bell, from my best cow. Now I will have to make another one for her.' He fondled the white soft skin of his bell-less cow while Surjeet Shona looked at her trophy, a handsome prehistorically shaped wooden bell, painted with a crude design of blue flowers. She shook it jauntily and waved to the boy, who was scratching his head with his flute.

Neel's expression was an instant dash of cold water. She felt her joy draining out. No word was spoken, but the contempt of that expression filled her with a mixture of fear, contrition and sadness. She knew she had overstepped some invisible boundary, taking her leagues further from her husband. 'I have seven-league boots on these days,' she thought. 'And they have a life of their own.' Before Neel revved up the engine she could hear the other characteristically liquid sound of these country tracts. The boy was propped up under a tree, languidly playing his flute.

Surjeet Shona dozed off, lulled by the intermittent sound of the bell bumping up and down on her lap. When she awoke the disjunctive feeling had left her and she impulsively touched Neel on the shoulder.

'Don't you like it?' she shook the bell gently. 'The sound is almost ... noble.'

With an effort, Neel smiled, turned to Surjeet Shona and patted her cheek. 'Enjoy it, Shona. But what will you do now? Buy a cow for it?'

❧

They reached the unmetalled red earth ghat road to Neterhat in the late evening, when the sun was low on the horizon.

'It won't take long,' said Neel. 'Not more than an hour.'

As he spoke, the sky darkened and heavy drops of rain spattered the windscreen. Soon there was a downpour and the road had turned into a river of red slush. The poor light was no help with the jeep skidding at every turn. 'We must keep going,' said Neel, and as Surjeet Shona prayed, there was a sudden whump and they came to a standstill. The engine roared and whined and the wheels spun, but the jeep stayed obstinately stuck. Neel got out of the jeep. 'Put the gear into second,' he ordered. 'The first's slipping. And start the engine when I tell you!'

Surjeet Shona slid into the driver's seat and watched Neel dragging broken branches from the roadside and stacking them under the front wheels, getting more and more bedraggled in the rain and slush. He waved to her and stepped aside, 'Go!' he called. 'Second gear!'

The wheels spun crazily again, spraying Neel with mud, and pushing the jeep deeper down into the bog. Steam rose from the bonnet as Neel strained to wedge stones under the front wheels. Surjeet Shona tried again, and with an almighty jerk and the sound of snapping twigs, the jeep surged forward on to the firm concrete of a bridge.

'Well done,' said Neel. He took over the wheel but the road beyond was steeper and at a sharp hairpin bend the engine began an alarming knocking. Neel was forced to try the first gear, there was a grinding sound, and the engine stalled. Nothing would induce it to start again and they were stuck at a steep angle in the middle of the hairpin bend with the rain lashing relentlessly at them. The car rolled dangerously back to a flatter area. 'Pass me the water,' he said. 'The engine's boiling.'

Surjeet Shona took out a half-empty bottle of drinking water. 'That's all there is,' she said. 'We could let the rain cool the engine.' But perversely, just at that moment, the rain stopped.

Night had descended and Surjeet Shona stood by the bonnet with a torch in one hand, balancing the water bottle with the other. Taking off his shirt and using it to protect his hand, Neel heaved at the burning radiator cap. It came unstuck after a mighty struggle, releasing a vicious jet of boiling water. Neel's hand was in the way and the jet hit it, scalding him painfully. Surjeet Shona screamed and jumped to Neel's help, letting go of the water bottle which spilled into the red slush. 'Oh God! Now look what you've done!' groaned Neel.

Surjeet Shona ignored the jibe and helped him back into the jeep. 'We have to wait for the engine to cool,' she said. 'There's nothing else to do.' They waited for the engine to cool down while Surjeet Shona ministered to Neel, cosseting him like a baby, anointing his hand with cold cream and admiring his shining mud-streaked body.

Help finally came from a group of road workers on their way up to Neterhat. They had a canister of water with them and cautiously filled it into the half-empty radiator where it bubbled and cooled down. Their reward was a free drive up to their destination which was blessedly near.

The cowbell had been lost in the melée, but Surjeet Shona didn't care. It had brought them nothing but ill luck and spoiled the sweetness of Topchanchi.

The next day at dusk, she and Neel drove out over the open fields of the Neterhat plateau, a vast landscape bathed in the light of a brilliant sunset. Oraon girls walked and sang arm in arm in small groups, their broad cheek-boned faces bronzed by the light, their short saris freeing their legs for graceful skips. Neel, whose hand was only lightly burnt, pulled Surjeet Shona out of the jeep, and arm in arm, they danced with the adivasi girls. Surjeet Shona felt she could touch the painted sky if she stretched out her hand.

But that very night watching the full moon through the open window of their bedroom, she could see, among a ring of squatting villagers ranged in front of Neel, one beauty, heart-shaped face shining like all the others in the moonlight, looking directly at him. Laser rays streaked between their eyes. The girl's sari had fallen aside from her shoulder and her naked breast was round and full, calling to Surjeet Shona's husband.

A familiar pain manifested in the pit of her stomach. 'Guru's early death fooled me about the nature of marriage,' she thought. It was a pain based on a deep fear, a familiar circular fear which she recognized, and she knew she had to free herself from the ridiculous and recurring dilemmas, the enigmatic bonds which sprang up so frequently between Neel and these sumptuous women. She thought back with incredulity of the intimacy of the red, wet womb of the jeep when she had ministered with such love and hope to Neel's wounded hand.

Surjeet Shona said nothing when Parasvanath Hill followed by the Barakar temples flashed by on their way back. Reminding Neel of his earlier assurance to stop and explore would only irritate him.

As remorseless friction attached itself to time, the pattern of their intimacy changed. Neel continued to gaze at Surjeet Shona sprawled asleep on the bed, but he stopped touching her so as not to arouse her. He rejoiced when she moved and fell into a newly perfect pose, but the feast was purely visual.

Later, Surjeet Shona was to come into bitter confrontation with Neel over her son's elite education in a boarding school near Shimla.

'A brown sahib, is that what you want *my* son to be?'

'I want a proper education for Gurdeep, he's my son!'

'Am I not his father now?'

'You may be …'

'*May* be? When I married you for your beauty, I did not expect such betrayals …!'

'I'm not a pin-up!' screamed Surjeet Shona. 'And who are you to talk of betrayals?' she added.

'Why am I saying all this?' said a voice inside her. 'It's unforgivable, what I said is unforgivable! Can't I hear him calling Gurdeep his son …' Fear gripped her. She lost her balance whenever she came into conflict with Neel and he brought out the worst in her, she could see it.

'You think I have no say in Gurdeep's future, in his upbringing, is that what you're saying …?'

Surjeet Shona could only make a painful apology. 'Sorry, I'm sorry!'

This threw up currents and the ill-matched pair went through a short harmony. But deep inside, both knew the marriage was doomed.

Surjeet Shona gave up joining Neel on his field trips in the fifth year of their marriage. When he stayed away an unnecessarily long six months in the Northeast, she was ready for a divorce. 'He must have been a tribal in his last life,' she said cattily.

❧

Gurdeep, buffered by the vastness of the Indian plains in his eyrie of a boarding school, wouldn't mind she convinced herself. He didn't ask about his stepfather's whereabouts on his annual holiday and Surjeet Shona waited till he was about to leave before breaking the news to him.

'Really?' was his laconic response. And though Surjeet Shona tried to say more she cautiously stopped when she saw his lack of interest.

'He wasn't even startled,' she thought. 'It isn't surprising though. He hardly saw Neel after he was seven.' Appearances were deceptive as she found out later.

The divorce was hard on Surjeet Shona. Neel had adopted a studied politeness towards her, and though her parents and other Rajmahalians stood by her as they would always as long as they lived, the loss and loneliness were hers uniquely. She retreated into the Guru Granth Sahib room again to nurse herself, sorely hurt.

10

Gurdeep Grows Up

Surjeet Shona shunned her constant array of suitors, convinced no spark could ignite her again. Any thought of going back to the Sharp's job drained her of energy. She concentrated on Gurdeep, and examined the possibility of other occupations. She tried painting, went riding, avoided parties and read voraciously. But there were terrible empty spaces when the book held in her hands would blur and thoughts of the failed marriage and loss of Neel would invade her like an attacking horde. When she slept her dreams were filled with the theme of Neel's betrayals. Those were the times she took refuge in the Guru Granth Sahib room, or more and more frequently, at the Petrovs' flat. Here, she allowed herself the dubious diversion of meeting people again.

When Doctor Ranji Talwar, a Calcutta consultant based in London's Harley Street, joined the queue of suitors, Surjeet Shona would eventually succumb. Much older, talked-of, the doctor courted Surjeet Shona aggressively, causing a flutter in their circles. She automatically resisted at first, but the doctor clothed his aggression in such gentle, adult and courteous attentions that his persistence paid. She toyed with the idea of moving to London with him, though she was still deeply wary of marriage. The house and ghosts were equally wary, but could do nothing when the doctor doubled his attentions as Surjeet Shona's resistance waned.

After several seasons Surjeet Shona found herself waiting expectantly for his next visit. She was nearly convinced he could provide her with the uxoriousness she craved. Eventually, she followed the doctor to London and moved in with him. Gurdeep would join them for the holidays, the arrangement seemed near perfect and Surjeet Shona settled tentatively into the business of housekeeping, taking pleasure in cooking for her attentive new lover. For a time she enjoyed the big city, the plays and concerts, the museums and parks, the bountiful shops. When she thought of it, she missed the rough exciting trips with Neel, dramatically at the other end of the scale, but she was determined not to allow herself any maudlin backslide over Neel himself, Neel the husband. She would take out her albums and look at the photographs, the tigress and her cubs, the young cowherd, the sunset over the Neterhat plateau. But when the photos of the Oraon women appeared she would feel an unpleasant heaviness. Then she would open up the albums with Gurdeep's pictures, their wedding, the motorcycle, and she would feel the same heaviness. There were no pictures of Martin to test herself with. 'That's the trouble,' she thought. 'There are parts of all of them I still feel for. At least. I think so. And I miss the Rajmahal.' She continued to avoid the idea of marrying Ranji even though she was at ease with him and enjoyed his mature, quiet company, even though he showed an unstrained affection for Gurdeep and the two seemed to get on well. But Surjeet Shona's mother's instincts wouldn't allow her a blind acceptance of Gurdeep's docility and she couldn't get over her uneasiness on this last score. And repeatedly, the heaviness would creep over her, mixed with a complete lack of anticipation. As if there was nothing left to be done. As if it were all over. There were no starbursts, no ecstasy. 'How far did all that take me anyway?' she consoled herself.

But the Ranji Talwar phase, too, was to end soon. The doctor would have looked after Surjeet Shona like a queen and indulged Gurdeep in every way, but he was work-conditioned long before the liaison. The demands of the taxing and specialized world of medicine with its frequent travel for conferences and seminars snatched away the advantages of eminence, and a heart attack killed him within two years of Surjeet Shona's move. She wasn't yet forty, and a twice-married woman, once widowed, once divorced, isolated yet again.

'There's some accursed fate chasing me,' she wept at the funeral. Gurdeep was with her, and though she held on to him she worried at his stoical behaviour. She was convinced the Rajmahal was her only faithful ally, her stability, and she went back bereaved a second time into its embrace. The house and the ghosts were overjoyed, but it was a dismal homecoming, and the charm of the Rajmahal failed to comfort Surjeet Shona this time around. Perversely, pictures of her life with the doctor kept interfering with her settling down and she was glad Gurdeep was out of this circle of gloom in his boarding school. But he was soon to become a difficult teenager and his visits home were filled with fractiousness and fights with his mother.

It was Ali Mallik who convinced Surjeet Shona that she should think of a change in the pattern. He knew of the difficulties with Gurdeep and saw Surjeet Shona wilting under the pressure.

'He misses a father,' she confided to him and Saira. 'I was sure I could deal with the problem, but it's gone out of my hands.'

'We had the same kind of trouble with Mumtaz,' said Ali. 'Although I was always here. Things normalized only when we sent him out to boarding school.'

'I didn't agree with Ali at first,' said Saira. 'I thought Mumtaz was going through the usual teenage problems. But it was the right thing, wasn't it? The boy's turned out a darling.'

'But Gurdeep's already in boarding school, a good boarding school. I sent him there because he didn't get on with Neel. Now he says he detests the place and can't wait to get out. And he says he hates Calcutta and the Rajmahal too. Sometimes I think he hates me!'

'It's the hormones,' said Saira.

'You have a brother in the US,' persisted Ali. 'Why don't you send him to school there. It might work. Try it out!'

The ghosts could come to no conclusion about the wisest course of action, and in their usual manner kept arguing in circles, while the house watched with impatience.

Gurdeep accepted the new move well and the relief of his agreeing with her for once readily convinced Surjeet Shona. She hoped her sibling would play the missing father role, and her sister-in-law would have to make up for her absence. There was also a twosome of cousins.

The arrangement worked well and this compensated partly for Surjeet Shona's loneliness and nagging feeling of guilt. She threw herself into activity and joined a group busy reviving traditional skills among silk weavers in the State. In time, the projects she started expanded successfully and she became fully absorbed in her work. She was drawn to other areas, and travelled all over the country. Some of the journeys would bring back the Neel period, and the contrast, without the old excitement, depressed her. But there was nothing to be done for it, and her work was her compensation. She joined the countrywide movement to keep traditional handicrafts alive and met powerful people involved in it. She became prominent in the field and was called to organize exhibitions and festivals abroad. Gurdeep continued to flourish in the States, and graduated to university. Surjeet Shona visited him often. But she could sense the underlying instability on his India visits, especially when the old hostility flared up as the visits extended. She tried her best, mixing these visits with travels and gatherings of Gurdeep's age group. But it was a losing battle. The ghosts, who were getting more and more disembodied and increasingly disinterested in the far away Gurdeep, were finding him a bit of a nuisance.

Surjeet Shona's worst fears were realized some years later when the Punjab cataclysm loomed and she learned that Gurdeep, now in his late teens, was involving himself with a separatist-funding group in the US, in complete sympathy with the demand for a Sikh homeland.

'You don't understand, Ma,' he said arrogantly. 'You have the taint of Bengali blood. You should hear the stories of discrimination against us poor Sikhs, then you may think again! I tell you, Khalistan's the only answer!'

'What taint? You have my Bengali blood too!' Surjeet Shona shouted back, during stormy conversations on the phone. 'What discrimination? What Khalistan?'

'Have you heard the Sikh jokes?'

'The Sikh jokes? You take them seriously? They're only jokes! I'm also Sikh and we tell the same jokes. We are proud of our sense of humour!'

'If I hear one more time that twelve o'clock has struck I will kill someone with my own hands!' stormed the boy. 'I tell you, Khalistan's the only answer!'

'Again Khalistan …!'

'I am what my Father was, Mother. I'm all Sikh! I'm ashamed of my Bengali blood! Have you forgotten the great Neel, your Bengali husband? Hindu bastard! And your other Hindu doctor!'

'Shut up! How dare you talk of them like that? Even if you didn't like Neel, Ranji was always so kind to you! I thought you liked him! And what is all this about Hindus?'

'They're all bastards I tell you!'

'How can you speak like that Gurdeep!' Surjeet Shona wept. 'Think of me at least! I'm your mother! You are all I have. And have you forgotten your grandmother?' She could hardly believe what she was hearing.

After a short pause, Gurdeep banged down the phone. But Surjeet Shona couldn't accept this without a fight, and immediately called back. She calmed down to an extent when her brother spoke to her instead of Gurdeep. 'Leave him to me, SS. Remember we love him. The other kids are here too. We are doing our best.'

But she couldn't help fretting. 'Is that same fate chasing my son too?' she worried.

When the Golden Temple was stormed and the bloodbath between militant Sikhs and the army turned the pool of nectar crimson, the tearing inside her astonished her. The Sikh ghosts were too agitated to see sense, and the other ghosts and the house could do nothing to calm them.

'I didn't know my Sikhness was so much in my gut! What's happening? What happened to Ma's side of things?' thought Surjeet Shona.

She couldn't stop the wrenching inside her, the feeling that the world was slipping away while the unperceived ghoul chortled and danced over a pool of blood. Visions flickered behind her eyelids when she slept and she woke up with starts, seeing Gurdeep sinking in that crimson pool with a kirpan in his raised hand. In a frenzy she booked a flight to New York, yet realized its futility even as she and Gurdeep continued their violent confrontation face-to-face. She came back after being assured by her brother that Gurdeep would get over it, but her crisis continued. She walked compulsively up and down the verandah with surges of revulsion going through her. Thoughts of the endless and ruthless militant killings preceding the excoriating attack on the Holy of Holies exploded inside her like her fists on the furniture and walls. Her mind went through re-runs of her love life. 'Doomed or disastrous,' she would moan. 'Nothing in between!' Sometimes the inner violence would recede and she would dwell on her Bengali family's history, on its swadeshi activity a century ago. Raja Sheetanath's involvement in setting up a National Bengali College, in organizing a mela for the sale of purely Indian goods and the fiery speeches he made in the countryside to arouse the villagers of Bengal to their heritage. 'How can I tear myself away from this fabulous history?' she would think. 'How can I separate my Sikhness from my Hinduness or my Brahmo Bengaliness or my Indianness? How can Gurdeep lose all that to narrow himself down to only one of them?' She was split, like her name was split sometimes. 'Split-reduced, down-scaled,' she thought, to 'Shona', the Bengali component of her name by Neel, and 'Surjeet', the Punjabi component by Ranji Talwar, to 'Shona-Baby' by the Bengali servants, and 'Surjeet-ji' by the Bhaiji. 'What should I, as a hybrid, then do?' she had asked Petrov long ago. And he had answered, 'Nothing, dear child, nothing. You are an important manifestation of what will inevitably happen after a hundred years, when every Indian is a hybrid like you and all the cultures fade out, and the not-this-not-that hybrid shines out like an arc lamp!'

This was one of the few times the ghost of the great Sardar Bahadur came over to visit his 'fifth rung', dragged by Inderjeet Kaur.

'You have to come!' she implored. 'I told you this mixing with Hindus would create trouble. As if she hasn't suffered enough already!'

'At that time you spoke of Bengalis, not Hindus. But yes, it is terrible what has been done to the Golden Temple and to us, shameful and terrible!'

'What she needs is a good loving caring Sikh husband!'

Inderjeet Kaur's ghost had forgotten her husband's version of 'loving caring' for the moment.

They hovered anxiously over Surjeet Shona, trying their best to caste soothing emanations over her. After a time, the Sardar Bahadur's ghost was impatient to get back to the Golden Temple. '"I-Say"! It is a matter of patience and time! What is the point of our hanging on here? It will blow over.' And seeing Surjeet Shona calming down he managed to persuade his wife's ghost to go wafting back to Amritsar with him.

But scant months later, after Prime Minister Indira Gandhi's assassination by her Sikh bodyguards, and the bloody reprisals against Sikhs in Delhi, even the Sardar Bahadur's ghost was disturbed.

'"Are-You-Listening"? Is this your blowing over?' said his violently agitated wife's ghost. 'You call this a blowing over?'

Surjeet Shona was frantically worried about her parents, who were in Delhi. She took the first flight out to find them sheltering in a Sheetanath relative's house.

The ancestor-ghosts who had hurried to Delhi subsided with relief. 'And who is giving them shelter for the present, tell me. "I-Say", tell me. Who?'

'I agree it is the Bengali side …'

'Not the Hindu side …?'

'But …'

'But what? Aren't they also part of our Surjeet Shona's blood …? Anyway, her father is there. What can you and I, poor ghosts, do for the child compared to a good, strong living Ohri?'

Gurdeep broke all communication with his mother, and Surjeet Shona had to get news of him through her brother. She heard that his soft young beard grew fiercer by the day, that he wore a saffron turban and attended Sikh gatherings with a kirpan slung over his shoulder, that he made heroic speeches. But she also found herself able to take stock.

Mumtaz Mallik was stationed in Delhi and spending time with him and his wife, Lalitha, her old Rajmahal friends and with her parents, she could find her bearings again.

'Tell me,' she queried, 'if it isn't better to have this richness of parts, this, this …' She was trying to put into words her dread of losing even a bit of her heritage and, with it, her son.

Mumtaz interrupted her. 'SS,' he said sympathetically. 'Your Sikh side must be in agony. And your feelings as a mother. But in the end, we know, all of us hybrids or non-believers if you like …'

'Non-believer in what?' interrupted Satinder, Surjeet Shona's father. 'I belong to a single, strong culture, and I married outside it. But I am a believer in my religion after all, and the storming of the Temple is deeply hurtful to me …'

'To me too,' said Surjeet Shona, surprising herself.

'Isn't that beside the point?' said her mother. 'What my daughter is saying is so clear to me.'

'The richness, none of the threads of the weave that makes us up, none, should be lost!' said Mumtaz with vehemence. 'Do you realize you are not only talking of us, more importantly, our children, but of our whole society …'

'I remember Uncle Osheem saying that we hybrids were "not-this-not-that", but what you've said is just the opposite …'

'Yes! We are both-this-and-that! We are all of it!'

'And my son, my son, what do I do about that?' Surjeet Shona thought.

But this wasn't the only time they had such discussions, and Surjeet Shona felt if she hadn't been able to restore herself in the comfortable downy basket of this drawing-room eclecticism, this active membership of the chattering classes, she could have lost her mind. 'I have this tendency to go berserk,' she thought.

She would only later come across Petrov's extended jottings on his 'hybrid' theory, his reverse-view on the 'inevitable and total miscegenation' of the subcontinent. The multifarious cultures will never lose their deep roots, he wrote now. Though they may shift and change and even cheapen. This will mean a loss in another direction, that is all too clear. It will mean the continued acceptance of imbalances. If the sheltered fortresses of the communities are infiltrated, it will be seen that they are never irrevocably breached, even if trapdoors are forced open or drawbridges let down for a moment. In this country, the unique bastion of a thriving, kicking archaic religion, and by 'archaic' I do not mean 'outdated' but 'ancient, original, aadi', it is unlikely even with all the forces of uniformization, hamburgarization, and globalization that a weakening will take place. Only a few flashes, only a top dressing of hybrids, sometimes more, sometimes less, but never enough for a final mix-up …

When she returned to Calcutta, the other Rajmahal families took over the therapeutic role. 'Don't worry, dear SS. Gurdeep will come back to you.' And using the same words as the Sardar Bahadur Ohri's ghost, they would say, 'It will blow over.' Behind their solicitude was the background of Surjeet Shona's cratered life, with which they were all familiar and the anxiety and puzzlement of the mansion.

In time, as the separatist movement subsided in an uncomfortable trail of violence and the uncertainty receded, Gurdeep allowed Surjeet Shona communication rights again. The next step was his return to his normal student life. Surjeet Shona kept her fingers crossed when he at last came home on a visit and talked of his studies and girlfriends like a normal person of his age. He laughed away his earlier madness as a phase, at the same time justifying it as caused by extreme provocation. 'But I can balance things in my mind now, Mother. I'm sorry. I know what you have been through.' When he hugged her Surjeet Shona couldn't stop her tears of relief. Gurdeep had taken a quantum leap into adulthood.

When he became a proper adult, he allowed his elitist upbringing to come home and married a WASP from Seattle. Surjeet Shona went to the US for a prolonged stay to join the flurry of a normal wedding, brushing aside concerns that a further hybridization had taken place. The reconciliation was complete and Gurdeep was back on course. With a wife and family responsibilities it would be difficult for him to lurch out so wildly again.

11

Ali Mallik's New Formula

The Malliks were growing old. And reluctantly, Ali Mallik found himself turning his gaze on himself and Saira, reluctantly because he was afraid to invite bad luck. Saira, his wife since the beginning of time and in at least the last six lives. Saira of the unsurpassable tall nobility, nose stone nestling by nostril, cigarette quivering in jet holder, gliding and swishing in exquisite saris… Perhaps that is what one always searched for, the other, the missing half. Were they lucky, the tender-hearted Saira and himself? Was he lucky, once he had her, not to have found it necessary to go on that restless search? Was that the ruby in the serpent's head, the nectar in the ocean of milk? Were they especially blessed, especially evolved, approaching nirvana? As if to mock at him, the man with the knife appeared again, and he was a wooden doll, with a key in his back instead of a knife, a wind-up toy walking stiffly down the road, trying to run beyond his mechanism's scope, and falling flat on his face just before the van reached him and swooped him up with a vice. 'Bleeding Hindus!' imploded the haemorrhaging Ali, realizing that nirvana would recede for the next twenty lives for the expression of that sentiment alone. 'Nirvana!' he scoffed. 'Me a Muslim and thinking of nirvana and past and future lives!' He worried again about the unexpected prejudices manifesting in him unannounced these days. How shaming if he couldn't one day stop himself from saying such things out loud? Where did they come from? Was it all a reaction to the Hindus' barely-concealed contempt for Muslims? Or was it himself, conditioned deep down by the violence of Partition, by the slaughter of one branch of the family, by overheard sentiments expressed by aunts and uncles, or by the post-conversion generations of his family? What had motivated the first convert to make such a big change? Was it conviction, based on true faith? Or was it greed, gain, sycophancy while the Muslim dynasties ruled, what? He wished he could get into the head of that first convert and re-live his life within him to find out …

Why, for instance, had he married Saira? Had he fallen in love immediately she was presented to him by his parents? Did he even faintly consider marrying a non-Muslim, a Hindu, for instance? Why did he always find himself appointing Muslim employees in the Rajmahal? His drivers, house servants, guards, watchmen were all Muslims, so far. Surely, it wasn't intentional. Wasn't it that word of such vacancies with a Muslim employer would circulate swiftly, engendering a rush from his community? So many would come flocking that Ali could scarcely blink before he had appointed one of them. Was that discrimination? Should he have done them the injustice of disqualifying them *because* they were Muslim? And should he then employ only Hindus, or reserve a certain percentage of jobs for them? Or make it strictly fifty-fifty?

Jainab was one of the earliest Mallik employees to join the Rajmahal, starting as odd-job boy and graduating later to the position of lobby guard. He was a stripling of fifteen when he came, but limited to a single seeing eye. In the socket of the other eye, lost through his parents' neglect of an infection, was a glass eye which he kept popping in and out of its socket, re-infecting himself periodically. Jainab spent much of his time lolling in a corner of the Malliks' inner verandah where he was sent to cut vegetables when he first started out. This was where Junior and Mumtaz, just five and two at the time, came on him.

'Who are you?' demanded Junior proudly. 'Beggars are not allowed in this house!'

Jainab was dressed in a frayed vest and torn pair of pyjamas though the Malliks would soon re-clothe him in some style.

'What beggar? I am cook's help!' said Jainab, equally proudly. 'Who may you be?'

'The owner's *eldest* son, who else? Everyone knows!'

Jainab crooked his finger at the pestilential child. To get him on his side was an automatic necessity.

'Come here!' he said. He reached out and caught hold of Junior's arm in a strong grip.

'Know what I am?' he whispered.

'Cook's help! You said so yourself!'

'That is just in name. Know what I am really? Know what is a magician?'

Junior swallowed. He had seen a magician once at a birthday party, putting swords through people and pulling rabbits and pigeons out of a hat.

'Magicians are not so dirty!'

'Beware! I am in disguise.'

'Show me your magic then!'

'Oh it is no big thing!'

'You are in my father's house! Show me! Now!'

Jainab lazily focused back on Junior and sighed. 'All right, small one. If you say so! Look here …' He passed a hand in front of his face, and his eye fell dramatically into his palm.

Junior backed away, staring at the small globe in Jainab's hand, the screwed up and reddened crater of his eye socket. Then he turned and ran while Mumtaz gurgled, undismayed but interested, to watch as Jainab's eye re-appeared magically in its socket. Over the years, Jainab would intrigue the children of the Rajmahal with this amateurish sleight of hand and other tricks, and the children would scream and scatter each time the glistening egg of his eye fell out. As time passed and Jainab's teeth were replaced by shining dentures, it was but natural that he should gurgitate and chase succeeding generations of Rajmahal children with his clacking dentures. When he was made a lobby guard it was added magic time for the children. The Rajmahal, which had been startled at first by the eye trick, looked on benevolently at these harmless jinks. It didn't know the egg resemblance would be drawn to its logical end at a much later date.

❧

Ali finally arrived at a solution to his dilemma, which was to appoint a Hindu every time a Muslim vacated a post, and vice versa. He didn't realize a feeling of insecurity would spread among the existing Muslim employees as they were replaced one by one. They saw their elder master as not only a betrayer of their community, but of going dangerously soft in the head. Jainab was by then the seniormost among them and their leader. Early on, he had managed to inveigle Ali into appointing a number of his relatives and friends and in time, had become the sole arbiter of employment in the Rajmahal. Naturally, he charged a fee for his good offices. This not only gave him his pre-eminent position in the house, but added substantially to his income. Ali's new formula meant an erosion of all this and Jainab felt denied and resentful. His loyalty to his masters stopped him from drastic action, and he watched the change with frustration.

The resentment mounted when the Rajmahal's Muslim chowkidar retired. Ali kept to his formula, and appointed a Hindu in his place, Vir Singh Rawat. Against the angry exhortations of Junior and the pleadings of Jainab, he specifically included the care of Pir Tasleem Ahmed's tomb among Rawat's duties. He was inspired by another tomb he had seen in the Punjab, outside a small town, Batala, the tomb of the one locally and lovingly known as 'Baba'. Before Partition, the Baba's devotees had been Muslims, Hindus and Sikhs. After Partition only Hindus and Sikhs remained, yet they continued to venerate the Muslim tomb, their devotions intensifying each time they had a sighting of the ghost of the Baba. And the caretaker was a Hindu. Ali couldn't know that the Baba's ghost occasionally came thundering across the country on horseback, over the rivers and plains, to honour Pir Tasleem Ahmed on his feast day, and that he was especially pleased to find a Hindu chowkidar, just as his tomb was cared for by a Hindu. The Baba's voice had gone unheard at Partition, and Pir Tasleem Ahmed's voice too would go unheard one day at the Rajmahal tomb.

Junior suggested the indirect method to Jainab, advising him to approach Saira, who had a soft corner for the amateur magician.

'I have something to say to you, Memsahib,' said Jainab. 'Something of great significance.' It was lucky the ghosts had all disappeared by then. Working through the turmoil of sorting these forces out would have left them in too much confusion. The house had enough to deal with as it was.

'I have to go out,' said Saira, as if he hadn't spoken. She intuitively understood what was on his mind, and didn't want a confrontation.

'Memsahib!' called Jainab desperately, following her out of the room. 'How can you allow a kaafir Hindu to look after our Pir's tomb? Allah will never forgive such disrespect!'

Saira began coughing and walked hurriedly towards the front door calling, 'Come on Ali! We're getting late!'

When Ali appeared, Jainab retreated into familiar deportment, standing by and opening the door for them.

'Where to, Sahib?' he questioned, with the irritating curiosity of an old and familiar servant.

'None of your business!' snapped back the mistress of the house. 'You just tell khansama to get dinner ready!'

Quelled, Jainab popped his glass eye out of its socket.

'Again?' scolded Saira. 'How many times have I told you not to do that! Burbak!' she added fondly while Jainab flowered.

The Muslims of the Rajmahal felt a thinning of their skins. Not only were they about to be outnumbered in their own stronghold, but here was a Hindu appointed in the most prestigious Rajmahal post. 'Allah will never forgive us!' they echoed, ignoring the reasoning voices of Ali and Saira. When either said, 'Allah is Allah to everyone. Not just to Muslims.' Or, 'The Pir's tomb is revered by all, including Hindus,' their skins turned thick again, their brains cloudy. Among themselves they murmured and stirred. 'It is not right, not right. What will happen to us?'

Their unrest was justified. And Ali, the house, the Pir and the Baba of Batala, if not Allah Himself, would be deeply mortified that it was the controversial chowkidar, Vir Singh Rawat, who was to betray their faith.

❦

Rawat's dwelling had been shifted by Ali to a new room built on the roof of the garage to free the narrow approach, which was blocked by his earlier godown, inducing precipitous turns, noisy honking, gear scraping, shouting and backing. Rawat's room and toilet were especially large, and with an eye to added rent, Ali had built a row of smaller rooms and toilets for the chauffeurs alongside. Things went according to plan and Rawat unhesitatingly moved into his new room, which he felt matched his prestigious position, followed by the lesser chauffeurs. But here the plan was stalled. Rawat was jealous of his attributes to power, not only as caretaker of the Pir's tomb but as possessor of the godown, and he had no intention of letting go of it. He took good care to leave behind the grave cloths, lamps and other accessories of the tomb and before moving into his new room placed heavy padlocks on the godown and unattached community toilet. 'This godown is a part of the sacred trust of my Pir-ji,' he sanctimoniously intoned. 'And no one has need of the toilet now.' Mischievously, because there was one other user of the toilet, Surjeet Shona's Sikh priest, the Bhaiji.

The chowkidar was adamant when the Bhaiji asked for access and even Surjeet Shona's admonitions went unheeded. She was forced to seek redressal from Junior, since his father had gone into semi-retreat.

'It's plain jealousy,' she told him. 'Because Bhaiji also has a religious role. The poor man has to go all the way up to the roof!'

'Well why can't you give him one of your loos?' said Junior brusquely. 'You have five! If he can have a room here why can't he have a loo as well?'

'Come on, Junior. Do you want the chowkidar to get away with this? Is that what you really want?'

Reluctantly, recognizing the common ground against Rawat, and conquering his natural perverseness, Junior agreed to send for the cantankerous chowkidar.

Rawat appeared through the garden gate, a burly figure in khaki, his head shaved with a knotted tuft springing up from the crown.

'I didn't notice his tuft before!' whispered Surjeet Shona to Junior. 'He can't be a Brahman, can he?'

'How do I know?' shrugged Junior edgily.

Sudden loud singing from the prayer room forced Junior to shout. 'What is this I hear, Rawat? Who gave you permission to place a lock on the toilet? You must open it! At once!'

'But that is impossible, Sahib!'

Junior would never get used to Rawat's oily familiarity. He gripped his chair arms. 'Oh I see! So the toilet belongs to you, does it?'

Rawat sighed. 'For us Brahmans, Sahib, all this is very difficult. First of all, you must understand that I have still need of old toilet while on duty in grounds. Necessary cleaning is done of dirty place by sweeper. Next, water is thrown to purify of defilement of sweeper's presence. All the time it is seen that he touches nothing. Even lock, I alone can open … Only I can use, or, of course, some other fortunate Brahman.'

Unnoticed by them, the music had stopped and the Bhaiji stood bristling outside the prayer room.

'Lies! He is lying, Surjeet-ji! He is no Brahman!'

'Bhaiji!' said Surjeet Shona sternly. 'Kindly go in.'

'How he was using same toilet as us before?'

'Bhaiji, I will talk to you later. Please go. Go!' repeated Surjeet Shona as the Bhaiji resisted.

Looking back furiously at Rawat, the Bhaiji ducked into the prayer room, though it was obvious his ear quivered behind the curtain.

'I am being paid to act over religious shrine and there is no other course for me but to accede to noble caste. My thread ceremony has been performed and my head arranged accordingly,'

Rawat said proudly, pulling the thread out of his shirt and twirling his tuft about.

'Rawat …'

''Pandey'!' exclaimed the chowkidar promptly. 'As befits Brahman status, I have taken superior name of Pandey, Pandit Pandey! This has been done after due consecration at temple.'

'But you are a Rajput!' said Surjeet Shona. 'That itself is a noble caste, the caste of the maharajas. There is no provision for changing caste! And why do you want to become a cowardly Brahman when you are already a warrior!'

'It is my fate,' said Rawat-Pandey complacently.

'The rites you are performing are for a Muslim saint, and Muslims are not caste-ridden kaafirs,' sniped Junior.

'But I,' declaimed the chowkidar. 'I am Hindu!'

'All right, all right,' put in Surjeet Shona again. 'What about Bhaiji? He too does the work of God, so then, he too must be a Brahman …'

'But he is Sikh, how can he be Brahman?'

'The mullahs also do the work of God …'

'Memsahib!' chided Rawat, thoroughly exasperated. 'They are Muslims, what are you saying?'

'This grave is that of a Muslim too …,' tried Surjeet Shona again.

'Oof Memsahib! How many times must I repeat …,' Surjeet Shona burst into giggles, 'that I am Brahman, enjoined to do priestly work!' roared Rawat.

'Out! Get out! Leave! At once!' exploded Junior, not appreciating at all that Rawat-Pandey's Chanakyan moves conclusively proved that the qualities of the Brahman need no sanction of birth. Looking unnaturally pleased, the neo-Brahman strolled out.

Junior turned his ire on Surjeet Shona. 'Stop your bloody giggling, SS! I'll get that fucking Rawat. Brahman my ass!' And he stomped away.

Surjeet Shona's giggles died down, but they had failed to acknowledge the dangers lying just under the surface in her country. The Rajmahal tried invoking the Pir to help with wise counsel. But the laconic ghost refused to enter the controversy. 'It is enough that my resting place has been honoured. I do not ask for more, and certainly not for trouble …' Poor Ali had spawned a Frankenstein and the wily chowkidar was soon to get carried away by his holy role into uncharted terrain.

Junior continued in a stream of rage. He ordered his guards, including Jainab, to break the lock on the toilet. But Rawat-Pandey was no pushover and the unsuspecting Bhaiji found, the very next evening, that there was a heavy new padlock on the toilet which he had been uneasily using. He crept hastily back to Jainab to whisper, 'Did I not tell you? It is locked finally!'

'We must break it again,' said Jainab intrepidly. 'That is Junior master's order!'

The Bhaiji was hopping up and down with the unstoppable demands of nature. 'I must go upstairs. Urinating just now is essential!' He disappeared with a cross-legged gait.

But Rawat-Pandey had organized a gang to stand guard over the toilet and when Junior's lock-breakers arrived with their implements there was an ambush. The eruption of noise brought out some of the mansion's inhabitants, including Surjeet Shona and Junior. They bumped into the aged Bhaiji who had just reappeared, relieved in one sense. Surjeet Shona wondered at the ease with which the small dispute had entered into this arena of violent conflict.

'Why,' she shouted to Junior over the noise, 'why all this? Can't you settle it some other way?'

'Please use the roof as before, Bhaiji!' she called imperiously. 'What is the need for this tamasha after all these years?'

The Bhaiji mumbled incoherently, but Junior wasn't ready to withdraw. There was still the major obstacle of the godown and Rawat-Pandey's ouster, which would bring such relief, not only freeing the godown for destruction and releasing the toilet, but allowing his replacement by a proper Muslim chowkidar. The business of the toilet had brought that into perspective. 'Why did I let things slide for so long?' thought Junior. 'You don't expect me to let that fool bully me, do you?' he sneered to Surjeet Shona. 'That chowkidar has to go!'

'See if it's so easy,' shouted back Surjeet Shona, though she thought to herself, 'Not that I would mind!'

They both knew Ali Mallik was also in the way, with his self-congratulatory appointment of a Hindu chowkidar and his light tread on Hindu-Muslim ground.

The belligerents were separated and sorted out with the help of the police. There were bloody gashes and bruises. No serious physical damage was done, but the question of harmony being restored was remote.

And yes, Jainab had lost his glass eye.

'My area record will be spoilt,' pointed out the police sub-inspector crossly. 'First Hindu-Muslim encounter I have witnessed after so many years.'

'You've got it wrong,' protested Junior. 'This is not a Hindu-Muslim encounter. After all, the Hindu chowkidar has been looking after a Muslim shrine, also for I do not know how many years. His quarrel is with a Sikh!'

The Rajmahal was weakening with age and it knew its attempts to sort out the situation would be hopeless.

'Enough is enough,' said Surjeet Shona. And at last she allotted one of her precious bathrooms to the Bhaiji. 'He's been here so long,' people said. 'He's grown up here. Come on, SS. Let the poor man have some peace!'

Surjeet Shona felt chastened. 'It should cool Junior down,' she consoled herself.

That evening, heavily band-aided, Rawat the neo-Brahman joined his wife at the evening puja in his garage-top room. Getting ready to prostrate before the household altar of Hindu gods and a terracotta replica of the Pir's tomb he said, 'We must propitiate the Pir to remember his servant. I have special need at this time.' His need was urgent, because he had heard that Junior Sahib, still on a roll, was about to demolish his godown.

It was Maudie Memsahib who saved him. She was to arrive the very next day in her wraith form, stunning everyone into inaction. Rawat-Pandey eagerly connived in her installation in the godown and Junior was pre-empted again. His frustration hit hysteria pitch.

The physical confrontation between the Hindu band, of Rawat-Pandey and his cohorts, and Junior's sidees created a base of unending rancour. Who could forget a blow, a fist jarring against a jaw, or a metallic implement impacting to split skin? And the resultant blood? How little it needed for the split skin and jarred jaw to release incipient messages implanted under that skin? So, one band was ever ready to spar with the other, ever ready to spill more blood, a society split like the skin. The sub-inspector should have realized the record of his jurisdiction was likely to break. It was a feature of the eternal division, based on the curious and confused miscalculations of bigotry. Junior's resolve to get rid of Chowkidar Rawat-Pandey had taken a leap into the darkness. It wasn't difficult to get to the denizens of that darkness and Junior was able to hire a minor gang, muscle men from an inner city gymnasium. The Rajmahal hoped Surjeet Shona would prove strong enough to somehow stem the deterioration. Although it was intrinsically lonely, not only at the desertion of the ghosts, but at the non-manifestation of its favourite inhabitants after death, it now felt sure the end was near.

When Surjeet Shona took up cudgels on behalf of Maudie and offered her toilet facilities as well, Junior's frustration ballooned and he was convinced of a sinister conspiracy. 'That do-gooding bitch must have a toilet-sharing mania!' he cursed, forgetting his own perverse injunction to Surjeet Shona to offer the Bhaiji relief. 'First she encourages that fat fraud by giving her toilet to the doddering Bhaiji, and now it's that old cow Maudie Jessop!' His mind seethed and his language reached its nonage nadir.

'Saala Hindu gatekeeper, Sahib, upto no good,' said Jainab, feeding his susceptible master. 'My cousin is waiting only to take same job into competent hands. Best reciter of Quran for Pir-ji's sacred tomb and he is strong, strong like ox. And true Mussalman, Sahib. Not like uncircumcized son of pig!'

The Bhaiji's need for a convenient relieving place had long been forgotten. They were on to something other, as the house discerned, and who could claim to have the answer to *that*?

12

The Immanent Junior

Ali Mallik, responding to the shifting balances in the Rajmahal, wondered if the long run of luck with his marriage could hold out.

'Saira,' he said. 'Look at our Rajmahal, almost empty! How much longer do you think we have? What do you think of our lives?'

'Sad,' said Saira immediately. 'So sad, so unfinished …'

'Saira!' sharply rebuked Ali, raising his voice higher than ever before with her. 'Think what you're saying, old girl.'

Saira stopped. 'I'm sorry, darling. I don't know what I was thinking. Forgive me.' She went across and sat by him. 'What is it?'

'I, I can't believe my ears. Say you didn't mean it. What did you mean? Haven't you been happy with me? Don't you still have your loving sons?'

Ali stopped his frightened outpourings and tried to analyse Saira's shocking words. She was sitting next to him, with her arm linked in his and her nearness helped.

'Fayyaz, unmarried, childless Fayyaz, living in sin, is lost to us, gone away to the unknown world of politics and ideologies, all of which we can only view from the outside,' Ali was thinking.

'Mumtaz is happy, and Fayyaz is loving when he comes,' said Saira, reading Ali's thoughts, which she could always do. 'You were right about our loving sons.'

Ali continued his thoughts, but spoke them out aloud, a transfer which was usual with his wife, so much at one with her as he was. And he voiced the unsaid fear which had always plagued them.

'What about Junior then?'

'Junior?' asked Saira softly. 'What about Junior? I know you don't mean his obsession with the Rajmahal,' she said, circumventing the obvious word, just as the papers did. '… rival groups clashed after a group from a certain community set fire to some dwellings …'

'What is it that went wrong, what is it?' said Ali.

'It doesn't matter, darling. There's nothing we could do.'

'There have been so many big ones, haven't there? The Partition and Khulna and Kashmir and the everlasting riots and flash points and the wars, and Bangladesh, and then, then, finally for our old lives, the destruction of the Babri mosque. And …'

'Darling …'

'And Bombay …? And my home …? Across the border? The other …?'

Ali Mallik referred to his home town, Dacca, capital of the East Pakistan he hadn't returned to at Partition simply because he was of a 'certain community'. And Dacca had erupted in fury at the destruction of the Babri mosque in India and the deaths and retaliatory deaths and bomb blasts that had followed in other parts of India, especially Bombay.

'And have you forgotten Calcutta and '46? And Noakhali? Have they dissolved in an acid bath leaving no trace? Oh it will come again, it will come again …'

Saira had no answer.

'Oh fuck.' said Ali bitterly. 'I used to dream …'

'I know.'

'The man-with-the-knife-in-the-back …'

'Shshshsh. You've known for a long time, just as I have. We won't see its end. That's not all …'

'It's Junior of course. Junior, Junior, Junior …'

They sat in silence and sorrow and Ali knew this was what Saira had meant when she had responded so spontaneously to his first question.

'My wonderful Saira,' he was thinking. 'My dearest. My most precious.'

And they were interrupted by a flush of love and endearments.

'That's what matters in the end,' said the Rajmahal with conviction. 'We could do with much more of that.' But then it too was suffering more and more from insecurity. 'Right?' it added, shakily.

And Junior? Did he deserve all this agonizing? Or was he just an unthinking and aggressive provocateur? A bad-natured loner deserted by his wife? Was it really so, again, unthinkingly important for him to get rid of that insipid structure on the drive and therefore Maudie, or de-Brahmanize the chowkidar for the sake of a toilet? Or for him to cross his father and the late Proshanto Mojumdar's lift desires, thus depriving them of freedom of movement? When he knew that he himself already had twinges in his deteriorating knees and shortness of breath? Why did he allow such matters to become obsessions, leading to blind rages and feckless machinations?

Even minor concerns such as his dislike of birds became phobias, as he took unsuccessful potshots at the pigeons with his air gun, cracking holes in the skylights. In a frenzy one day he dragooned all hands, making them shout, wave brooms, shirts, sheets and arms from the lobby floor and on the stairway. The pigeons, flapping noisily and hysterically, swooped up the well of the stairs and through the open skylights releasing into the air in a burst. At the signal, the skylights were banged shut and all that was left was a flurry of dismembered feathers. But a covey was found mysteriously re-settled under the high ceiling the very next morning, to the approval of the Rajmahal, which empathized with the pigeons, though it had mixed feelings about the mess they caused. It was discovered that the servants who were superstitious about pigeons had secretly opened the skylights at night. 'One day there will be stalagmites and stalactites of pigeon shit in the lobby,' swore Junior, when he saw the pigeon-wallah carrying out cartloads of droppings. 'The fumes from it are going to poison us all. It's raining pigeon shit.' The guards took to keeping umbrellas ready to protect the tenants and their guests and the pigeon-wallah found his work increased with its additional load of little bald baby birds, which kept perishing after endless plunges. Helpful Surjeet Shona offered to try out the droppings as a fertilizer for her garden. 'If guano works why not this?' she said, and suiting action to word made her grumbling gardener use it in the flower beds with inconclusive results. When the vultures circled, Junior allowed their presence to possess him and in an unconscious imitation circled round and round the room with flailing arms while he tried to work out solutions. After their flight, Junior was the most relieved, though he still had nightmares about them. He tried to smoke out the last stubborn pair on top of the raintree, but vultures not being wasps ignored all such attempts. Their droppings adorned the tree and with the erosion of these droppings, the tree was losing its foliage.

'It will surely die,' the gardener told Surjeet Shona. 'Their excrement is spoiling the vegetation.'

'I'd rather they left than the pigeons,' said the Rajmahal.

❦

It was typical of Junior to start fizzing when, for the very first time, he heard one of the Hindu groundsmen, Ramnath, addressing old Jainab as 'Jai Ram', turning the Muslim name into a salutation to the Hindu god.

'Ei Ramnath,' called Junior in ire. 'Why are you calling Jainab "Jai Ram"? You can't say a simple Muslim name or what?'

'Arrey na Sahib. Then ask him why he calls me "Ramjaan"? Why he cannot say Ramnath?'

'What?' said Junior. 'Say that again. What did you say?'

This suddenly became very important to Junior. It was to mark a break in his thinking and slow down his subsequent actions. It was to revolutionize our Saira and Ali Mallik's Junior, the essence, the boiled down sour milk, of their agonized deliberations.

'I am telling you, Saheb,' Ramnath's high-pitched voice cracked. He cleared his throat lowering the pitch, which started climbing again word by word. 'Why?' he said, in the declamatory tone a parliamentarian would be proud of. 'Why he cannot call me "Ramnath"? Ha? Ha? He has some problem or what? He cannot say good easy Hindu name like "Ramnath"? He must make me some Muslim, some "Ramjaan Shamjaan"...' He started choking.

'Incredible!' Junior's cussed bent of mind was stalled, intrigued by the nuances inherent in this slippage. 'Yes, yes?' he said.

'Just like lying Hindu, mocking me that I am Hindu when I am true Mussalman, haj what is more,' burst out the indignant Jainab.

'*Lying* Hindu he says? *Lying* Hindu. Is it not known to all that Mussalman always trying to make all others into Mussalman? So he calls me "Ramjan". Ask him. Ask him if he did not do it first of all. I am, bas, following only. And still I am to blame?'

Junior had received quite a battering in his life. Under Ali's tutelage he had become a competent lawyer, but his embitterment had crystallized when he had been appointed for the Muslim plaintiff in a Hindu-Muslim conflict. Whether he would win the case or not was irrelevant, but he was forever branded as a 'communalist', a fanatic and a closet Pakistani. The injustice of this branding turned Junior, already an introvert, super-sensitive to the rest of the world. Everything became coloured with the poison of prejudice and in time, as a defence, he convinced himself Muslims were superior to Hindus in all aspects, with biased comparisons ranging from the absurd to the sublime. He compared the rich non-vegetarian fare of Muslims to the watery vegetarianism of Hindus. The generosity of Muslims to the penny-pinching of Hindus. The equality among Muslims to the caste system of Hindus. And at the lofty end, the monotheism of Muslims to the pantheistic idol worship of Hindus. Junior twisted himself into a self-righteous bigot. His general sourness afflicted his looks, including the elegance which characterized the Mallik men. When his wife left him his sourness was curdled further by bitterness.

Junior, though so hard in his dealings with others, was like putty with his wife, Nadira. She was quiet, traditional and pretty, given to instant obedience with Saira and Ali, but transfigured when she was alone with Junior. Saira didn't know this and often wished Nadira would laugh and joke, act bitchy, anything to show more spirit. But Nadira stayed adamantly docile. Saira had nightmares that Junior was beating and torturing his wife. She rushed out of bed in a frenzy one night and threw open their bedroom door. The two were fast asleep and Junior had his arm protectively around Nadira. It took Saira and Ali some time to realize that Junior worshipped his wife and it was the cold and mysterious Nadira who was keeping them all guessing. When she walked out on Junior with her children to return to her parents in Dhaka, Saira felt a sense of déjà vu. Nadira had made up her mind when Junior told her she must stop using make-up and keep her head covered in public. 'Next it will be a burkha!' she icily said. And when he came back from the courts in the evening, a shocked Ali and Saira were waiting to tell him the news of her departure with the children. Junior locked himself into his bedroom and stood holding on to a shelf, with eyes screwed tight and teeth clenched so hard that the tip of a weak tooth snapped off. He sleep-walked to the bathroom to rinse out his mouth and taking the sharp scrap of tooth in his hand pressed it between forefinger and thumb, producing a pinprick of blood, as if this small pain would bring Nadira back. The Rajmahal lamented, though it wasn't surprised. Expert witness, it had overheard Nadira whispering complaints to its walls and into the phone to her mother and seen her withdrawing into herself. For all his bluster and manly airs, Junior hadn't managed to draw Nadira to him.

The blow turned him half crazy and he tautened and hardened himself more against the rest of the world. Saira and Ali understood some of the torment he was going through and they didn't try to stop him when he crossed the border to Dhaka in a desperate attempt to cajole Nadira back. Nothing would shake her, though she agreed to send the children to India at distant intervals. Neither Saira nor Ali could do anything about the unfortunate tendencies which Junior displayed in more and more marked fashion from now on.

❧

After all this time, it was the decrepit innocent Maudie's attack on him which had started the process of change in Junior. Surjeet Shona did him the injustice of believing his cruelty had driven Maudie back to drink and to turn her suicide gun on him. And Junior did himself the same injustice. 'My harshness gave Maudie that push!' he insisted. But it was unlikely that looking at semul flowers and birds could have bewitched her permanently out of alcoholism. Or despair. The flowering season of semuls is so short. They didn't stop to think that it was his sudden appearance which had deflected her gun from herself and saved her. But Junior was to put himself on trial, finally leading to his self-conviction and sentencing. The internal trial meant another period of suffering for him and still no inkling of the conflict was allowed to show.

A further burden borne by the Malliks at the time was the decline of their other daughter-in-law, Lalitha. She was diagnosed with a brain tumour and Mumtaz, desperate for his family's support, went willingly back to Calcutta.

'At least Mumtaz has come back to us,' sighed Saira.

'Yes, now,' said the Rajmahal bitterly. 'Now when Lalitha is nearing the end …'

Lalitha's terminal illness exposed other weaknesses. Junior was incapable of expression, but he could easily see that Lalitha's 'Hinduness', or her being from Kerala, made no difference to the closeness in the family or to the universal pain of loss.

Saira need not have wept over Junior. The change was both imminent and immanent. Junior was thrown back into his immanent self when the absurdity of old Jainab and Ramnath's unflinching name-calling dawned on him after the paving of Maudie's crisis, Lalitha's impending death and his own brush with it. Having convicted himself, he fretted over his sentence in that uncharacteristic gush of self-mortification. And it had to be, of course, to withdraw the case against poor broken down Maudie who was laid up in hospital again.

The old Anglo-Indian lady was speechless with delight when Junior gave her the news. She took his hands in her gnarled grasp, 'And just imagine, I used to think you were so wicked!'

Junior patted her brusquely, still unused to his new role. 'I'm getting another flat for you Maudie, because the Rajmahal has to be pulled down.'

'Oh but where's the money?' wailed Maudie.

'Didn't I tell you I'd do it? Just leave it to me!' He couldn't help the aggressive tone, his kindness would fit him ill for some time. But inside, he felt as if a fresh breeze was blowing through him. He vowed not only to get her a flat of her own but to add a topping to the money that was due to her. That and the other major self-sentencing, to give up the Rajmahal, the source of his power and the base of his defeats and frustrations. At last he would readily accede to the brokers of good sense and sell out, slake off all the stale, crusty, accretions of that old building. He would free his parents by moving them to a garden house and himself from the posturing of all these years which he had worn like a suffocating hairshirt. To sell the Rajmahal was to him like betraying himself, because it might provide the tear in the hairshirt through which his febrile inner surfaces would become visible. But it would lead to his punishment-salvation. And the mansion's doom.

The Rajmahal shuddered repeatedly, weakening with every shudder, squaring its age-sloped shoulders to face up to the inevitable. Demolitions were in the air and it uneasily awaited the beginning of the end, the bringing-down of the godown. But Junior's past couldn't allow him such a facile passage. The twister of violence had been whirling itself into a nice potency ever since the Bhaiji, prompted by that very, if not 'same', Junior, had been forced to defy Chowkidar Rawat-Pandey. And that defiance would prove costly.

13

Twice-Married, Twice-Bereaved

The rumblings of the Rajmahal volcano could no longer be ignored. Feelings between sections of the mansion staff had hotted up with the goading of Junior's musclemen. The neighbour, who couldn't forget the breaching of his wall to make room for the tomb, had passed on his ill-feeling to his son. And the son was kept fully informed of all the goings-on. He had no hesitation creeping in through the new breach created by the city toughs and the volcano was never allowed to go extinct. Though Junior had dismissed the toughs by then, their links with the staff were already well forged. And the two teams placed themselves knowingly on the summit of the volcano.

Surjeet Shona found herself inextricably linked to the situation. Not merely because it was her Bhaiji who was involved in the initial problem. But for other, more vital reasons.

Surjeet Shona's weavers' organization and other projects were well set, run by dedicated younger workers and her presence had become nominal. Between a few conferences and seminars, melancholy time hung heavy on her hands and her Rajmahal altruism became a compulsion.

The Rajmahal, a sentimentalist if anything, had enjoyed Surjeet Shona most when she had been immersed in Martin, the phase Surjeet Shona considered her berserk phase. It watched her reactions with interest when Martin Strachey came down for his parents' funeral. He had climbed high in British academic circles, his eminence resting on original researches into Calcutta, the city he had abandoned and with it his parents. 'His wife hasn't come because she's too ashamed,' thought Surjeet Shona, her heart full with the poignancy of the old couple's end, and for her ex-lover's feelings. But there had been too much in between and Martin was too crushed by the manner of his parents' deaths to feel anything but penitence and grief. And though Surjeet Shona admired his fine greying, the roughening of his skin contradicted by the refining effect of the present pain, no vestige of that searing affair threw threads between them. The other Rajmahalians, inarticulate, their age an upsetting reminder, attended the funeral with ashen faces. Surjeet Shona could see the affected Martin struggling with his emotions, but there was no help for him. 'He must feel everyone's accusing eyes on him,' she thought. 'What a burden he'll have to carry.'

The Rajmahal looked on Surjeet Shona, this original daughter, with pensive love. 'Neel was wonderfully interesting and a Calcuttan. But he was a bastard. And the doctor may have been more suited, but he took on too much for his age. It's a good thing she didn't marry him. But how can she be protected? She's so messed up and independent and always trying to do good! I wish she would simply go back to her original self-centred self. Poor little thing.'

Surjeet Shona was neither poor, in another sense, nor little. And though the mansion may have been wise, its assumptions about the 'real' Surjeet Shona took it into difficult terrain beyond its scope. Though to do it justice, it was remarkably flexible for such a rigid thing as a building.

Where the Rajmahal found Surjeet Shona's altruism unnatural, the Gulianis were simply suspicious. Especially after Surjeet Shona agreed to help them redo their flat.

'What she is getting out of this helping us?' sniffed Mrs Guliani. 'What she thinks she is getting?'

And when her husband rebuked her too quickly she shot back, 'You are paying for her work or what? How much you are paying?'

In another context, Guliani couldn't help agreeing with his wife when they discovered Surjeet Shona's close involvement in all the mansion's goings-on.

'Always here, always there,' said Mrs Guliani. 'No one can live without her or what?'

'Who knows?' shrugged Guliani disparagingly. 'As long as our work gets done.' Inside he was as puzzled as his wife. 'What has she to do with all these people, these Petrovs and Maudie Jessop and all the others? And why is she so ready to help us too?' He wondered if she was getting a cut from the interior decorating firm working for him. 'No,' he thought. 'She's too stinking rich as it is.'

'It's just loneliness,' temporized the Rajmahal. 'Everyone gets lonely when there's no one else in the house.'

While Surjeet Shona ministered to the Petrovs during their last days, she would go on to the verandah where the old Russian sat cross-legged on his divan, his loincloth hanging about his haunches almost indistinguishable from the folds of his skin. She would look at his skeletal form, the skull-head enlarged on the shrunken body, the brittle, feather-light and rigid ribcage rising and falling as the frail lungs pumped. Then the ghoul would rise up from the pit of Surjeet Shona's stomach, scratching, hurting the sore spots in her intestines, trying its best to raise them into ulcers, a process that had begun those many years ago. The tears had decreased and dried gradually, recurring only at decreed intervals. But it was during her son Gurdeep's wedding that they appeared without cause, the ghoul coming to reside within her permanently and slumbering, awakening unannounced.

She wondered if it was the lowered resistance of a weakening body, or the accumulation of sorrows which lay the base of weepiness in the elderly. She recalled her indifference to such manifestations in others, assuming the elderly must be mawkish and soft in the head. That she should weakly shed tears at her son's wedding or Osheem Petrov's frailness or a leaf falling on green grass, was an indication of another her, another Surjeet Shona who had as a robust young woman wept only at her own concerns and sorrows. Wasn't it beginning to feel perversely pleasurable? 'What beauty there is in sorrow, in death,' the philosophers said, yet under the sentiment lay knowledge, the knowledge that perfection and perpetual bliss must evade one till the end. So her tears were for everyone, embracing the world and fearfully yet pleasurably waiting for the ghoul to reach out for her.

The tears threatened to turn into a flood after Maudie Jessop's crisis, and Surjeet Shona, who was apprehensively waiting for the hot flushes of menopause, theorized that the flushing of tears was a substitute. 'You get caught anyhow in the end,' she lamented.

She had been battling the underlying fear of the 'down-scaling', the one-way concertina of life, the folding in with deceptive coos, squeezing and compressing one for the final plucking out by the ghoul. The Rajmahal would be disappointed to know that she felt her sense of urgency had led to impotence in the end, that her activities were insignificant, a speck of a life and that if she did simply nothing but sit and drink like Maudie, it would make little difference.

When Lalitha was brought back by Mumtaz for treatment, Surjeet Shona was glad to have him in the Rajmahal. The gravitation of their English lovers towards one another all those years ago, leaving them both rejected, formed an unexploited link. Lalitha sat up with them and they could see her straining to join the conversation. But the deterioration was pitilessly swift. Often, she would slump over, in the grip of a malignant slumber induced by the jealous proliferating cells. When she returned to the Rajmahal after radical surgery she had already left them in a sense, her mind slipping away and her body helpless. As the process drew on, a desperate Mumtaz sought his sanity in the ground floor Ohri flat. It was during one such visit that he noticed Surjeet Shona's tearfulness and put his arm around her. 'Come on, SS. You're the strong one. You can't fold up on us like this. What's the matter?'

What could Surjeet Shona say, when she herself couldn't qualify the 'matter'. But the little incident launched her on her dream phase. When she had the first of these dreams she woke up and rocked herself till she was calm. 'What was it?' she wondered. 'Was it sorrow? For what? Why am I so filled with this sorrow? Did I have a bad dream?'

She couldn't remember. And these days she woke up often with that experience of deep sorrow. A moment later, it was replaced by a sense of anticipation and joy, and Mumtaz sprang to life in her thoughts. Mumtaz, strong, tall, with his normally twinkling eyes shadowed with the fear of death, another link between them. Were the tears for her past trials, all the deaths, her son, or the tragedy of Lalitha's present? She quickly got up, eager to be with Mumtaz again.

The Rajmahal could see Surjeet Shona's metamorphosis and, like the ghosts, would have pinched itself if it could. It would have cheered too, but the time wasn't propitious with all the deaths and Lalitha's ebbing life. 'Dear Surjeet Shona, she deserves another chance,' it said. And it keenly observed her awakening.

14

Heavenly Hetaerae

Surjeet Shona lies on the grass under the raintree. It is a broiling summer day and the sun scorches everything that allows it access. She lies in deepest, soothing yet dark, dark shadow, saved from this access by the raintree. She is naked, her body almost white in the gloom and she looks up at the leaves and flowers of the raintree with its pink silken tufted panicles and lifted up leaves horizontally fusing to shut out the sun. She closes her eyes and sees the inhabitants of the mysterious black green of the tree, mythical pale beings draping languid limbs from the branches and resting their wings against the trunk, cloudy hetaerae of the sky gods. Underneath her deliciously freed body is the feel of the damp grass, and now and then when there is a movement of air, the leaves stir and the stored water showers her with icy drops. She sees the facade of the Rajmahal in negative imprint on her inner lids, black in the glare beyond the tree with white rectangles where the chiks lie lowered on each verandah. And framed within one of those rectangles is the shimmering figure of a man. Surjeet Shona's desire grows for that man. She arises, stretches, caressing her flawless body with her hands and walks out from the shade into the sun, turning herself into a torch in the white light. She looks up at the man, shading her eyes with one hand and waving with the other. In a moment, he is with her under the dark of the tree, his body transformed to pale nakedness. Languidly they embrace, exchanging sweet kisses. Then the man takes Surjeet Shona's nipples, still burning from the sun, between his gentle teeth, one by one while he mounts and enters her and the hetaerae shake the branches to loosen the tufted flowers on to the lovers.

Surjeet Shona wakes up in a fever of arousal aware that the shadowy man, that shadowy lover, is none of the previous inhabitants of her dream world. But Mumtaz. The verandah on which he stood was on the top floor, the Mallik floor, the matching flat to hers on the ground floor, the two balancing ends holding that crazy collection of inhabitants together. Does Lalitha not matter then, Lalitha who is such a close friend and confidante? Then why after all these years, when she is almost fifty, is she having the dreams of a virginal teenager with Lalitha's husband as the desired other?

Surjeet Shona left her bed and, clothed, drifted on to the verandah, down the steps and into the garden and glare of her dream, towards the raintree, under which she had just lain in that dew of heavenly arousal.

She had inherited some of the detritus of the Rajmahal. The abandoned wrought-iron lift, the birdcage, lay at one end of the verandah, modified, filled with plants, and the two marble ladies of the lobby stood hidden in the shrubbery outside. Junior, hyped by prudery, had provoked his sequestered father. 'They must be removed!' he had exhorted. Ali was admittedly disgusted when his son had taken him on to the landing and pointed out the once-pristine ever-young and elderly figures clothed in pigeon droppings. And the other desecration committed on them, their nipples and area between the legs, blackened, accentuated by the repeated and surreptitious finger-rubbing of drifters. Even the mansion had been feeling uncomfortable for some time.

'What will happen to the fountains?' Ali had protested.

'The fountains can stay,' Junior had said. 'We'll convert them into normal fountains. We'll even allow them to play. But this disgraceful exhibitionism cannot be tolerated anymore. How could you, as a Muslim, tolerate it in the first place?'

Surjeet Shona's garden became the repository of the statues, though she promised to position them discreetly. She had them cleaned, nullifying the offending stains with bleach and detergent. When they reappeared after a few days in the sun, she hoped the dappling of the shrubs would camouflage them.

She hesitated as she moved out towards the raintree. Since Petrov's disappearance it had frightened her to look at it, and though they were mostly gone, a pair of vultures had stayed to build a giant nest on top of the tree. Her attention was first drawn to them when she saw them noisily copulating on that remote summit. Then they took up residence, huge even at that height, altering the profile of the raintree. She walked part of the way down the lawn without raising her eyes, and saw that the ground under the tree was caked with droppings.

She was repelled. 'To think I lay there in my dream! Why such a cruel dream, why?'

She turned her back on the tree and looked up at the mansion, shading her eyes with her hands. The chiks were down as in her dream. But there was no figure on the Mallik floor. She went back to the verandah and lowered herself on to a reclining chair. The tree was within sight minus the pale hetaerae, only the vulture couple, making a majestic tableau on their high stage. She shut her eyes, but all she could see on her throbbing eyelids was an ugly face. Ever since Surjeet Shona's affliction by her fear, it had manifested as a series of merging and changing aspects, mostly faces. In the early days, while she and Martin were locked in those terrible ecstasies, the faces would appear inside her eyelids when they closed. Later, when the conflagration in Punjab was at its height, and her break with her son at its most painful, the crimson vicousness of the pool of nectar was there in her eyelids, tiny bloody eyelid pools which carried the shadow of the giant ghoul in all its aspects. And it was always distorted, whether with a satyr twist of the lips or a sharp arrangement of the facial bones or the elongated cynicism of the God of Death. So this melting and changing image became almost like Surjeet Shona's familiar, except that she was no witch and the image came unbidden and always with its wake of dread. So was it with Petrov's vultures … It was natural to believe, once his body had vanished, that the vultures had carried him off and devoured him in some hidden charnel house. Surjeet Shona pictured this charnel house as the top of a tall tree, it had to be that same busy raintree, with a whole world being enacted on its spreading and complex summit, a pre-after-life world. There the vultures pranced with spread wings in a hideous danse macabre shrieking harshly while they fought for poor broken Petrov's meagre remains. She lay on the chair with her eyes closed, allowing the faces to change and coalesce till they ceased. Her eyelids grew blessedly quiet and she became aware of the loud cawing of roosting crows. When she lifted her eyes to look up again, it was dark and the vultures had gone. And then she saw them in flight against the twilit sky, and her fear evaporated. Ordered by nature to associate with rotting carcasses and the raw, red insides of once living beings, they had been transformed into phenomenal creatures of the wind, full of grace and mystery.

❦

Whenever Lalitha improved slightly through the rough progress of her disease, Mumtaz would come alight with hope. Surjeet Shona would feel the joy of her dream lover working in herself and wonder, what did she want? Was it Mumtaz, was it not? It was too early to say and she herself was the first to admit that dreams were hardly the thing to go on.

Lalitha died, too young for death, her face still unlined, her hair still black. 'Her cropped hair,' thought Surjeet Shona. 'Her beautiful hair, tragically cropped for that ruthless carving up.'

She and Mumtaz spent time on either side of Lalitha's hospital bed, watching her die, her eyes only sometimes open with their light dulled. Surjeet Shona could see Mumtaz growing gaunt, grey-faced, his shoulder bones jutting out. She couldn't dissociate him from her dream-under-the-raintree Mumtaz, he was that Mumtaz. Was it love which gave her such pleasure to keep looking at his downcast face, the fuzz of grey hair withdrawing from the temples yet forming a high thick crown which occasionally let out a strand, the long bumpy nose and wide lips, and sometimes catch his eye? Or was it just the dream remembrance which made her long to run her fingers over the vulnerable collarbone and neck and down that gaunt body, once so robust and strong? Many came, Lalitha's children, Ali and Saira Mallik, Fayyaz. And Junior, who was given to standing grimly at the door. Once, when Lalitha had almost fallen off the bed in a fit, Mumtaz had burst out at the dark figure of his brother, 'Get out! Get out Junior! Standing over her like a djinn! How can she ever get well?!' Junior had dropped the curtain which he was holding aside and vanished, never to come to Lalitha's room again till the end. But it hadn't helped. Nothing had helped. And Mumtaz had later apologized to an expressionless Junior.

After shouting at his older brother, Mumtaz had buried his face in the comatose Lalitha's side and wept, and all Surjeet Shona could do was swallow and put her hands on his shoulders, helpless and angry.

'Come on you monster!' she had called silently to the ghoul. 'You've had your fun! Get on with it!'

When Lalitha died, late one evening, everyone was in the room, down to the servants. They stood there in spaced-out silence, their sharp shadows slanting in paralleled abstractions under the glare of the light. No one thought to stop them as they came in one by one, sombre, awed at the thought of looking death in the face.

'She is brain dead,' whispered the doctor monitoring her.

Surjeet Shona could see Lalitha breathing, watched the monitor screen of Lalitha's heartbeat, the painful, jagged, jerky graph, pulling itself along its rocky path. Then the pik, pik sound stopped and became a long, even eeeee … not even a wail, because it had no changing cadences, just a dead, flat, inert eeeeee … The graph had stopped jigging and also drew itself straight, flat, inert, a path out of life into the black, illusory space of the inner machinery … 'He was right, Uncle Osheem was right. It's the little differences, the changing pressures shutting and opening the valves, forcing the graph to jump up and down, that give us life. When that restlessness goes, there is only nothingness.' The machine was switched off. In the silence, a daughter threw herself on her mother's body and wept noisily. Mumtaz was sitting by the bed with his face hanging low, his hand clenched over Lalitha's. And the others just waited. 'While the ghoul grins!' thought Surjeet Shona. She closed her eyes too and tried to imagine herself dead, but all she saw were the ugly faces swimming in the two little red eyelid pools.

'The day those images disappear for good, my brain will also die,' she thought.

❦

It was summer when Lalitha died, and even after she was brain dead, holding her heart-live hand, Mumtaz felt her sweat, or was it his own, dripping from his brow on to her.

His voice broke, 'How can it be when she's still sweating?' he asked the doctor. 'Open your eyes,' he begged softly, desperately sealed into the closeness he had built up with Lalitha over many years. 'Open your eyes. 'Litha. Look at me. 'Litha. Open your eyes.'

Tears slowly dripped, like Mumtaz's sweat, from the onlookers' eyes as they saw his grief, and heard the scattered sniffling and Lalitha's rasping breath which made the quiet, pik-pik-ing hospital room quieter. Spaced out with the others in that oblique design of parallel lines were Saira and Ali whose tears were for their son, Fayyaz and Junior's for their brother, and Surjeet Shona's for her love Mumtaz, and her friend 'Litha. But for most of the others it was like watching a film, which they imagined to be connected to their own lives because it was happening in the same room with them. They also knew in their heart of hearts that their tears were not of grief but of the many catharses that take place in a life without affecting one personally. It was poignant, because it concerned someone not meant to die at that age, leaving behind such a heartbroken husband. And they acted their parts in that film, feeling the necessity of their separate roles.

❦

After Lalitha's death, whenever she could tear herself away from the Mallik flat where Mumtaz was sunk in terrible grief, Surjeet Shona again found herself spending time in the Guru Granth Sahib room. She listened to the verses of the Gurus of the Sikh progression, and to the poetry of the Sufi and Bhakti saints embodied in the sacred book.

> The wick is dry, the oil runs out,
> The drum is still, the dancer sleeps,
> The fire burnt out, no smoke ensues …
> The string has snapped, the lute is mute …
> O Kabir, he who has conquered the five sins …
> To reach the highest seat, he has not far to go.

To Surjeet Shona the simpler yet inspired sentiments of the hymns, full of the joy of devotion, calling with unquestioning faith in the name of the Supreme Being, were detached from the reality of grief.

> Of his bounty one cannot write too much …
> God is master, God is truth
> His name spelleth love divine …

Yet both were part of the same created world which Mumtaz wanted to escape and which the hymns together celebrated and transcended. She thought of the idea that rebirth was undesirable, that merging with the Supreme Being was the ultimate goal.

Rebirth undesirable?

'How can that be?' thought Surjeet Shona. 'How can rebirth, or birth for that matter, be undesirable? Why has this beautiful world been created then? Do we run away because of a momentary unhappiness? If the "highest seat", the ideal is achieved, and all animate beings merge with the Supreme and there is no more rebirth, then why this world with all its fabulous beauty? To go back to Uncle Osheem's idea of that little difference, that disharmonious conflict, does even "God" need it so badly that he has to create the world as we know it, the undesirable world from which we all must escape, working towards our non-return? If he is "God" can he not, much more easily, retain his wholeness, instead of sending all those parts of himself out into the world? Is it because it is a world of such intricacy and beauty that he too has forever been filled with desire for it? Seduced, by his own creation?'

She was going through such pain with Mumtaz steeped in the depths of sorrow, which she too had known in great measure, over and over again. Had she, at any time, wanted to end this life of hers? Perhaps intermittently, yes, perhaps. She watched Mumtaz calling out incoherently, pleading to join Lalitha. There was a scale, where things were weighed, wasn't there? In the balance. So then, could one say, the pain and sorrow outweighed the happiness? Was the pain, caused by her great fear of Death, enough to outweigh the happinesses of her life and thus push her into the arms of that very Death willingly? Could she ever countenance suicide, like Maudie, and the Stracheys and Mumtaz in his frenzy? The scales must have tipped over during those intervals of berserk sorrow following the blows of her tragedies, but in the end, would she say the result was a permanently tilted scale?

'No,' thought Surjeet Shona with conviction, 'those scales will never be still enough, never stabilize enough, to tip over forever. We're kept guessing, and that is what makes life, the a-rhythmic tilting and lifting. In any case Uncle Osheem,' she said, addressing Petrov in an imaginary monologue, 'please tell me why most creatures, from ants to elephants, and including us poor humans along the way, have such a strong life-instinct, fight death so automatically and implacably? Why does the orderly State have laws which punish murder but not self-defence? Doesn't all this give Life the place of winner? The orderly State protecting life, the orderly State punishing the taker-of-life, the orderly State protecting the defender-of-life? So. Isn't it better not to wonder any more, but to get on with the business of life. And living?'

She felt a surge.

She could see Mumtaz coming out of his despair, with his mother's nurturing and the bright potential of herself in the Rajmahal.

And as if to ready herself, Surjeet Shona began significant preparations. She was almost as normal, courageous, sexy, sensual, frank and healthy as she had been when she had first come to settle in the Rajmahal, and she was no self-sacrificing martyr, 'termartyr', as her father taunted anyone that way inclined.

Appraising herself in the mirror she approved of the stylish, shoulder-length hair, with its beginnings of soft grey, and the allowed luxury of tinting to minimize the grey. Her Chinese hairdresser was especially attentive.

'Her beauty will finish off if she dezzint hurry! Why you wasting time, eh? You can make some chappie happy still!' And after the cosseting at her weekly session she would say, 'See, I make you so young. Lookit dat body. Come on, SS. When you going to bring de good news, eh?'

The Rajmahal looked on morose and loving. 'Will the games never end?' it thought. But on the other hand it also realized that loneliness was unanswerable.

15

A Love Story

To Mumtaz that season was bonded to the lurking unpleasantness of a certain summer in his childhood. A hot, humid, windless summer, when the children of the Rajmahal, normally so vividly active, were overcome with a torpor which they threw off only towards evening, when the South breeze started up from the sea and the humidity turned cool against their melting bodies. They changed playgrounds over the years. The Maidaan, where the activities were endless. Or the zoo, where their favourites were the magnificent white tigers of Rewa. Or the pontoon restaurant on the Strand, where after a boat ride, suspended within the limpid orange and red skywater of the sunset, they would eat ice-cream and cake. Or sometimes the Lake Club, with its sloping lawns, its shed housing those impossibly elegant racing boats, when they would go for dinghy rides around the mysterious islands of the Dhakuria lakes and climb into the cement loudspeaker which broadcast ragged cement music at regatta time. Magical regatta time, when racing boats were taken out on the shoulders of muscular oarsmen who would row obediently and gracefully to the rhythmic 'in-out, in-out' of the coxes, slumping over their oars and almost tumbling into the water with exhaustion at the end of a race. The star skull oarsman was Jimmy Sen, unbeatable, hero-worshipped by the children. Towering, hefty, unshaven, Jimmy Sen was their invincible Tarzan-Roy-Rogers-Captain Marvel that summer. Standing on the upstairs terrace, the Rajmahal children's screams would rise shrilly over the adult voices. 'Jimmy! Jimmy! Jimmy!'

The Lake Club was the very same club contemplated by Proshanto Mojumdar while he swam in forbidden waters at the all-white club. This club was closed to white people, started as an alternative serious rowing club for Indians forbidden entry into the older Calcutta Rowing Club. Here was Martin Strachey, allowed into the Lake Club premises (for non-whites only), a child after all, but not his parents, who would wave in a friendly way from the Calcutta Rowing Club (for whites only), which jutted out at right angles to the Lake Club. The clubs were notionally separated by a cantilever bridge over a stretch of deep water, a well-proportioned and elegant steel bridge which was out of bounds, cut-off from both clubs by barbed wire fences. The bridge was open to the public, and thronged by crowds dressed up for their outings in colours never seen in either privileged club, munching peanuts, moori and channa from paper packets, their children holding on to balloons and ice-sticks. The attraction in that out-of-bounds stretch was the view of the large, fat, speckled fish which moved in shoals, in and out of the shadowy water in sudden rushes at the eatables thrown at them. The Rajmahal children managed to get those fish to come to their side too, and threw them genteel crumbs begged from the club cook. But they couldn't see the fish clearly because of the interfering fence and sloping grassy bank. Those were the idyllic times.

The bad time started that summer with Mumtaz fracturing his arm. He and half a dozen others were plunging uncontrollably up and down on a slanting tree branch on the Maidaan, swifter harder, shouting breathlessly, when it snapped. Mumtaz, who was perched on the highest point at the tip found himself pinioned on the ground with an excruciating pain tearing through his right arm which had fractured in three places. His young bones repaired rapidly, but he was never able to play more than a weak game of tennis afterwards, destroying the promise he had so far shown.

Meera Petrov was the only insider Rajmahal girl child that summer, and she was hardly recognized as such because she was such a tomboy. So when she came forth in a two-piece dress with her flat midriff bared a good four inches and her almost-as-flat chest hidden behind an entrancing top with wide frills, the surprised boys were taking in hissing breaths before they knew it. Meera, brown-haired, golden-skinned, was in the ultimate state of pre-puberty perfection, and that day, she had applied a light gleam of lipstick and a dash of pale blue eye shadow. In a sudden realization of the effect she was having, she preened, swaying her hips as she walked in a manner which was to become a habit but was, that day, all new. The boys, smitten as if with one blow, were anxiously trying to please her. Mumtaz was filled with a desire to place his hands under the frilly top and on that flat chest and felt an acute sense of frustration with his arm in plaster. That was the summer Ali and Saira decided to shepherd the children to the Lake Club as often as possible and keep them under their watchful gazes because of Mumtaz's accident. He couldn't show off his non-existent rowing skills in the fixed punt, he couldn't clamber in and out of the loudspeaker. All he could do was to sit in the broad-bottomed dinghy to be taken out on the water by an obliging majhi, or hand over to bare-midriffed Meera his share of crumbs to feed the cuddly fish. Meera was enjoying herself, trying to make up her mind whom to favour, Martin or Mumtaz, setting the tradition for their future rivalry. The other possibility was Junior, but he was already forbiddingly distant. Meera's younger brother Boris, whose friends were Fayyaz Mallik and the Norman boys, was disgusted and couldn't believe what was happening to his sister. In the end neither aspirant succeeded. They were standing at the barbed wire fence, looking over at the all-white club, arguing about segregation, when Meera, fired by her new powers, said, 'Well. It's just as bad here, not allowing palefaces.' And to the shock of the boys she began climbing the fence. 'See if they can stop me. I'm both. A paleface and an Indian.' She went cautiously, placing her feet and hands carefully between the barbs and steadying herself by holding on to a post. But her weight loosened the strands and in a moment she had slipped, landing astride the barbed wire and goring herself before she fell off. The frilly top caught and tore and that desirable not quite flat chest was exposed. But Mumtaz was too shocked to appreciate this, his fear exaggerated by the terrible commotion from the lake. Jimmy Sen, who had been practising solo, going all-out in a powerful burst of speed, had had his spine rammed into by the pointed bow of another skull, novice-propelled and racing against the one-way rules. The dazed children had been hurried away by the Malliks before Jimmy Sen was brought in, but for a long time Mumtaz imagined the blood gushing from a hole which went right through his hero's body. Jimmy Sen had taken years to regain partial normalcy and start rowing again. By that time Meera had gone away to boarding school and Mumtaz was getting ready for Cambridge. The loss and memories associated with that summer surfaced at Lalitha's death, from which he felt he would never recover.

His mind crawled along morbid, enervating grooves, embellished by the image of his dying wife's black silver-sequinned hair flaring on her still pillow and her dusky, emaciated, precious face.

'What's the use?' he said to Surjeet Shona. 'It's better to go sooner than later, without suffering. Look at Mother. Smoking obstinately and coughing her guts out.'

Surjeet Shona put her hand on his arm and said, 'She'll be okay, Mumtaz.' And again she said, 'She'll be okay,' her heart pulling, and she put her arm around him and her head on his shoulder. He was so diminished with loss that he had become cadaverous and ugly. His nose was enlarged between the gaunt cheekbones, his forehead dwindled though the hairline had gone so far back it had actually expanded. And the remaining hair, still thick, had whitened.

He could see the top of Surjeet Shona's head, an upper view of her nose and the slanting curve of her parallel eyebrows and eyelids, eyelashes. 'Forgive me,' he said haltingly and lightly pressed her hand.

❧

'Darling, what are we to do?' Saira wailed, wringing her hands and pleading with Ali. 'No one deserves to suffer like that boy.'

'SS,' she said. 'You must come more often to see the boy. You're his only hope.'

'What do you mean?' said Surjeet Shona, speaking too fast. 'Why don't you summon his other friends? All of us can do something by being with him.'

'It's only you who can save him, darling,' said the distraught mother. And she prayed to the nameless God with whom she chatted sometimes in her head. 'Please let me see him normal before I go.' These consecrated chats were never smooth, interrupted by Saira's racking cough. As if to invite disaster, she would immediately light a cigarette, while taking up her interrupted chat with God. 'Sorry. I can't help it. Haven't I reached a respectable enough age?' This would be uttered in a mental wail, similar to the wail with which she pleaded with Surjeet Shona. 'Save my boy, SS. You're the only one who can.'

Ali and Saira discussed Surjeet Shona. 'She's in love with him,' Saira said. And when Ali asked her what they should do, she said, 'I'm trying my best, Ali. We'll just have to wait and see.'

Surjeet Shona was feeling her way slowly, awkwardly, urged on by the Rajmahal. Saira brought Mumtaz down to her flat and left them alone whenever she could. But Mumtaz was unresponsive.

Robi was squatting by Surjeet Shona's side during one of those visits, when she lighted on the subject of Petrov's disappearance, still a burning issue at the Rajmahal. In her desperation to arouse Mumtaz she said the first thing that came to mind.

'Do you think Uncle Osheem was pushed over the roof, Mumtaz?'

'Don't be absurd, SS! Your imagination's running wild.'

'Nothing like an absurdity to bring some life back into him,' thought Surjeet Shona.

'Anyone could have done it, one of the servants, an old enemy ...'

'And this person decides Osheem's a menace at this time, when he's reached a hundred ...'

'He wasn't a hundred ...'

'Ninety-nine then,' said Mumtaz rudely. 'At least! And how exactly would this mysterious killer have done it?' Surjeet Shona signalled to Robi, who had opened his mouth, to keep quiet. 'Trundles all the way down by the rusty stairs, undetected,' continued Mumtaz, answering his own question. 'And then *vaporizes* Osheem. And, incidentally, have you asked yourself why someone should want Osheem dead?'

Robi was holding his head and he burst out irrepressibly. 'It is I who left Shaheb,' he said, tears streaming down his cheeks. 'I left him alone. After all these years, I only allowed those vultures to get hold of him.'

Surjeet Shona and Mumtaz knew his reference was to real vultures, not the human kind.

'You left Uncle Osheem alone that night, Robi?'

'I left him, I left him, oh, I left him! I did not want to say. But, yes. I, I, Robi, whom he saved from the clutches of Death, I left him to the mercy of Death's knaves!'

'It's all right,' comforted Surjeet Shona, 'we understand. Don't worry about all that. Of course we understand. Uncle Osheem himself talked of Jom and his netting and noosing and hooking us all with his weapons.' She looked at Mumtaz. Would all this talk of death be too much?

'When did you leave him?' asked Mumtaz keenly. 'Was it night or day? Was it dark?'

'How can I forget,' moaned Robi. 'It was before omaboshyo night. Such a night, such darkness.'

'Do vultures work by night?' wondered Surjeet Shona aloud.

'But when I came back, from, from that bathroom, it was dawn Shona baby. And the vultures had done their work. They had been waiting. Did we not all see them long beforehand, waiting, waiting?'

'Just a minute.' said Mumtaz loudly. 'Have you ever heard of a vulture attacking living creatures? Even if they are old and helpless?'

'There must be a difference between scavengers and birds of prey,' said Surjeet Shona, suddenly as frantic as Robi to save Petrov's dignity. 'Robi,' she asked, 'did you ever see vultures taking away live creatures, even weak and old creatures?'

'They are cowards, Shona baby. How can they?'

'So then,' said Surjeet Shona, 'we come to the inevitable conclusion: that Uncle Osheem died, and they, the waiting vultures, carried him away ...'

'Do vultures carry away carcasses ...?'

'I do not know,' moaned Robi.

'It's all right, Robi,' said Mumtaz kindly. 'There is no shame in that. You must know the Parsis give their dead to the birds in places called Towers of Silence.'

'The Tibetans leave their dead on hilltops for the birds too,' said Surjeet Shona, trying to make herself feel better. 'It is an air burial, and that too is natural and noble. God made those birds for this task, Robi, to transform death through their bodies back into life. You have to remember it is natural.'

Surjeet Shona, glancing sideways at Mumtaz, thought, 'It won't be so easy to forget. Not in the Rajmahal with death all around us in such frightening disguises.' And this was the first time she felt like leaving. 'We must get away,' was her clear thought. 'We must transfer ourselves to the living world and before, not after, our deaths.' The Rajmahal winced. This was also the time when she would make the traitorous remarks. 'We have to get out of this houseful of near-skeletons, look at the Rajmahal, falling apart like a dehydrated skeleton itself.' The time when she could see with X-ray eyes into the spaced-out network of rusted girders and worn walls enclosing worn inhabitants. The time when she would stroke the pillar against which she stood, and place her cheek on it to say, 'sorry'.

❧

Mumtaz responded at last to the forces of time and the gentle pressure of the Rajmahal's most intrepid woman, his mother. He began to drop in often at the Ohri flat without devious persuasion.

This was the time, too, that Surjeet Shona found it propitious to make preparations and take special care of herself. 'There's no escape,' she half-lamented half-rejoiced when the almost-forgotten flooding with joy and desire alternated with panic. 'It's happened again.' She remembered a comment in Petrov's diary, about a contradiction involving pain and pleasure: a lover giving pleasure yet inflicting torture. Whose presence is intense delight and whose absence intense pain. 'I'm letting myself in for it again.'

She was walking up and down on her verandah talking aloud to herself when she stopped short at the sight of Mumtaz in the doorway. Her heart thudded. 'Intense delight,' she thought.

'Talking to ourselves, are we?' said Mumtaz. He sat back and stretched and said, 'Heard the latest?' He had filled out to his original stature, lost the gauntness and the diminished look on his face. 'They're wondering if Maudie's gun belonged to Shudo Mojumdar. Poor old Maudie. She keeps saying it was her husband's.'

'Really! But didn't Shudo notice?'

'Who knows? He's not here to be asked.'

Robi was squatting by Surjeet Shona as was his wont. He coughed delicately. 'Shaheb. They have been saying ...'

'Who has been saying ...?'

'The servants, Mojumdar Shaheb's servants have been saying, when the dog died there was too much blood ...'

Mumtaz sat up. 'And, what else are they saying?'

'They found small pieces of brass, like ...'

'Bullets?' exclaimed Surjeet Shona and Mumtaz together.

'You mean Shudo Shaheb shot the dog!?'

'Who knows, Shaheb. It bit him once.'

'Ho, ho,' said Mumtaz. 'What next?'

'But surely Proshanto Shaheb must have been angry.'

'That they do not say ...'

'Pro said nothing, did nothing, and Shudo stayed on with him ...?'

'It could be that Pro simply forgot,' said Surjeet Shona.

'How can you forget such a thing? Would you forget if someone killed your dog?'

'He was senile, Mumtaz. You didn't know. You didn't live here. Pro forgot everything towards the end. He lived in a dream world of his own. Things that happened in the present vanished as soon as they were over …'

'But then, that man Shudo's dangerous!'

'He is bad man,' said Robi. 'They are also saying …,' he stopped suddenly.

'Come on, Robi, Tell us! What are they saying?'

'They know he had one gun, Shaheb. They are saying he tried to, na, na, na …'

'Harm Proshanto Shaheb, is that what they're saying?'

Robi was holding his head and moaning, as was also his wont. 'They are bad people too, those servants. Stealing from their shaheb, cheating … Na, na. It is nonsense …'

Robi got up, disgusted with himself, and left.

Surjeet Shona was incredulous. 'Mumtaz! Could Shudo have killed Pro?'

'There you go again! Next you'll say he pushed Petrov off the roof!'

'Shouldn't we find out …?'

'SS, SS! Do you realize what you're saying? Pro died a normal death, there must be a doctor's certificate or the police would have been here. In any case, his body's gone, not even the ashes are left. You can't investigate a murder without a body, darling!'

Surjeet Shona flushed.

'I know what you're thinking,' teased Mumtaz. 'Exhume the dog, that's what you're thinking!'

'Oh no,' said Surjeet Shona in a turmoil. 'It's ridiculous, what a ridiculous idea!'

'Full of holes,' said Mumtaz mischievously. 'Bullet holes … Dig up a long-buried dog's remains to find out if its owner was murdered by his brother who had no motive. It's Rudro who's inherited, SS, not poor old Shudo! And while we're about it, shouldn't we consult an ornithologist?'

'Now what?'

'Aren't you interested in the habits of the great Indian vulture?'

Mumtaz smiled and Surjeet Shona smiled back at him. Mumtaz put out his hand and gently tweaked Surjeet Shona's cheek. Then he took her hand and pulled her upright close against himself, and then, very slowly, very serious now, looking into her eyes, he brought his head down to hers till their lips touched. The kisses, so long awaited, were sweeter than Surjeet Shona's wildest dreams.

'My own SS,' murmured Mumtaz, holding her tight against him.

Surjeet Shona joyfully responded, savouring once more the hardness of a man's body, this man's body. Mumtaz began to uncover her breasts, following the sequence of Surjeet Shona's dream.

'Not here,' she said, and she led him inside.

There followed such a passage of absorption and rejuvenation for the lovers that they became blind to everything around them. It was difficult to say who was happier, the Rajmahal or Ali-Saira. Freely and guiltlessly happy, Surjeet Shona wondered, like Ali, why this hadn't happened many years ago, many many years ago. 'But then, there was Martin, wasn't there? And all the others. And 'Litha …' She and Mumtaz both knew such an ideal matching those many years ago was irrelevant when the now was so perfect.

'SS,' Mumtaz said to her one afternoon, when they were lying on her bed, sealed by their sweat, as if they would never be parted, 'You are my wife. You always were …'

Surjeet Shona murmured, flowering to the feel of his fingers moving on her hair in slowest, gentlest strokes. 'Don't say anything.'

She had a blurred, warm feeling imbuing her whole body, in a layer just under her skin, that she and Lalitha were one person and that Mumtaz felt this too. And in a layer under that layer, she knew and knew Mumtaz knew, this was the way to deal with his past love and her past friendship for Lalitha and the happiness the little Keralite had created around her and with them during her life. She turned her face to Mumtaz's and ran her fingers along the shallow lines etched in crooked horizontal bars along his brow, then around the expression of pleasure in his eyes, along the ridge of his long, bumpy nose, down the naso-labial lines and along the bow of his lips. And Mumtaz returned her touch for touch with his fingers, along the frown lines on her forehead, her long eyebrows, the wrinkles by her eyes, along her eyelashes, forcing her to close her eyes, along the ridge of her nose, the curve of her cheekbones, the edges of her lips. Then their erotic trembling fingers met at the tips, and joined, pulling them closer and closer till their lips were touching again.

'You are my wife, my beautiful wife, you always were …' Surjeet Shona knew she could resurrect his wife for him, be that resurrection. Expressing sorrow, exhibiting it, to the one she loved and who loved her, his passionate solace, his kisses on her lips and the salt of her tears tasted through his tongue on hers … Happy, shared sorrow …

16

The Scarlet Net

Old Jainab, uneasy after the loss of his glass eye, was restless. The shakiness of age addressed him directly through the wrinkled, quivering, empty socket and all attempts to get him fitted up again failed against his logic.

'I am blind after the loss of the old,' he categorically stated. 'Allah has divested me of my sight!'

Ali Mallik grumbled. 'He's crackers. He thinks he can see with a glass eye. You'd think he was a hundred the way he carries on. Would you imagine the bally chap's much younger than I am?'

Ali had a blind spot to the visible signs of his own ageing. It was true there was no tangible change in his skeletal appearance, apart from an increased hollowness of the cheek and a ptosis affecting the left eyelid. But age, like the Calcutta monsoon, doesn't allow for easy resolution, and, intangibly, Ali looked his age and therefore older than Jainab.

❧

Galled beyond reason by his eye's missing 'sight', the old magician went hunting. And the hunting ground had to be the scene of habitual assault, the dank smelly corridor between the godown and garages, the location of the Brahmanised toilet. The Rajmahal sighed. Delighted as it was by Surjeet Shona's new lover, its instincts clearly indicated big trouble ahead.

'Where is it, where is it?' intoned Jainab, clacking the false teeth he had pushed loose in his mouth.

It was dark and he searched among the weeds and cracks in the paving with a torch, his face close to the ground. Something white and shining near the wall caught his single eye, and he bent over for a closer look. And that was Old Jainab's last act in this life. With a sickening sound, his head was smacked against the wall, coinciding with his curdling scream for help. The Rajmahal braced itself. No one could explain, or admit to knowing enough to explain, what really happened. Of the two chief protagonists, Junior and Rawat-Pandey, neither was on the premises at the time.

When Mumtaz came running down armed with a curtain rod, Surjeet Shona tried to stop him.

'Get out of the way, SS,' he called excitedly, pushing her away.

And he rushed blindly and foolishly into the smelly, mysterious passage where all the evil of the world was that night concentrated and where all the rites of the dark phase of the moon had been performed from ancient times, long before the mansion's existence, centred in a venom pit.

Indescribable wracking sounds. Rushing feet, a scream, conjoined screaming, fearful din of violence. Surjeet Shona running towards it all. The godown an impossible barrier. Pushed out again by a narrow, seething mass. Wrenched out of the way by an arm. Feeling, more than hearing, a vibration deep inside. Mumtaz. Oh yes, Mumtaz ... in unspeakable pain.

Ali and Saira come running stiffly, half falling down the stairs. They see the police arrive and the bodies carried out. They see their middle and lately bereaved, just-found-happiness-again son, Mumtaz. And his new love Surjeet Shona. Shaking, standing by them with her hands tightly covering her eyes.

'Don't hide from it,' snaps Saira. 'Go on. Open your eyes. Look girl. Look my darlings.' She coughs and weeps in spasms, spitting out phlegm and blood.

'Look after her,' Ali to Surjeet Shona, whispering. He quells an old man's tremor. 'Bring her with you later. I must go.'

Ali Mallik's ptosis blinds his eye, an apology to old Jainab for his mockery. He hobbles quickly and painfully to the ambulance and gets in behind the stretchers on one of which lies Mumtaz, still alive. While Surjeet Shona thinks, 'It's me of course. Something always happens when I'm with a man.' Pinioned in the rigid hold of shock, she is powerless to follow her injured lover.

When Mumtaz had floated by under the high light hanging over the Rajmahal drive, she had looked at his face through her fingers, in obedience to his mother's injunction. 'Look my darlings,' Saira had cried. Surjeet Shona could see his face very clearly, through the crystalline lenses of her faultless eyes. On that face was a fine, lacy tracery of blood, a tattered scarlet net.

Junior finds old Jainab's dentures in the morning, in the passage. The grisly dentures grin back, pleased never to go to work again, never to enhance the smile of the old magician again. Then Junior notices a little circular disc, winking in the sunlight. He approaches it, picks it up – a piece of glass, black, with bluish wisps cunningly worked into it, and it pricks his finger releasing a tiny speck of blood. On the ground is left behind a space, inside a circle of white powder, such as could have been formed by the ferocious crushing-into-dust of an eggshell. Or a glass eye. Junior remembers ragged Jainab's arrival at the Rajmahal and the first trick he performed for them a long, long time ago. He remembers how he shared that moment with his little brother, Mumtaz. And he prays, 'Let my kid brother live. Oh Allah, please let him live!'

The police arrest everyone in the lethal fracas, chauffeurs, guards, other staff, city musclemen, neighbours' men. All the people prised out from the passage are bundled into a Black Maria. Except for the absent chief protagonists, Chowkidar Rawat-Pandey and Junior. Many have been injured, old Jainab has been killed outright. But only Mumtaz, the outsider, the intruder, is critically injured. Who knows who is guilty, when lips are universally sealed? But at last and with finality, the chowkidar's Rajmahal days are over.

'Let me de-frock him so that my Pir can have a proper guardian,' says Junior to his father.

'You have carte blanche, my boy,' replies Ali at last. 'Oh yes!'

But the chowkidar hasn't lost his Chanakyan skills, and this final joy is denied to Junior. Even as they speak, he is heard trumpeting that his youngest son, the apple of his eye, has landed a prime government job. By reason of his status as an untouchable.

'What the hell!' rages the impotent Junior. 'What happened to his Brahmanhood?'

The chowkidar has bribed a petty official and his son is in possession of a stamped piece of paper which certifies him unquestionably as a Shudra, the lowliest of the castes at the head of which tower the lofty Brahmans. His Shudra status gives his son instant access to a reserved job, in government service.

'Sir,' says the shameless fraudster, circumspectly divested of his top knot and sacred thread. 'I, henceforward to be addressed merely as Valmiki, come humbly to take your leave. I am old now, just like this old building. And my Pir-ji has need of a younger and fitter servant. And in any case,' he sighs. 'I can no longer hold such a sacred charge, belonging as I do, with my son, to the lowest of the low. If I have in any way committed wrongdoing, I crave your forgiveness.'

The Bhaiji's voice rises joyously from the room of the Guru Granth Sahib:

'… the wondrous task is done
Satisfied are all desires
Filled is the World with joy
All pain ended
Complete, pure, eternal …'

Not long after, the Rajmahal is vacated by the remaining inhabitants and sold. It is destroyed, including that rooted carbuncle,

Rawat-Pandey-Valmiki's godown, eradicated in such a savage and surgical manner it hardly feels the pain. Surjeet Shona stops by one afternoon and steps into the space of clean new light between the two adjoining properties. She steps straight through the non-existent wall with its non-existent iron rails and barbed wire, from the pavement into the non-existent garden. Opened out like this, the ground looks diminished, impossible to imagine the scale of the building once standing here. Surjeet Shona's feet sink into the pink and beige rubble of brick and plaster, by shards of high-quality glass with peacocks' tail eyes which look up at a dark, cloudy sky. The raintree is back to full green strength, its leaves drooping in the sunlessness. A chowkidar appears by her side and notes the direction of her gaze.

'There were once vultures on this tree, Memsahib. A pair of vultures. The police came and fired their guns at the tree top, through the gaps, not at the vultures themselves you understand, for that would be inauspicious. Again and again they fired. And that is when the great birds left.'

There isn't a pigeon in sight either. The mansion's memory is seeping away through its heart, brain stone into Surjeet Shona's hand which has picked up the stone, trying in vain to pass into her emotional body. The tremors of its expending power force it to slip from her grasp to fall soundlessly on to the ground, yet shatter to a powder which will never be re-constituted. The new building, many floors high, will be filled with hard squares of brightly lit offices and hard bright machines and will remember nothing. Only the Pir's grave will remain, Surjeet Shona can see it, protected by Junior's wall bulge, behind a wilting dust-shrouded hedge-maze. It will evolve again into a centre of congregation, devotion and strife. And near it is that old pit, swirling with venom.

17

Memory

Surjeet Shona remembers one by one and over and over her marriages and the deaths of her men. 'I won't send for Gurdeep. I will not!'

Will Mumtaz live or die? Will she lose her fear of that ghoul, transcend it? Hasn't she talked to Mumtaz of the now because of that fear? Will Mumtaz live or die? Will he live or die?

When she visits Mumtaz in the hospital with the distraught Saira that night, she finds everyone from the Rajmahal present, thronging the corridors. Old Jainab's body has been taken away, but his relatives are there, wailing and beating their breasts. They come crowding around Surjeet Shona. As if she can bring him back to life.

She breaks away and finds herself in Mumtaz's room. Saira, who has reached there before her, is standing with bowed head near her prone son. She looks up. She knows Surjeet Shona is the one who matters.

'Go to him, darling,' and she retreats to cough and cough painfully, while Ali puts his arms around her and tries to help her with a glass of water. There is a flurry and Junior is there. He dashes forward, sees Surjeet Shona and holds back. He huddles with his parents and others of the family and they dumbly watch Surjeet Shona sleepwalking towards Mumtaz. They register this is the first time they have seen her looking ugly. And they remember how Mumtaz grew ugly before their eyes as Lalitha slowly died. Surjeet Shona's hair is flattened in parts, standing up in others, its white spreading dramatically. Her salwar-kameez is askew and she appears too thin, shapeless. It is almost impossible to look at her face, the loosened, trembling lips, the softening jawline, the deepening lines. The conspirators, Gravity and Time, have been presented with another victory. Abruptly, as sometimes happens.

Surjeet Shona is afraid to speak. Or look at Mumtaz. Her eyes gaze about the room. Avoiding the bed scrupulously. She looks at the ceiling, white, dead white, in one corner a small patch with loose plaster. Her eyes reach a ceiling fan hanging down in the middle of the room, on an extra long rod. This is an old building with high ceilings. She looks down the wall to the right of the room. 'It must be a thick wall. These old buildings have such thick walls.' She moves forward slowly all the while. Then she stumbles. Her eyes fall on an edge of white. Where she can see a hand. 'Mumtaz ...?' The hand is lying palm-down and the top is covered with plaster. Out of the plaster emerges a long tube culminating in a suspended bottle. Her eyes swivel out and away from the bottle. Then like a pendulum, towards the figure on the bed. They stop at the face. All that is visible of it apart from the hand. The body is under a sheet. The head swathed in bandages. The central portion of eyes, nose and mouth uncovered. The eyes closed. The fine lacy tracery of blood, the tattered scarlet net, has been cleared. Leaving a crazy pattern of cuts and contusions. Surjeet Shona's hand touches the free fingers. And Mumtaz opens his eyes and looks straight at her.

Her heart melts and lightens through a rainbow burst with the flash of his mischievous eyes. 'SS.' Almost inaudible. 'How good of you ... Always ... so good ... My 'Litha's friend ... 'Litha ...' And, alarmingly to everyone who immediately rushes around him, his eyes fill with tears.

Surjeet Shona feels a familiar twisting pain in her centre. Her heart turns to cold dark stone. She is intimate with the nuances in Mumtaz's eyes. And she knows. Instantly. Much ahead of the others. That Mumtaz has entered a time warp. Pitilessly drawn back by the allure of his long and deep marriage. To Lalitha. That a wedge of his life, the crucial wedge preceding the incident, has been neatly sliced out of his memory …

'If he dies,' she thinks, 'I will have to live with the memory of that last gesture he made to me. Of his pushing me away. "Get out of the way, SS!" he said. "Get out of the way!"' Surjeet Shona leaves her lover's limp unremembering fingers with a stunned expression.

'Ali, Ali. Can it be …?' Saira, whispering.

'The boy will go through his suffering all over again …'

'I thought, wasn't he, SS, weren't they …?' Fayyaz.

'She hasn't realized it yet. SS hasn't realized he's going to go through all that pain again. All she knows is she may lose him. That's all she can think of.'

'We lost little 'Litha. Little warm 'Litha, our dearest son's dearest love. And he nearly lost his reason. Then SS came and saved him …,' Ali's voice breaks.

'He may lose his reason completely. Now …'

'Darling …'

'Wait. Let the doctor …'

'We *must* tell him! We *must*! We can't let him forget …'

The doctor looks at Saira with a frown and Ali shushes her again. Surjeet Shona stands against the farthest wall, her eyes wide open and dry, glittering, unfocused on the doctor's intent form. Then the doctor calls and the family circles the bed. Surjeet Shona, statusless, falters and keeps her distance. Out of Mumtaz's sight.

The doctor whispers with the family. Surjeet Shona moves closer, turning her glittering eyes on Mumtaz. His eyes are closed again.

Ali and Saira circle Surjeet Shona in with them. The doctor stands watching.

Mumtaz opens his eyes and smiles at his loved ones. Then grimaces with pain. 'Darling,' Saira again. At a loss for words. 'How, does it, are you … how do you feel? Tell us … do you remember?'

Mumtaz's eyes move desperately from figure to figure. Dilating. Rolling about. Demented.

The doctor gestures at them to stop, move back. Whispering, 'Later. It's dangerous now. Later we will have to gently probe his mind to bring back the past. Now. He must rest. Please. Never try to force him.' Mumtaz is unconscious again. The doctor soothes them. 'It's all right. That's the best way for him to rest …'

It comes to be known that the re-visitation of that extreme loss may prove not only tragic, but hazardous in Mumtaz's frail condition. 'His memory may come back. Such things have been known to happen.' They know the doctor is being kind. Every attempt at reminding Mumtaz, even gently recounting small episodes from the past, is met with the demented rolling eyes and the swoon. And Mumtaz drifts incoherently in and out of consciousness-in-a-time-warp, bordering death.

Memory can do many harmful acrobatics, denying an inconvenient fact which simply ceases, never was … In this arena of memory and forgetting, truth and hallucination, people often cannot place themselves or identify their own roles … Surjeet Shona reads Petrov's passage on memory again and again through the sick wrenching inside her. 'Does Mumtaz not want me in his deepest self? Was our short span of love an inconvenient fact which has simply ceased? Oh Uncle Osheem, why did you not comment on this grotesque edge, this extreme of forgetfulness? Who do I look to now, what do I do to bring Mumtaz back?'

'Are you thinking what I'm thinking?' whispers Ali to Saira.

'You know I am, darling. We're all thinking the same thing.'

The 'inconvenient fact' imagined by Surjeet Shona is something other for them. All, every one of them, want Mumtaz to forget the other way around, to forget Lalitha. It is the remembrance of *her* that is inconvenient, not the living, not Surjeet Shona.

'What a tragedy for Lalitha's memory and our grandchildren, that we should wish this.'

'And what a tragedy for SS and Mumtaz that we are forced to make such a wish!'

'Only the return of his memory can save him. Only remembering he's in love with SS.'

'He can fall in love with her again, can't he?'

The family clings together and Surjeet Shona is pushed to stay as close as possible to Mumtaz. She looks long at his eyes behind which his loss spreads like the waters of the ocean, into which she feels she can plunge dangerously any moment. The eyes return her look when they are open, but without recollection of that essential period. 'Will I lose this last, this best love once and for ever?' Can anything, should anything, be 'once and for ever', when the world so consistently denies permanence? Is it of any use to try and pass back into him the currents of their new love, willing him to forget one way and remember another? Or fall in love again? If he, and she with him, knowing its surreal wastefulness, can traverse that terrible terrain of anguish … again? Either way lies their salvation and their tragedy. If Mumtaz's memory comes back, the cruelty of that repeated grief-in-a-time-warp will haunt him. And if he falls in love with Surjeet Shona again, there will be that gap, that forgotten period … And they will both feel forever uneasy, both betrayed and guilty.

Surjeet Shona can't keep away from the hospital. But should she confuse Mumtaz, while he wonders, 'Why, why is SS waving her face in front of me with such persistence? What is she to me …?'

Should she not free him, let him go back to his Lalitha? And his ugly, ditto-grief?

Isn't association with her, Surjeet Shona, pre-ordained to end unhappily?

Does she have the right to engage him in this fierce tug-of-war?

But then, should she wish him back to Lalitha, back to the dead?

Can she wish that on him and such a sacrifice on herself?

Ask no more, Surjeet Shona, lest thy head fall off!!!

Trussed up with the cutting rope of this tug-of-war, she strains to break free. While the love that surrounds Mumtaz waits, with its breath held.

❧

And then one day, Mumtaz opens his eyes and smiles. 'SS. Is it you? You look so tired. What has happened?' His gaze drifts about the white hospital room.

'Mother!' he exclaims. 'Father!'

Saira and Ali come tentatively up to him. Afraid. Will those eyes start their wild staring, their dangerous rolling again?

The eyes are quiet, normal and one by one they let go their breaths. Held for so long.

'Darling …,' says Saira, then stops as Ali darts her a warning look. The parents embrace their son gently and are surprised at the firmness of his return embrace.

Junior bustles out of the room after directing meaningful looks at them. They wait. Mumtaz has closed his eyes again. Was it a temporary break? No one speaks.

The doctor comes in with Junior and approaches Mumtaz.

Ali holds Saira, who is silently sobbing. She starts coughing and Ali ferries her to the back of the room, where Surjeet Shona stands alone. Tears streaking her face. Ali pats her on the shoulder. He has two women to comfort.

Then they hear Mumtaz talking in a normal voice. Surjeet Shona suddenly grows younger. She becomes the recognizable, the younger Surjeet Shona.

'Doctor! What's wrong with me?' the voice of the cheerful, normal Mumtaz.

And then, wonder of wonders. 'SS,' softly, 'SS. Have I been giving you a rough time? What happened? Did anyone get hurt?'

Surjeet Shona comes up to him. The tears still mark her face, but there is a spring in her step. She speaks as softly as Mumtaz. 'You,' she says. 'You were the one hurt.' She can't stop her hands from trembling and Mumtaz catches them and puts them to his lips. He looks deep into her eyes and Surjeet Shona feels dizzy. She is certain sorrow doesn't exist, never existed, never will exist. There is a fireworks display in her head. She stoops to touch his lips with hers, gently places her cheek against his scarred healed face.

Then he says, 'Jainab. Jainab's gone isn't he?' His expression droops and there are gasps all around the room.

'Ali, Ali, he's relapsing,' cries Saira in a panic.

'Oh, I'm all right. Don't worry Mother!' Mumtaz makes to get out of bed and is stopped by the doctor.

'Just a minute young man!'

'Young man? I'm in a time warp, am I?!'

The doctor ignores the question and examines him. The others look at one another, acknowledging the irony of Mumtaz's words.

The doctor tells them Mumtaz will be well and ready to leave soon. He tells them Mumtaz's memory has possibly been restored fully. Except for the period between the injury and now. It has been neatly sliced out.

'And if he remembers later?' asks Saira.

The doctor smiles at them. 'Does it matter?' he asks. 'He is quite strong already. He will cope.'

Suddenly, all the conundrums cease to exist, never were. The period now cut out of Mumtaz's memory has no importance. Even if he remembers his grief-in-a-time-warp, his repeated anguish. Even if his heart twinges for Lalitha occasionally.

'How can we ever thank you enough?' Saira sobs happily.

Mumtaz is discharged from the hospital. He wants most to be with Surjeet Shona. He has no recollection of his regression. No one tells him of it. His children mill around him. His brothers. His parents. They tell him of his precarious condition. His life teetering on the brink. But nothing of his earlier memory lapse. He listens to all this with Surjeet Shona by his side. Often holding her hand as if holding on to reality. Sometimes he hesitates. Seems to frame a question, but doesn't.

He has moved into a bungalow with Surjeet Shona. It has no resemblance to the Rajmahal.

Healing takes place of the many wounds. There is happiness. Even when Mumtaz has headaches, moans, occasionally shouts in his sleep, reliving the sliced out period of his hospitalization at times and calling as he did then for Lalitha. And Surjeet Shona takes it without fear. Fear has left her. Death has become so familiar, almost like a friend. She sees Mumtaz's nightmares as a subconscious healing. The work going on at night to free him during his waking hours. And maybe, maybe, to free him altogether one day during his lifetime. And hers. Surjeet Shona's spirit is bright and shining, true like the best of metals, forged and tested in the furnace.

Credits

Pages 13 and 282: The Sikh hymn is a translation, with help from friends, of the hymn contained in the Guru Granth Sahib, which was read on the occasion of the installation of the Book on 16 August 1604, in the Golden Temple, in the presence of Guru Arjun Dev.

Page 32: Adapted from a translation of *Nil Durpan* by Michael Modhushudon Dotto, *Modhushudon Rochonaboli*, Horof Prokashoni, 1973, Page 211. The original play, in Bengali, was by Dinobondhu Mitra. There is some confusion over whether the translator was Modhushudon Dotto or Rev. Long, a missionary.

Page 46: *Hobson Jobson* is the alternative name of *A Glossary of Anglo-Indian Colloquial Words and Phrases*, an amusing compilation used by the British during colonial times, by Henry Yule and Arthur C. Burnell, published in 1886.

Page 97: *The Book of Famine* – Saeed Ali Khoja's comments on famine in India and some inputs on Russian and Central Asian connections with India are from, *India and Central Asia in Modern Times – Historical, Poltical and Cultural Links from the Early 19th Century*, by Prof. Devendra Kaushik, 1977, Delhi.

Page 114: Quotation from *The Viceroy's Journal*, by Lord Wavell, ed. P. Moon, (Oxford 1973), entry for 20 October 1944, p: 93.

Page 133: Story of Lebadeff from *Links,* an Indo-Soviet publication, brought out in 1987 after Gorbachev's visit to India in 1986. Lebadeff's story is well-known among Bengalis, especially among Kolkata's theatre-going and academic circles.

Page 143: *The Book of Hope* – Descriptions of Maudie's wedding, merchandise, automobiles and some artefacts have been adapted from news items, advertisements, etc. in the archives of *The Statesman and Friend of India* of the early part of the twentieth century.

Pages 197: The boatman's song is by Rabindranath Tagore, translated from Bengali by Kamalini Sengupta.

Page 265: The quotations from the Guru Granth Sahib are taken from Appendix 5 of *A History of the Sikhs*, Volume I, Second Edition, by Khushwant Singh, Oxford University Press. Kabir section, p: 311 and Nanak section no. 4, p: 314.